Beyond the Primal Addiction

Written by experienced practitioners in the fields of addiction and psychoanalysis, and illustrated by a range of moving vignettes, this groundbreaking book examines the psychological foundations of addiction in the areas of food, sex, gambling, internet usage, shopping, and work.

This book not only explores the roots of addictive behavior, explaining why popular treatment options such as the 12-Step Program often fail, it also provides insights for emotional resolution and strategies for behavioral change.

Beyond the Primal Addiction seeks to understand rather than pathologize addictive behaviors, now so pervasive in contemporary societies. It will be essential reading for psychoanalysts, psychotherapists, and other mental health professionals, as well as their clients.

Nina Savelle-Rocklin, PsyD, is a psychoanalyst specializing in eating disorders. She hosts a radio program on LA Talk Radio and is regularly featured in magazines, summits, and podcasts, including *Psychology Today*, *Real Simple*, The Dr. Drew Podcast, and more. She is the author of *Food for Thought: Perspectives on Eating Disorders*.

Salman Akhtar, MD, is Professor of Psychiatry, Jefferson Medical College, and a training and supervising analyst at the Psychoanalytic Center of Philadelphia. He was the recipient of the 2012 Sigourney Award for Distinguished Contributions to Psychoanalysis.

D1729650

Beyond the Primal Addiction

Food, Sex, Gambling, Internet, Shopping, and Work

Edited by Nina Savelle-Rocklin and Salman Akhtar

Routledge
Taylor & Francis Group

LONDON AND NEW YORK

First published 2019
by Routledge
2 Park Square, Milton Park, Abingdon, Oxon OX14 4RN

and by Routledge
52 Vanderbilt Avenue, New York, NY 10017

Routledge is an imprint of the Taylor & Francis Group, an informa business

British Library Cataloguing-in-Publication Data
A catalogue record for this book is available from the British Library

Library of Congress Cataloging-in-Publication Data
A catalog record for this book has been requested

ISBN: 978-0-367-15069-3 (hbk)
ISBN: 978-0-367-15072-3 (pbk)
ISBN: 978-0-429-05481-5 (ebk)

Typeset in Times New Roman
by Apex CoVantage, LLC

Chapter four is reprinted, with its author's and publisher's permission, from *Psychodynamic Psychiatry* 43:1–25, 2015.

Printed in the United Kingdom
by Henry Ling Limited

To

David Rocklin and Muge Alkan

The objects of our dependence

"Masturbation is the one major habit, the 'primal addiction,' and that it is only as a substitute and replacement for it that the other addictions – for alcohol, morphine, tobacco, etc. – come into existence."

Sigmund Freud, 1897b

Contents

Acknowledgments

Six distinguished colleagues and two outstanding graduate students have contributed to this volume. They put in a lot of effort, sacrificed time, and were always patient with our requirements, reminders, and requests for revisions. Dr. Ariela Green helped one of us considerably by locating some important bibliographic references. Jan Wright prepared the manuscript of this book with her usual skill and diligence. To all these individuals, we are very grateful.

Nina Savelle-Rocklin and Salman Akhtar

About the editors and contributors

Salman Akhtar, MD, is Professor of Psychiatry at Jefferson Medical College and a Training and Supervising Analyst at the Psychoanalytic Center of Philadelphia. He has served on the editorial boards of the *International Journal of Psychoanalysis*, the *Journal of the American Psychoanalytic Association*, and the *Psychoanalytic Quarterly*. His more than 300 publications include 89 books, of which the following 20 are solo-authored: *Broken Structures* (1992), *Quest for Answers* (1995), *Inner Torment* (1999), *Immigration and Identity* (1999), *New Clinical Realms* (2003), *Objects of Our Desire* (2005), *Regarding Others* (2007), *Turning Points in Dynamic Psychotherapy* (2009), *The Damaged Core* (2009), *Comprehensive Dictionary of Psychoanalysis* (2009), *Immigration and Acculturation* (2011), *Matters of Life and Death* (2011), *The Book of Emotions* (2012), *Psychoanalytic Listening* (2013), *Good Stuff* (2013), *Sources of Suffering* (2014), *No Holds Barred* (2016), *A Web of Sorrow* (2017), *Mind, Culture, and Global Unrest* (2018), and *Silent Virtues* (2018). Dr. Akhtar has delivered many prestigious invited lectures including a Plenary Address at the 2nd International Congress of the International Society for the Study of Personality Disorders in Oslo, Norway (1991), an Invited Plenary Paper at the 2nd International Margaret S. Mahler Symposium in Cologne, Germany (1993), an Invited Plenary Paper at the Rencontre Franco-Americaine de Psychanalyse meeting in Paris, France (1994), a Keynote Address at the 43rd IPA Congress in Rio de Janiero, Brazil (2005), the Plenary Address at the 150th Freud Birthday Celebration sponsored by the Dutch Psychoanalytic Society and the Embassy of Austria in Leiden, Holland (2006), and the Inaugural Address at the first IPA-Asia Congress in Beijing, China (2010). Dr. Akhtar is the recipient of numerous awards including the American Psychoanalytic Association's Edith Sabshin Award (2000), Columbia University's Robert Liebert Award for Distinguished Contributions to Applied Psychoanalysis (2004), the American Psychiatric Association's Kun Po Soo Award (2004), and Irma Bland Award for being the Outstanding Teacher of Psychiatric Residents in the country (2005). He received the highly prestigious Sigourney Award (2012) for distinguished contributions to psychoanalysis. In 2013, he gave the commencement address at graduation ceremonies of the Smith College School of Social Work in Northampton, Massachusetts. Dr. Akhtar's books have been translated in many languages, including German, Italian, Korean, Romanian, Serbian, Spanish, and Turkish. A true Renaissance man, Dr. Akhtar has served as the Film Review Editor for the *International Journal of Psychoanalysis*, and is currently serving as the Book Review Editor for the *International Journal of Applied Psychoanalytic Studies*. He has published nine collections of poetry and serves as a Scholar-in-Residence at the Inter-Act Theatre Company in Philadelphia.

Lance Dodes, MD, is a Training and Supervising Analyst Emeritus at the Boston Psychoanalytic Society and Institute, a member of the faculty of the New Center for Psychoanalysis (Los Angeles), and a retired assistant clinical professor of psychiatry at Harvard Medical School. He has been the Director of the Substance Abuse Treatment Unit of Harvard's McLean Hospital, Director of the Alcoholism Treatment Unit at Spaulding Rehabilitation Hospital (now part of Massachusetts General Hospital), and Director of the Boston Center for Problem Gambling. He is the author or co-author of many journal articles and book chapters about addiction and the author of three books: *The Heart of Addiction* (HarperCollins, 2002), *Breaking Addiction: A 7-Step Handbook for Ending Any Addiction* (HarperCollins, 2011), and *The Sober Truth: Debunking the Bad Science Behind 12-Step Programs and the Rehab Industry* (Beacon Press, 2014; senior author). Dr. Dodes has been honored by the Division on Addictions at Harvard Medical School for "distinguished contribution" to the study and treatment of addictive behavior, and has been elected a Distinguished Fellow of the American Academy of Addiction Psychiatry.

April Fallon, PhD, is the Faculty Chair and Professor at Fielding Graduate University, and Clinical Professor in Psychiatry at Drexel College of Medicine. She received her baccalaureate degree from Allegheny College (1975) and a Doctor of Philosophy in Psychology at the University of Pennsylvania (1981). She has received numerous awards for her teaching of psychiatric medical residents, including the Psychiatric Educator 2012 from Philadelphia Psychiatric Society. She has co-authored five books with Virginia Brabender: *Models of Inpatient Group Psychotherapy* (1993), *Awaiting the Therapist's Baby: A Guide for Expectant Parent-Practitioners* (2003), *Essentials of Group Therapy* (2004), *Group Development in Practice: Guidance for Clinicians and Researchers on Stages and Dynamics of Change* (2009), and *The Impact of Parenthood on the Therapeutic Relationship* (2018). She has also co-edited an additional volume, *Working with Adoptive Parents: Research, Theory and Therapeutic Interventions* (2013). In addition, she has researched and written on the development of disgust in children and adults, body image and eating disorders, the effects of childhood maltreatment, and attachment and adoption. Dr. Fallon maintains a private practice in Ardmore, Pennsylvania.

Lawrence Jacobson, PhD, was born and brought up in London, England. After earning his BA in Philosophy, Politics, and Economics at Oxford University, he moved to New York City and obtained a Doctorate in Clinical Psychology at City University of New York. He encountered a range of fraught but fascinating clinical and societal situations as a psychologist at Bronx Municipal Hospital in the 1980s and as Senior Psychologist and Acting Clinic Director at Manhattan Family Court. At the time he also served as Assistant Professor of Psychiatry at Albert Einstein College of Medicine. In the early 1990s he completed psychoanalytic training at the White Institute in New York City, where he is a member of the faculty and supervisor of psychotherapy. He has also been a clinical supervisor at a number of doctoral programs in the New York City area and served on the editorial board of *Contemporary Psychoanalysis*. He has written numerous articles on, among other issues, the intersection of group and individual processes and the intersection of contemporary culture with psychoanalytic culture and practice. A particular interest of his has been the clinical and theoretical handling of the changing sexual mores and activities of the last couple of decades. He is in private practice of psychoanalysis, psychotherapy, and supervision in New York City.

Stanley Kletkewicz, MA, is currently a doctoral student in Clinical Psychology at Fielding Graduate University. He is a licensed professional counselor. He has completed a Master's in Psychology at Fielding Graduate University and a Master's in Counseling at Biblical Theological Seminary. Before his work in the field of counseling psychology, as a volunteer, he developed and implemented programs geared toward reducing recidivism with inmates in a federal prison. His work resulted in recognition from the Federal Bureau of Prisons as Volunteer of the Year. Previously, Mr. Kletkewicz spent over 25 successful years in wholesale distribution, leaving that industry as Executive Vice President of a large, New Jersey-based distributorship. He is developing ways to integrate his years of executive leadership and business experience with his current counseling position in order to provide a unique experience for his professional clientele.

Jean Petrucelli, PhD, is a clinical psychologist and psychoanalyst; Director and Co-Founder of the Eating Disorders, Compulsions and Addictions Service (EDCAS); Fellow; Supervising Analyst; Teaching Faculty; Conference Advisory Committee Chair and Founding Director of the Eating, Disorders, Compulsions & Addictions one-year educational certificate program at the William Alanson White Institute for Psychotherapy and Psychoanalysis. In addition, she is an Associate Professor for New York University's Postdoctoral Program in Psychotherapy and Psychoanalysis; Adjunct Faculty, Institute of Contemporary Psychology; Associate Editor for the journal *Contemporary Psychoanalysis*; Editor of five books, including winner of the American Board and Academy of Psychoanalysis (ABAPsa) 2016 edited book *Body-States: Interpersonal and Relational Perspectives on the Treatment of Eating*

*Disorder*s (Routledge, 2015); *Knowing, Not-Knowing & Sort-of-Knowing: Psychoanalysis and the Experience of Uncertainty* (Karnac Books, 2010); and *Longing: Psychoanalytic Musings on Desire* (Karnac Books, 2006); co-editor with C. Stuart of the book *Hungers and Compulsions: The Psychodynamic Treatment of Eating Disorders and Addictions* (Rowan & Littlefield, 2001; re-released 2009); and most recently, co-editor with S. Schoen of *Unknowable, Unspeakable and Unsprung: Psychoanalytic Perspectives on Truth, Scandal, Secrets & Lies* (Routledge, 2017). Dr. Petrucelli specializes in the interpersonal treatment of eating disorders and addictions and lectures nationally and internationally. She is in private practice on the upper west side in New York City.

Ricardo Rieppi, PhD, is a psychologist in private practice in New York City and is completing his psychoanalytic training at the NYU Postdoctoral Program in Psychotherapy and Psychoanalysis. He currently serves as an Advisory Board Member for *The Candidate Journal*, Chair of the Candidate Outreach Committee (of Division 39 of the American Psychological Association), and Steering Committee Member of the Psychotherapy Action Network (PsiAn). He has co-authored several papers, ranging in topics such as ADHD treatment and socioeconomic status, schizophrenia and stigmatization, and psychological factors affecting blood pressure. His clinical interests include relational psychoanalysis, affect regulation, gender, and culture.

Richard Rosenthal, MD, is Clinical Professor of Psychiatry and Co-Director of the UCLA Gambling Studies Program. He co-authored the American Psychiatric Association's diagnostic criteria for pathological gambling; initiated and was co-investigator for the first genetic studies; was on the committee that developed the national certification for gambling counselors; and was a member of the National Academy of Science's Committee on the Social and Economic Impact of Pathological Gambling. The National Council on Problem Gambling awarded him their Research Award, and their two highest honors, the Monsignor Joseph Dunne Lifetime Award for Advocacy and the Dr. Robert Custer Lifetime Award for Direct Service. Dr. Rosenthal is a graduate of Cornell University and the Albert Einstein College of Medicine. After completing his psychiatric residency at Mt. Sinai Hospital in New York, he served in the Navy as Chief of the Neuropsychiatric Unit at the Marine Corps Recruit Depot in San Diego. Discharged with the rank of commander, he moved to Los Angeles and entered private practice. He is a board-certified psychiatrist and a Distinguished Life Fellow of the American Psychiatric Association. Dr. Rosenthal is a graduate and faculty member of the New Center for Psychoanalysis. His 55 publications have been cited almost five thousand times. In addition to his work on gambling, he has written about wrist-cutting and self-mutilation, the etymology and conceptual history of addiction, transitional phenomena in the treatment of borderline personalities, and a series of literary studies, most notably about Dostoevsky.

Nina Savelle-Rocklin, PsyD, is a psychoanalyst specializing in food, weight, and body image issues. She is the author of *Food for Thought: Perspectives on Eating Disorders* (Rowman & Littlefield, 2016), and wrote chapters in two psychoanalytic books, *Freud and the Buddha* (Karnac, 2015) and *Mistrust* (Karnac, 2017). A recognized expert in the field of eating psychology, she has written guest articles and appeared in many national publications and summits, including *Psychology Today, Redbook, Los Angeles Times, Real Simple, Beverly Hills Times, Huffington Post, Prevention, Refinery 29, Healthline*, and more. Dr. Savelle-Rocklin also presented at the American Psychoanalytic Association's National Meeting in 2014. In addition to her Los Angeles-based private practice, she hosts a radio show on LA Talk Radio, has an interview show on Focus TV Network, and writes an award-winning blog, *Make Peace with Food*, which incorporates psychoanalytic concepts, principles, and ideas. She is dedicated to bringing psychoanalytic principles to the general public.

Charles Wisniewski, DO, is currently a Child and Adolescent Psychiatry Fellow at Drexel University College of Medicine. He completed his adult residency in Psychiatry where he served as Chief Resident. He received a Bachelor's in music at Boston College, a Master's in Medical Sciences at Boston University School of Medicine, and his medical degree at Rowan School of Osteopathic Medicine. During his residency Dr. Wisniewski served as Wellness Chair for Psychiatry and was a member of the University Wellness Committee for Drexel. He is also an instructor for junior psychiatry residents and medical students. He has begun incorporating his music skills and training into his clinical practice and has presented his techniques at local professional meetings and at national APA meetings. Since moving to Philadelphia, he has been a part of numerous bands that play at local venues in the city and is involved in local arts programs. Dr. Wisniewski hopes to continue to develop techniques in music medicine with a younger population in his fellowship and afterwards in his practice.

Introduction

The founder of psychoanalysis, Sigmund Freud, famously acknowledged that all psychoanalytic treatment can accomplish is to transform "hysterical misery into common unhappiness" (1895a, p. 305). The implication of this admission was that no human being could escape a certain minimum baseline of unhappiness. Thirty-five years later, Freud (1930) stated that a modicum of emotional discontent is inevitable since one cannot avoid being a victim of cruel acts of nature, betrayal by friends and relatives, and gradual deterioration of the body. And, of course, Freud was hardly alone in concluding that a certain amount of emotional suffering invariable accompanies human existence. Buddha's First Noble Truth embodied this very realization, and Henry David Thoreau (1854) grimly declared that most men lead a life of "quiet desperation."

Just as human unhappiness is ubiquitous, so are human attempts at thwarting or minimizing it. Over centuries, myriad measures have been devised to reduce personal helplessness and discontent: belief in God, determined efforts to tame the forces of nature, retreat into solitude, recourse to the omnipotence of creativity, idealization of love, absorption in work, and use of mood-altering substances. The last-mentioned has become a consuming topic (pun unintended) of medical concern, scientific research, psychiatry, population health studies, movies and plays, civic policy making, and tabloid sensationalism. This current highlighting of man's need to obviate his existential dysphoria by using alcohol, opioids, marijuana, and other such substances must not make one overlook that human history is replete with evidence that such addictions have existed from times immemorial.

However, the story of man's search for active euphoria or mindless oblivion involves means other than using psychoactive substances as well. Ordinary life activities such as eating, shopping, reading, surfing on the internet, having sex, and working can all get libidinized and pulled into the psychic centrifuge of addiction. These "addictions without substances" (Fenichel, 1945) can also serve as psychic retreats from emotional suffering, though, regrettably, causing further pain themselves.

The book in your hand addresses this very issue. It is titled *Beyond the Primal Addiction* to highlight the astuteness of Freud's (1897b) observation that masturbation was the "primal addiction" (p. 272) and all addictions followed from it.

The essence of this proposal is that addictions involve a radical turning away from actual object relations, and utilizing one or the other form of self-stimulation as a remedy of inner turmoil. And, as stated earlier, this self-stimulation might come from substances or from emotionally hyper-invested activities. The latter mentioned have, however, remained under-investigated. This book rectifies such omission in psychoanalytic literature and does so with the help of a comprehensive and convincing etiological overview, illustrative chapters on six specific "behavioral addictions" (food, sex, gambling, shopping, internet, and work), and a concluding summary. Its aim is to enhance therapeutic empathy with people having such maladies and to arm clinicians to help them better.

Prologue

Chapter 1

A general psychoanalytic theory of addiction

Lance Dodes

Addiction has been widely misunderstood and inappropriately treated for virtually all of human history, because of a failure to appreciate its psychological nature. Although there are physical aspects of drug addiction, a great deal of evidence shows that these are not a factor in either its nature or cause (Dodes, 2002, 2009). Indeed, despite its many superficial forms including both drug and non-drug foci, addiction is a single psychological symptom and a subset of the psychological symptoms we call compulsions.[1] Failure to appreciate this has led to labeling each type of addictive behavior as if it is a separate diagnostic entity. Thus, an addiction involving compulsive use of alcohol became "alcoholism," while addictions involving other drugs became "substance abuse disorders," and non-drug addictions focused on gambling, eating, and sexual acts were each given a diagnostic label as though they were distinct. Balkanization of addiction has overlooked the clinical fact that people commonly shift their addiction – i.e., the focus of their compulsive behavior – from one area to another, or have multiple foci of the addiction ("multiple addictions") simultaneously. Of compulsive gamblers, 30% to 40% have alcoholism, for example, and a familiar addiction history seen in gambling clinics is the person with polydrug abuse in teen years, moving to alcoholism in his twenties, then to compulsive gambling in his thirties. Most important of course is that the psychological mechanism behind all of these foci, when understood, is seen to be the same.

In this chapter, I will briefly review psychoanalytic theories of the psychological nature of addiction, before describing a current view about which I have written for many years, and its implications for treatment.

Theories of addiction

Modern psychoanalytic views of addiction began in the 1960s with development of the "self-medication" concept of drug use (Krystal and Raskin, 1970; Milkman and Frosch, 1973; Khantzian, 1978) (note that all early writers wrote only about addictions focused on drugs, not considering that their ideas applied equally to non-drug addictive behaviors). The original version of the self-medication hypothesis was that people used particular drugs in order to alleviate their most troubling emotional states, for example, using stimulants like cocaine or amphetamines for depression. While this idea fit some instances, it overlooked the fact of people changing their use from one drug to another of a completely different or even opposite effect, such as cocaine to heroin, or using them simultaneously. This hypothesis also did not fit the fact that people with entirely different emotional problems all used the same drug: alcohol. The fact that people can and do switch from drug addictions to non-drug addictions like compulsive shopping, internet games, eating, and so on, also suggested that the "choice" of a drug, as the focus of addiction, could not be explained by its physical effects.

However, the self-medication idea was useful in a different way. It pointed to the psychological nature of addiction, specifically its use as an ego function to manage emotional distress. This was an important improvement over earlier psychoanalytic, and popular, ideas that addiction represented simply gratification of a wish in the context of lack of mature ego functioning.

From a treatment standpoint, thinking of addiction as an ego function began the movement away from believing that people with addictions were unsuitable for psychoanalysis, or any psychodynamic therapy. If addiction were a maladaptive ego function rather than a sign of severe or primitive character disorder, there was no reason to separate "addicts" from anyone else, when determining optimal treatment.

Over the next couple of decades others made significant contributions to understanding the psychology behind addictive behavior. Wieder and Kaplan (1969), Wurmser (1974), and others described the use of drugs as an object substitute. Kernberg (1975) wrote of addictive behavior as a reunion with all-good self and object images. In these formulations, the capacity to keep, use, and control a drug has meaningful properties as a replacement for unavailable or inconsistent others, especially major early figures.

Khantzian (1978) and Khantzian and Mack (1983) considered a deficit psychology to explain drug users' frequent failure to take good care of themselves. They described a "self-care deficit" arising from failure to internalize a group of functions that includes the ability to anticipate danger, and enough self-concern to lead them to protect themselves. While people with addictions do regularly fail to care for themselves via their addictive behavior, such failure is true of every pathology to some degree; the maladaptive nature of repeated neurotic and characterological symptomatology is what distinguishes it from what is considered healthy function. The idea of a self-care deficit is not peculiar to addiction, therefore, but its value may be in helping to understand why some people with addictions (or any destructive behaviors) take longer than others to seek help.

Wurmser (1984a) emphasized the importance of primitive superego function in addiction. He described the use of drugs to create an identity free of the tyranny of an archaic superego. This concept fits well with those people who feel compelled to return to their addictive behavior when flooded with guilt.

The significant role of narcissistic fragility in addiction was another contribution by Wurmser (1974), who wrote of a "narcissistic crisis" in drug abusers.

He wrote of the collapse of a grandiose self or an idealized object leading to an intense "addictive search." Kohut and Wolf (1978) similarly referred to addictions as "narcissistic behavior disorders," within their framework of a deficit psychology in which drugs served as part of psychological structure. McDougall (1984) described the use of drugs and other addictive behavior as ways to "disperse" emotional arousal to avoid affective flooding, particularly in more primitive people.

Each of these early psychoanalytic theories has merit in that each offers a rational basis for specific instances of addiction. However, they apply to different individuals. For some people with addictions, archaic superego pressure precipitates an intense need to be freed from guilt. For others, the loss of a significant person, or the chronic absence of needed emotional objects, leads to substitution by an always-available and controllable object that then becomes compulsively sought. For some, it is the collapse of a grandiose self. For still others, it is affective flooding not well explained by one of the preceding.

A comprehensive theory

Over the past almost 30 years, I have suggested a way to understand addiction that provides an underlying basis of earlier views (Dodes, 1990, 1996, 2002, 2003, 2011). This theory has three parts, as follows:

1   Every addictive act is preceded by a feeling of helplessness or powerlessness. In classical language such states may be called "psychic traumas"; the imposition of a state of helplessness on the ego when it is overwhelmed by a drive/ affect that it cannot manage without excessive anxiety (Freud, 1926). Addictive behavior functions to repair this feeling of helplessness. It is able to do this because taking an addictive action (or – importantly – even just deciding to take this action) creates a sense of being empowered, of regaining control over one's emotional experience and one's life. This *reversal of helplessness* can be described as the psychological function or purpose of addiction.

    It is important to add that people suffering with addictions tolerate the usual experiences of helplessness in life just as does anyone else. It is only when the meaning of a situation produces a sense of *overwhelming* helplessness that it precipitates the insistent drive to repeat the addictive behavior. In order for conditions to lead to feeling overwhelmed, the meaning must be of central importance to the overall psychological issues of the person. This has major implications for treatment, since it means that exploring the issues that precipitate addictive feelings may be a kind of royal road to the critical issues for the entire psychotherapy. Correspondingly, exploration in psychoanalytic or psychodynamic therapy will allow anticipation of future addictive urges, with the possibility of mastering the behavior.

2   States of overwhelming helplessness are inherently narcissistic injuries, since the ability to be powerful over oneself and one's internal state, to regulate one's mood and one's sense of inner safety and reliability (Spruiell, 1975),

are central to the nature of healthy narcissism. A consequence of narcissistic injury is the production of narcissistic rage (Kohut, 1972). It is this rage at helplessness that is the powerful *drive* behind addiction. In fact, it is the very properties of narcissistic rage – especially an extreme intensity that overpowers ordinary judgment – that gives to addiction this most defining characteristic (I will return to this later).

3   In addictions, the emotional purpose and drive, as above, are always expressed in a substitute action (a displacement). It is this displaced act that we call the addiction. As mentioned previously, we name addictions by the form of this displacement: when the reversal of overwhelming helplessness, driven by the narcissistic rage it produces, is displaced to drinking alcohol, we call the resulting compulsive behavior alcoholism. Another way to say this is that without displacement, there can be no addiction. This has important treatment implications, since when patients are able to undo their displacement and take a more direct action to reverse their feeling of being utterly trapped, they have found a way to replace addictive behavior. This makes sense since the addictive behavior was, to begin with, a replacement for direct action that had been psychologically forbidden or inhibited. The following are clinical vignettes illustrating these ideas.

Clinical vignette I[2]

Mr. S was a 40-year-old man in psychoanalysis; he was not an addict in the usual sense, but his difficulties with smoking cigarettes illustrate clearly the issues I am trying to highlight. His father had been a violent man, and his mother had been passively compliant with his father's violence toward her; Mr. S described her as being like a "vegetable." As a child, Mr. S had regularly sought refuge from the "crazy adults" by hiding in a secret place in the cellar of their house, where he felt both safe and in control. At the time of this vignette, he had been in analysis for two years. He had previously stopped smoking and now spoke of his renewed craving for cigarettes. In the analysis, he had recently been feeling increasingly dependent, and very uncomfortable with what he considered to be "surrendering" – to the process, or to me. He said about his craving for cigarettes: "I wanted the comfort of it, I wanted to do something ... it's paying attention to the anxiety and unhappiness, even if it's destructive." Asked what he would have been doing about these feelings by smoking, he said: "Soothing them, maybe; that's not right ... it was a powerful urge, I felt frustrated." Several sessions later he returned to his urge, saying "there's a compulsion, it seems a gesture of defiance, but totally displaced ... it's a certain kind of 'fuck you to the world' feeling ... maybe it's a reflection of anxiety about the project [a big job he had been preparing at his work]. It's getting close and isn't ready yet ... I really don't feel in control." I commented that he had been saying he didn't feel in control in several ways, and perhaps cigarettes were a way to be in control. He said: "I know it's a pleasure, but that's not enough [to explain his intense desire]." I agreed with him. Mr. S continued: "I guess [in smoking] I regain some control over the crazy world; it would be better to throw dishes!" He was surprised at his remark, and after a brief pause, added: "I guess it's a way of letting out some rage."

I agreed with him again, and suggested that smoking for him could be driven by rage about not being in control, and would express that rage, as well as resolve the feeling of being out of control, through an action which would yield a sense of taking back control. I commented that this could seem confusing since, overall, resuming smoking certainly would mean being out of control, but looked at very closely, it means just the reverse. Mr. S thought about this aloud a few minutes, then said, "Somehow I feel a great sense of relief right now." He went on to speak of his efforts to be in control of his life through not only cigarettes, but also alcohol (he had been a moderately heavy drinker) and food. We were then able to consider a wish he had expressed that week to change several appointment times for the following week, as an analogous effort to retake control in the analysis, where he had been feeling frighteningly out of control.

This man made it clear that his impulse toward addictive behavior was a "letting out some rage" about feeling that he was not in control, and simultaneously was a reparative effort to regain mastery, arising in the setting of intensified dependency and anxieties about "surrendering." His initial thoughts about his craving were from the side of external reality, or from superego pressure, i.e., that it would be very foolish to smoke. As is usual with addictive behavior, this approach neither aided his understanding nor reduced his craving. Interpreting the unconscious dynamic behind the craving dissolved it, however, and led to further exploration of his feelings of helplessness and his indirect means of managing them. He did not resume smoking at that time.

Clinical vignette 2

Mr. C, a 52-year-old man whose advancement in his career as an architect had been severely hampered by his chronic alcoholism, entered psychotherapy after a previous psychoanalysis 20 years earlier. He described an early history of intense envy of his older brother, whose aggressiveness and creativity had stood in contrast to his own sense of having been a compliant, good boy. Paradigmatic of his experience was the story told by his mother that when she had caught him masturbating at age three and had told him to stop, he had done so immediately, in contrast to his brother. Characteristic, too, was his experience, as a child, of letting other children painfully bend back his fingers without defending himself.

In his analysis with a woman analyst, he never revealed the extent of his angry, critical feelings toward her. When she became aware that he drank heavily, he reported that she told him to stop drinking; he did so immediately, but the transference meaning of this was never addressed. After the analysis, he resumed drinking. His drinking was secretive in general. He attempted to conceal it from his wife, drinking in his car or when she was away or asleep. These attempts were never ultimately successful, and his wife was quite aware of his heavy drinking and experienced it as anger directed at her. (This is characteristic of the accurate perception by others of the addict's underlying affect, though without a real understanding of its basis.) His secretiveness was expressed as well in the current therapy, in which he again did not at first reveal his critical or angry feelings, but, it later came out, had a number of devaluing fantasies about my professional ability and my sexuality. His inhibitions were reflected in several ways. As a child he had slept with his mother after having nightmares, until he was 12 years old, and recalled seeing his mother naked in silhouette once, when she stood in her nightgown in front of a light. Later, he developed an inhibition in regard to looking. His analyst had discussed with him his failure to notice her habitual knitting while she sat in analysis. In the current therapy he failed to notice my analytic couch in the room; and while sitting a few feet away at a concert by chance, he failed to notice me. His inhibition of aggression, as in his allowing his fingers to be bent back, expressed itself in adult life, among other ways, through involvement with a con man that he permitted to steal from him.

When he began therapy, he was still drinking. Strikingly, he recognized that he was an alcoholic, paid lip service to the need to stop, and described himself as feeling guilty about his drinking, yet had no guilty affect at all. When this was pointed out in an exploratory, nonjudgmental way, he began to speak of a feeling that no one was going to stop him in his drinking, that in fact there were many complaints he had about how he was being treated in a variety of contexts, and that in general he lived with an angry feeling that he had put up with enough. On one occasion early in the treatment when he drank, he said he had the thought, "the hell with it," and added he felt "entitled ... I deserved it." When he was questioned about this entitlement, he associated to an occasion when he had bought the wrong item at a store at age seven and his mother had unfairly scolded him. He said he had always thought he had felt guilty then, but in retrospect he saw that he had been very angry and had had the secret thought that he was right in his rage: he was entitled to be treated better and to be enraged, though it had to be kept secret.

On another occasion when he drank, he spoke of feeling that he had been let down. It became clear that one area in which he felt this was with me – after I had challenged his intellectual acceptance of his alcoholism. His association on this occasion was to an incident when he was four years old and had visited his father's business. He had called out proudly to his father, who was leading a meeting. His father had been angry and afterward had spanked the boy. His father's puncturing of Mr. C's exhibitionistic narcissism, and of his wish to join with his father whom he idealized, was an empathic failure that had been re-experienced when I challenged his offer of his prized intellectual understanding. His subsequent drinking was a response to this narcissistic deflation and reflected his rage and reassertion of his potency. Mr. C's final drinking episode in his therapy occurred when he had felt devalued and powerless in response to a combination of my informing him of my vacation, his wife's leaving on a trip, and criticism of his prowess by a colleague at work. He associated to a man confined to a wheelchair who had been ignored as unimportant by Mr. C's older brother. It was possible at this time to clarify with him his rage at feeling that he had been placed in a powerless, helpless position, and the value of his drinking as seizing power over his experience, while also defying those (his wife and me) he felt were devaluing him.

Clinical vignette 3

A business owner who had a history of alcoholism had been robbed for years by his son's embezzlement from the family company. When he discovered that the son's thefts from the company were far greater than he had known, he ended many months of sobriety in a two-day alcoholic binge. Investigation in treatment revealed the long-standing helpless rage he had felt about his son's thefts, a helplessness that was linked to his internal moral prohibition about firing his son. He finally said that he had the thought, "The hell with it," drinking was "the only thing left that I could do." His drinking was a form of reassertion of an internal sense of power (doing the only thing that he felt he *could* do) against his helplessness, and it was fueled by his rage at this helplessness. The immediate consequence of his drinking was that he felt better (i.e., he felt no longer threatened by the narcissistic traumatization of helplessness) and he had no conflict about drinking at the time he drank; the drinking was ego-syntonic. However, this action to assert his power was displaced from a realistic focus, necessitated by his inhibition about taking action against his son. The addictive behavior was therefore an unconscious compromise formation, in which he gave up realistic action, although he consciously experienced his behavior as purely gratifying.

Clinical vignette 4

The patient was a 32-year-old married woman in psychoanalysis, with a history of chronic alcoholism. She was drinking excessively and self-destructively when the analysis began but had no idea why she drank and was highly self-condemnatory about it. In the course of the first year of treatment, the analysis of her drinking episodes revealed their connection with unexpressed and almost entirely unconscious rage, mostly toward her husband. While she was expressing her rage via her drinking, she maintained an outwardly passive acquiescence to repeated slights and insults from him. She felt devalued in her marriage as if she were a child, and injured and trapped. In this, she appeared to recreate her childhood conflictual relationship with her father. The resulting compromises in her marriage were chronically unsatisfactory and her self-abnegation in her life was juxtaposed with the return of an enraged drive for mastery (with multiple roots) displaced in the compulsion to drink. She continued to drink intermittently through the first year of analysis. The following material from that year illustrates the compulsive nature of her drinking with its requirement of displacement.

Two months into her analysis, she reported drinking for the first time in several weeks. She said, "I had no time with [her husband] Marty; I'm angry about that. He's spending a lot of time with [a visiting female cousin]. I'm jealous; he never took off time from work for me. I felt relieved when I made a drink – it felt good. But when I was drinking it, I can't say I felt better. I can't say it's a pleasurable thing because it's really not, but there's some part of me that wants the drink." She then described having another drink, and added, "It's an obsession, it's not because it's pleasurable." She finished by saying, "Now I feel, 'you've had your fling, now you've got to get back on track.'" In this hour, she described her drinking as driven and a relief but not pleasurable, similar to compulsions in general.

In a number of following hours she spoke of her anger with her husband. She said, "If I don't deal with the anger I drink or I explode, You'd think my feeling good when I succeed in not drinking would reinforce not drinking, but then something happens and [referring to her staying up late drinking] I need space and time to do what I want to do." A bit later, she told me that she had called to complain about excessive demands on her time by the local PTA, something she noted she would never have done in the past. When she did this, she did not drink.

Soon after these hours and while she was still not drinking she developed a new transient symptom, a parapraxis. She said that Marty had given her a letter to mail but would not tell her who it was for or why it was important. Although it very soon was clear that she was furious at the thought that he was treating her like a child, she had not recognized her anger at the time. She had (instead) dropped the letter and lost it. When she later found it, she lost it again. As we explored the determinants of this she said, "I should have torn up the envelope." The situation here was just like those in which she had felt compelled to drink, but she instead developed a new symptom to manage her unconscious rage. The analysis of her parapraxis and the analogy between this and her drinking helped clarify how her addictive behavior was similar to other unconsciously determined symptoms.

A week later, again speaking of her drinking, she said, "It's something I can do." She began to speak of how unreasonably angry and cold her father would become and how much Marty was like him. Two hours later she spoke of how "automatic" was her drinking, how driven from within, and she associated to antecedents of this drivenness in childhood frustrations in which she wouldn't dare to express an opinion that differed from what was expected. These hours, in which she associated easily from her alcoholism to the emotions in her present and her past life suggest how completely the analysis of her drinking was integrated into her analysis as a whole.

She became more aware of the function of her drinking as a displacement of her rage, and the relief she experienced from drinking as a sign that it served to repair her sense of helplessness to act in forbidden ways. She eventually could say of her drinking, "I'm tired of appeasing Marty.... I want to say to him 'I don't want to do what *you* want any more.... Drinking is something you're not going to take away from me.'" Here she was consciously referring to her husband, but the transferential meaning of her statements was rising to the surface.

Not long after, she canceled an hour and in the following session began to speak of how hard it was to come in for analytic hours. She said the struggle to come in was like the struggle over whether to drink and that she "gave in" to staying home. I wondered with her whether she didn't "give in," but rather she triumphed. In response she said, "Yes! I felt that I took control of my life. I didn't want to come!" She laughed briefly. I said that this seemed a nervous laugh, nervous about her taking the control she was talking about. She said, "I *am* nervous about taking control, even if the control is an escape. It made me feel good to decide not to come. *It wasn't a good decision but it was a decision*." I underlined the importance of this statement. I said that she often felt she wasn't empowered to make the decisions, and that the significant point she was making was that the decision was *hers*, regardless of whether it was "good" or not. I added that the importance of making a decision of her own for herself applied to both staying at home and to drinking.

A short time later, she missed several hours. When she returned the next week, she said, "I hate coming four times a week. I resent it; I hate dealing with my problem. When I call and say I can't come in, I feel I'm in control." I agreed. She said, "I feel out of control when I come in.... What's the point of coming when I'm so upset? Why?" She raised her voice at that point, something she rarely did, then said, "I don't want to come here and yell." I asked her why not. She said, "Because I need to be in control, not overwhelmed, not crazy.... Why do you want a pressure cooker person?" She began having a series of dreams about her husband leaving her, a part of whose meaning (in addition to its transference relevance) was her wish to be rid of him as she became increasingly aware of her anger. Characteristically, the wish was expressed in her dreams as his acting upon her rather than her acting upon her own unacceptable feelings. The following hour she spoke of alcohol not being enjoyable, but said, "Just the idea of someone taking it away makes me panicked."

Her drinking continued intermittently, but she reported that her husband had noticed a change in her attitude and behavior with him. It appeared that her drinking, as with any compulsion, might not be fully eradicated until the deeper roots of her neurosis were analyzed. However, her addictive behavior was no longer a mystery to her, as its function as a displacement of her rage associated with conflictually self-imposed helplessness was made clear.

Discussion

1   For all of history, addictions have been separated from other forms of psycho-logical symptomatology because of the belief that addictions had to do with the effect of drugs: their physical properties or the allure of physiological pleasure that was magnetically attractive to hedonistic people. Understanding that addiction is neither more nor less than a psychological symptom com-prehensible in ordinary psychological terms, and having nothing to do with the physiology of drugs or the notion that addiction is a search for pleasure, allows addiction and its treatment to be included with every other aspect of human emotional life.

In particular, addictions have been separated from compulsions (in spite of their obvious similarities) because addictions have been seen as ego-syntonic – actions people wanted to do – whereas compulsions have been seen as ego-dystonic – things people wish they didn't feel the urge to do. But addictions regularly become ego-dystonic over time, as we know, and com-pulsions may become ego-syntonic: people accept or even value compulsive behavior. People who are pleased with their compulsive neatness are one example. Beyond this, in practice, addictions and compulsions often trans-form into each other, as in the case of people who stop their ego-syntonic use of drugs only to find that they now suffer with a compulsive need to clean the house which is unwanted and ego-syntonic (cf. Dodes, 2002). Ego-syntonicity is simply a superficial quality that ought to have never separated some symptoms from others.

The error of thinking addictions are searches for pleasure has added to moralizing about them, as well as leading to the view of people with addic-tions as psychologically sicker than people with ego-dystonic compulsive behavior. From a psychoanalytic standpoint, this separation of compulsions and addictions has been fostered by a view that compulsions represent a compromise formation, like other neurotic symptomatology, but addictions do not. Even when the field moved from viewing addictions as the unbridled search for pleasure in people with limited characters, to realizing that they could be seen as ego functions, there was no clear recognition that addic-tions, like compulsions, exist precisely because of an internal compromise. They are a compromise between the need to directly act and inhibition of taking a direct action to satisfy a wish or drive. For example, Wurmser's description of addiction as freeing oneself from the tyranny of an archaic superego can be understood as reversal of the helplessness imposed by superego constraints on the ego or self, yet simultaneously an incapacity to fully overthrow the superego by taking a direct action. The compromise is seen in the displacement that creates the "addictive" (compulsive) behavior, in this case displacing a rebellion against the superego to a distant act.

The mechanism of addiction I am describing applies equally to situations of overwhelming helplessness arising from the other areas highlighted by psychoanalytic theorists: loss of relationships (leading to a compulsive search for an object substitute), loss of needed grandiosity or a needed omnipotent object (leading to a compulsive search to feel re-empowered via a symbolic triumph, as in winning a bet, or a completely controllable affective state via a drug), affective flooding, and so on. The compromise in these cases is often required by inhibition of a forbidden rage toward those who have abandoned the person, or incapacity to bear grief, among other possibilities. This compromise is identical to that seen in compulsive acts, in which a seemingly incomprehensible repetitive action is a displacement from forbidden direct expression.

The important treatment implication of the sameness of addictions and compulsions is that people with addictions are as amenable to psychoanalysis or psychodynamic therapy as anyone else (Dodes, 2003). The suitability of any one person for psychoanalysis depends on his or her overall suitability for psychoanalysis. As always, it is the capacity to do psychoanalytic work that is the criterion for suitability, not the form of an individual's symptomatology.

2   While there is an inherent narcissistic fragility in people suffering with an addiction, as shown by their narcissistically enraged reaction to certain situations of helplessness, it is important to recognize that those suffering with addictions do not, as a group, have a narcissistic personality disorder. The degree of fragility in people with addictions is often restricted to the areas that produce the addictive symptom. The presence of an addiction symptom is therefore independent of overall character. People with addictions run the gamut of mental health and are no different from those with any other "choice" of symptom. Since addictions may be understood to be a subset of compulsions, it is unsurprising that like compulsions, they may be present within any character structure or level of emotional function.

3   The rage that accompanies narcissistic traumatization has been well-described by Kohut (1972). In my view, his description explains the most defining characteristics of addiction. He wrote that narcissistic rage is set apart from other forms of aggression by its "deeply anchored, unrelenting compulsion" (p. 380), its "utter disregard for reasonable limitations" (p. 382), and its "boundless" qualities (p. 382). These characteristics are identical to those that describe addiction. There is also a characteristic loss of ego autonomy in both narcissistic rage and addiction. (This loss coexists with the active functioning of unconscious elements of the ego, i.e., the psychological mechanism I've described. It is the coexistence of elements of function and

loss of function that results in the paradox of simultaneously seeking control, psychologically, while being out of control in external behavior and conscious experience.) Kohut further pointed out that "narcissistic rage enslaves the ego and allows it to function only as its tool and rationalizer" (p. 387), and that in chronic narcissistic rage "conscious and preconscious ideation, in particular as it concerns the aims and goals of the personality, becomes more and more subservient to the pervasive rage" (p. 396). Substituting "addiction" for "narcissistic rage" in these statements creates a perfect description of the acute and chronic addicted state. This is not a coincidence, as in my view it is narcissistic rage (at overwhelming helplessness) that gives to addiction its most salient features.

4   Awareness of the role of displacement in creating addictive behaviors assists both patients and therapists in tracking changing symptoms during treatment. When shifts occur from one addictive focus to another, both patient and therapist can understand what is happening and not fall into the error of assigning a new diagnosis.

Further treatment implications

Referring "out"

Because addictions are as suitable for psychoanalytic or psychodynamic treatment as any other compulsive behavior, it is almost always a mistake to refer patients with addictions to outside "addiction counselors" for auxiliary treatment. A well-trained psychotherapist who is familiar with the nature of addiction as discussed earlier, is the best person to treat most people suffering with addictions. Few of the treaters who call themselves addiction counselors are well-trained in human psychology, making their approach unhelpful or even potentially destructive of psychotherapy. Despite this, sometimes highly competent psychoanalysts and other therapists send patients elsewhere. One reason is they underestimate their ability to treat the symptom. But another common factor is countertransference negative feelings about "addicts." Keeping in mind the psychology of addiction as I've described is an aid to managing or even eliminating such countertransference.

Referring out has several unintended consequences. It gives patients the message that their addiction is different and unrelated to the rest of their emotional lives, undermining their understanding of it. It gives patients the message (whether countertransferentially accurate or not) that the therapist views addictions as something repulsive, or beneath their consideration. By extension, this means to patients that they are repulsive. Referring treatment of an addiction to others also critically loses the valuable opportunity to work with the precipitants of addictive thoughts, the factors that arouse feelings of overwhelming helplessness, which are always central to the psychology of the whole person.

Although it should not be necessary to say, it is of course never appropriate to refuse to treat a person until they stop their addictive behavior. This is as absurd as telling patients they must stop being depressed before they can be treated for their depression. The single exception to this rule occurs when people need to be medically treated, e.g., by detoxification, before they can begin therapy.

A corollary is that continued addictive behavior should be expected during therapy, just as other symptoms recur in the midst of treatment. Beside the fact that addictive thoughts or actions are important opportunities to improve understanding of the emotional factors behind addiction (including factors in the transference), treatment simply does not depend on sobriety. (Clearly, in an emergency the therapy must be placed on hold. A person who is continuously drinking may need a brief hospitalization for detoxification, for instance.). Termination is decided on the same basis as for any patient: assessment of progress in the work of psychological growth and of the likelihood of continued benefit.

While an exploratory, not judgmental or policing approach should be taken, including exploration of the key moments when addictive thoughts recur, it must be remembered that some patients may perceive lack of pressure to stop their behavior as a failure to care about them. Therapists must be alert to this possibility and take it up with patients, as an important and useful area to explore. In some cases, a therapist's not pressuring or policing a patient may need to be explicitly discussed to prevent development of an unspoken negative transference based on a perception that the therapist does not care enough to protect the patient.

Denial

A common difficulty encountered in treating people with addictive behavior is their minimization, or complete denial, of the severity of their symptom. It is important to appreciate that people with addictions are no less able to view reality than anyone else. "Denial" reflects just a defensive position, against shame, or against a (projected) expectation of judgment by others, or against a perceived threat to continuing an addicted behavior that is felt to be needed. It is often useful, therefore, to explain to patients that at the heart of addiction is a healthy core; a need to protect against utter helplessness, which is normal and essential. As an example, I sometimes note that those people who survive best when faced with literal helplessness, as in concentration camps, are those who find a way to maintain some sense of autonomy and power, by subtle forms of resistance or other means. But those who passively accept their helplessness become depressed, and some die. Hence, the only problem with addictive behavior is that it is not a good way to express that healthy drive. (This is a way of phrasing the displacement nature of addiction.)

Approaching patients this way, explaining the healthy core of addiction, is both a help against shame as well as evidence that the therapist is genuinely not judgmental about addiction. With this approach, my experience is that "denial" often disappears. It is as though patients say, "If my addiction is just a basically healthy response to feeling trapped, then there is no need to deny it. Sure, I've got *that*."

Informing patients of a psychological view of addiction may also assuage patients' expectation, and fear, that this therapy will be like others they've had, and that like those, their behavior will become the narrow focus of the therapist ("Let's keep a record of each drink and see if we can get that number down!"). I do not suggest lecturing patients, but people with addictions often have strong preconceptions based on previous experience with counselors as well as the pre-dominant social stereotype and views associated with 12-step programs, that can interfere with viewing their behavior psychologically.

Diagnosis

From a psychological standpoint, diagnosis usually depends on the intrapsychic factors behind behavior rather than the behavior itself. Sometimes, people have excessive and harmful behavior that is not an addiction, though it looks like one. For example, adolescents may take drugs in a repetitive, excessive, and dangerous way but for non-compulsive/addictive reasons, such as striving to be accepted as a member of a peer group, or expressing autonomy and defiance as part of development. The way to accurately diagnose an addiction is to investigate the precipitant to episodes of the behavior. If the behavior is an effort to manage the kind of power-less feelings I've described – i.e., it is a compulsive symptom – it is reasonable to describe the behavior as a true addiction. Making the diagnosis allows appropriate treatment decisions. A person with non-addiction reasons for repetitive hazardous behavior will need a different approach than someone with a true addiction (for a discussion of non-addictive causes of repeated excessive behavior, see Dodes, 2002).

Viewing addiction as a psychological symptom avoids the trend to label people with several diagnoses just because they have several displacements. The term "dual diagnosis" also no longer makes sense when it is used to mean a combination of anxiety, depression, and addictive behavior. Clearly, these are all connected with each other and their connection is exactly what is important for patients to understand for their overall treatment and for treatment of their addiction. "Dual diagnosis" is a reasonable term to apply to people whose compulsive or addictive symptoms exist simultaneously with a genuinely separate biological diagnosis such as schizophrenia or bipolar disorder.

An example

Psychotherapy or psychoanalytic treatment must address addictive symptomatol-ogy at the same time as addressing everything else about the individual. In this work, it is helpful to focus attention backwards in time from the earliest moment that a thought or urge toward an addictive act occurs. This moment of feeling powerless obviously precedes the addictive action, and may have occurred hours or occasionally days before the act is performed. Over time, patients, and their therapists, can become extremely good at recognizing this issue and using it to predict future addictive urges (many case illustrations of this, involving multiple foci of addictive behavior, are described in the books previously cited (Dodes, 2002, 2011) and elsewhere (Tepper et al., 2006)).

It is clear from the displacement nature of addictions that if a more direct action can be taken to reverse overwhelmingly powerless feelings, there would no longer be an emotional need for the addictive act. Discussing and discovering possible more direct ways to manage the helplessness behind addictive urges is very often helpful in treatment. It is not only practical, but exploring these options opens up investigation of the reasons (inhibitions, fears, fantasies) for not pursuing them. With awareness of how their addiction works in them, patients often come up with their own ways to manage addictive urges well before the underlying issues are worked out. Here is a brief example (excerpted from Dodes, 2002):

Clinical vignette 5

M was a woman who subserviently followed her husband's orders, often followed by taking Percodan she kept for that purpose. On one occasion, her husband called her to say he was bringing home a group of business associates for dinner, and directed her to prepare a fancy meal, something she hated. She reported that she meekly agreed, as usual. Immediately upon hanging up she felt a nearly overwhelming compulsion to take some of her pills. At this point in her treatment she had reached a good understanding of her emotional pattern of use and had, in fact, been able to turn down a request to manage the cash register at a forthcoming PTA event. But this was not the PTA, and she could not bring herself to call back her husband and tell him she was not going to entertain anyone that evening. However, she came up with a solution that I heard about at our next appointment.

"I didn't use any Percodans," she said with some pride, after she had told me about the conversation with her husband.

"How did you do it?"

"Well, I knew I had no chance to stay out of the medicine cabinet if I didn't do something about the damned dinner. Then I thought of it: Why should I make the dinner? I called up a Chinese restaurant and ordered take-out! As soon as I did it, the urge to use the pills just vanished!" She smiled a little, then looked serious. "I know I have to do better for myself," she said. "But I didn't use any drugs."

In this example, the patient was well aware that doing "better" for herself would have meant taking a more direct action, such as her initial thought of calling back her husband and refusing to comply with his order. But in finding a more direct action, even if not the most direct one, to undo the intolerable helplessness she felt, she did not need the usual displacement. Over time, she would need to work through her need to place herself in such a belittling relationship, but for the time being she regained control of the addiction symptom that had been part of her maladaptation.

Concluding remarks

Addictions are neither more nor less than psychological symptoms, a subset of those we call compulsions. This simple fact has been misunderstood throughout human history, for several reasons. Primary has been the obvious physiological effects of drugs. Until the advent of modern psychology, physical effects of drugs were thought to explain addiction, when coupled with moralistic views of human behavior. People did harmful things to others, therefore they must be bad. The drugs they use make people feel high, so addicts must be seeking that high: they're hedonists. They can't control themselves, therefore they are psychologically primitive. Sadly, the notion that people with addictions are seeking pleasure has recurred in modern form in the widely popularized neurobiological idea that addiction is a form of reward-seeking. That view is completely incompatible with clinical facts (for instance, soldiers with heroin addiction in Vietnam were found to not use heroin again when they returned home. According to the popular "chronic brain disease" view, they should have developed a chronic neurobiological disease and not been able to stop [see Robins et al., 1975]. Likewise, patients placed on high-dose narcotics for pain ought to all become addicts, and nobody ought to be able to stop addictive behavior with talking treatment). But between wishes to explain addiction in non-psychological terms, and popular ideas that it is a spiritual disease, even well-trained psychotherapists have often failed to appreciate that they are the best people to treat people with this common symptom, so long as they understand how it works.

Notes

1 Compulsions with a psychological origin, including addictions, must be distinguished from the repetitive behavior produced by the biological entity, "Obsessive-Compulsive Disorder."
2 The clinical vignettes in this chapter have been excerpted from earlier publications of the author: Clinical vignette numbers 1 and 2 from Dodes (1990), numbers 3 and 4 from Dodes (1996), and number 5 from Dodes (2002).

Six syndromes

Chapter 2

Food addiction

Nina Savelle-Rocklin

People who binge or relentlessly overeat often believe that food is the problem. They describe themselves as "chocoholics" or "foodaholics" and fear they will always struggle with what they call an "addiction" to food. Many report that they never consume sugar or white flour. They think the only way to stay "clean" (as they put it) is to avoid all problematic or forbidden foods. Inevitably, they binge or overeat, experiencing intense feelings of shame and labeling themselves as hopeless addicts.

Yet, is food addiction a valid concept? In the last few years, there has been a great deal of media coverage of this topic. Last year, I posted in a public Facebook group that with respect to binge-eating, psychological triggers are far more influential than the food itself. One reader took offense, writing that it was "a proven fact" that sugar is as addictive as heroin. This person is not alone in her hyperbolic assertion that sugar and heroin are equivalent. Lately it seems that the notion of food addiction, especially sugar addiction, is accepted by the general public as scientifically factual, as is the idea of "detoxing" from sugar. This notion of detoxification is also false, since any food eaten, even pure protein sources, can be turned into sugar in the body through the process of gluconeo-genesis, a metabolic pathway that results in glucose being generated from non-carbohydrate foods.

The premise of a recent bestseller (Taubes, 2016) is that sugar is not only addictive, but is the principal cause of obesity, diabetes, coronary heart disease, and many other fatal diseases. This book and others (Jacoby and Baldelomar, 2016; Zinczenko and Perrine, 2016) assert that sugar is poisoning us, making us obese and unhealthy. Studies from the fields of neurology and obesity research have come to divergent conclusions. Some researchers (Spring et al., 2008; Avena et al., 2008; Corsica and Pelchat, 2010) believe that food may be considered addictive. These studies make a case for the reward theory of food addiction (Gearhardt et al., 2009; Volkow et al., 2013) correlating specific foods with increased dopamine levels. Dopamine is the chemical that mediates pleasure and motivation in our brains. The basic theory of food addiction is that sugar and other foods activate the release of dopamine. People eat sugar, get a dopamine rush and feel good, and then have to eat increasing amounts to get the same experience they previously felt with less. Food addiction theory points to these changes in the brain, specifically higher levels of dopamine, as evidence of addiction.

A plethora of other studies, though, refute these claims (Albayrak et al., 2012; Ziauddeen et al., 2012; Ziauddeen and Fletcher 2013; Pressman et al., 2015; Westwater et al., 2016), deducing that there is little evidence to support the idea of any food as physiologically addictive, including sugar, which is the substance most often labeled as addictive. Nutrition researcher and neurobiologist, Stephan Guyenet (2017), reminds us that diet and lifestyle factors such as excess calorie intake, physical inactivity, cigarette smoking, alcohol, and illegal drug use contribute to obesity and other noncommunicable diseases. He further notes that these diseases are not all correlated with sugar intake, and points out that sugar intake has actually been declining in the past two decades, the same period in which both obesity and diabetes rates have dramatically increased.

Sugar does change our brains, as do certain drugs. Spending time with friends, playing games, having sex, shopping, and any other pleasurable activity also raises the dopamine levels in our brains. One study proved that listening to classical music has the same impact on our brains as cocaine (Salimpoor, 2011). Our brains also react differently to sugar than to drugs like cocaine or heroin. In research studies with rodents who were given cocaine (Di Chiara, 2005; Avena et al., 2008) their dopamine levels surged but did not return to baseline. The rodents needed more and more of the drug to maintain the baseline dopamine levels. That is not what happens with sugar or any other hyper-palatable or so-called "addictive" foods. After ingesting sugar, dopamine levels surge, yet later return to a baseline level and stay consistent.

Also, the studies that confirm that rats show more addictive behavior for sugar than for drugs such as cocaine and heroin are misleading. Humans are motivated by psychology as well as biology, but rats are motivated by survival. Rats do not turn to food to soothe hurt feelings, to numb themselves or distract from the painful exigencies of life. Rats are primarily food-seeking, and sugar is food. Naturally, they choose sugar over drugs like heroin or cocaine. Benton (2009) examines the animal model of sugar addiction and finds it baseless, deducing that there is no support for the notion of sugar as addictive.

Margaret Westwater and her colleagues (2016) also find little evidence to support sugar addiction in humans. They suggest that "addiction-like behaviours, such as bingeing, occur only in the context of intermittent access to sugar. These behaviours likely arise from (intermittent access) to sweet tasting or highly palatable foods, not the neurochemical effects of sugar" (p. 1). Westwater also differentiates between sugar per se, on its own, and sugary foods, which usually contain fat. She makes the point that most people do not eat spoonsful of sugar, but rather have food that contains sugar. The researchers also note the difference between cravings for food and for drugs. "Food cravings are relatively short-lived and subside with fasting as opposed to drug cravings, which persist and do not lessen in intensity with abstinence" (p. 65).

Similarly, another study (Marcus et al., 2017) concludes,

> Sugar does not seem to contribute to weight-gain more so than other sources of energy in the diet. Instead, the current scientific community nowadays seems to reach consensus that "food addiction" (and its role in weight gain) might be better explained by "eating dependence" as a result of the unique individual experience with food and eating (instead of being caused by a specific food).
>
> (p. 70)

Of course, self-described food addicts do not always identify sugar as their "drug" of choice. In the same study that refuted sugar as an addictive substance, Markus and his colleagues identified the types of foods that are most commonly associated with addiction-like behavior. Their research showed that "high-fat savory" foods are more likely to trigger addiction-like behavior. In fact, only one person in 20 reported addiction-like behavior for "mainly sugar-containing" foods. People have cravings for various types of food, some craving chocolate and others pizza, and they may find it difficult to eat those foods in appropriate quantities, yet that does not constitute a physical addiction. There are other reasons for this inability to stop eating a particular food. There is also a link between dieting and binge-eating (Polivy and Herman, 1985; Polivy et al., 2005). When people rely on willpower, telling themselves they cannot or should not eat a particular food, they are more likely to binge on that food later. Sometimes this is because deprivation leads to wanting more of what they cannot have, and sometimes it is a means of managing anticipated future deprivation. Many patients have said something along the lines of, "I'm going to eat this whole pizza, because after this I won't be able to eat pizza for months." Additionally, there is a link between the anticipation of dieting and binge-eating (Urbszat et al., 2002). The anticipation of deprivation of specific foods, as well as the actual deprivation experienced through restriction or dieting, therefore leads to overeating or bingeing. This highlights the importance of unconscious psychological motivations with regard to bingeing.

Clinical vignette I

Ruth, 45, considered herself a food addict. She felt discouraged by her lack of control over food at night. Single, never married, and relatively new to the Los Angeles area, she had not formed any meaningful friendships in the area. Nor was she dating, believing that nobody would be attracted to her at her current weight.

Ruth easily made healthy choices at breakfast and lunch. Only in the evening, when she was home by herself, did food become a problem. She described how in those dark hours, an emptiness came upon her, slowly expanding until it was an unbearable void. When we explored that internal void, she spoke of a childhood marked by desperate loneliness, and I had the sense of her being enveloped by forlornness. But Ruth was not interested in talking about the past. From her perspective, the problem was in the here-and-now. I suggested that it was not a matter of control; I believed that her relationship to food was expressing something that her mind could not process or tolerate. When she was alone at night, she felt the echoes of that childhood loneliness and emptiness. By stuffing herself until she was full, she symbolically filled that emotional void with food, unconsciously swapping emotional emptiness for a full stomach. Instead of feeling emotionally uncomfortable, she experienced only the physical sensation of discomfort.

Ruth had been focusing on what she was eating instead of identifying and processing what was eating "at" her. The problem was not food, but rather her intense emotional hunger. Ruth looked dazed at this notion. "So, I'm not a food addict?" She considered this and sighed in relief. "All this time I thought there was something wrong with my brain that made me eat."

We are in the midst of a cultural zeitgeist that increasingly privileges biology over psychology, and this extends to research in binge-eating. One recent study (Kessler et al., 2016) finds that binge-eating disorder "may be related to maladaptation of the corticostriatal circuitry regulating motivation and impulse control similar to that found in other impulsive/compulsive disorders" (p. 223). I believe this view of disordered eating as a brain-based illness is myopic. Yes, we have brains, the organ that is the physical control structure of our bodies, but we also have *minds*, which refers to a range of mental processes. Our minds allow us to think, feel, imagine, believe, remember, and perceive, on both a conscious and unconscious level. Our brains do not operate alone, nor do our minds function independently of our brains. Research that focuses exclusively on the brain as the primary source of the behavior ignores the powerful influences of the unconscious mind, as well as the familial, social, cultural, and other influences that impact our brains. People turn to food for a reason – for comfort, to alleviate anxiety, to distract from painful or upsetting thoughts, to sleep, symbolically fill a void, or calm down. Eating is a way of managing difficult internal states. It's the mind's way of protecting itself.

Another reader who responded to my Facebook post about the importance of psychological motives related to binge-eating shared that she had initially joined the "sugar is like heroin" message, which she believed actually caused her to binge on sugar, further reinforcing the idea that she was an addict. Then she noticed that her children had no problem eating sugar, "sometimes in small amounts, sometimes larger, and sometimes they couldn't care less about it, and I realized I was the exact same way when I didn't try to restrict it. I cautiously began allowing myself to have it, and it hasn't been a problem and I finally feel empowered around it, instead of like a scared victim" (Facebook post, personal communication, 2018). She further noted that when she started allowing herself pleasurable activities through the day, then, "bingo, sugar wasn't a thought."

This aligns with my clinical experience treating individuals who struggle with binge-eating. Most enter treatment believing themselves to be sugar addicts, unable to keep cookies, candy, ice cream, or anything with sugar in the house, lest they consume it all. By the time they leave therapy, they are able to eat sugary foods in moderation, often without giving it another thought. Their brains have not changed, but their minds have undergone a structural transformation. Of course, the science makes little difference to patients who experience intense powerlessness and helplessness over their eating, and are preoccupied with food, often to the point of obsession. They eliminate what they consider forbidden foods, only to end up bingeing and feeling terrible. As one patient put it, "I may not be addicted to food but I sure feel like an addict."

When it comes to eating issues, food actually serves as a temporary solution to the problem. Only by decoding the symbolism of eating and identifying the underlying conflict or deficit that is leading to the behavior, can permanent change be created. From this vantage point, the psychoanalytic perspective can be helpful and transformative.

An historical perspective of addictions

Early psychoanalytic theory offered what Khantzian (1995) deemed a "collective unempathic if not pejorative view of addicts" (p. 17. Classical theory viewed addicts as driven solely by pleasure, linking addiction with the gratification of frustrated drives (Glover, 1932; Radó, 1933). Problems in the early oral stages of development, which roughly corresponds to the first year of life, were seen as inhibiting the ability of addicts to deal with frustration. Glover (1932) noted that drug addiction serves defensive functions, such as "to control sadistic charges, which, though less violent than those associated with paranoia, are more severe than the sadistic charges met with in obsessional formations" (p. 315) and to protect against psychotic reactions during times of regression. Around the same time, Radó (1933) writes that, "not the toxic agent, but the impulse to use it, makes an addict of a given individual" (p. 2). In his earlier writings, Radó (1926) views addicts as having poor frustration tolerance, which leads them to drugs and alcohol as a way of re-experiencing what he called the "alimentary orgasm" (p. 408) and avoiding depression. This "alimentary orgasm" refers to a general feeling of well-being throughout the body, an experience that originates at the mother's breast, since feeding is bound up with a blissful sense of security and warmth. Radio suggests that ingestion of narcotics recapitulates this experience, which addicts prefer to give to themselves by taking drugs rather than depending on another person.

By the mid-century, the psychoanalytic view of addiction had evolved to include broader, less pathologizing perspectives. Addicts were no longer viewed from a drive theory perspective of being pleasure seeking. Instead, they turned to drugs and alcohol as a means of self-regulation, whether to manage painful affects, including aggression (Khantzian, 1974) and anxiety (Goldstein, 1972). Krystal and Raskin (1970) posit that addicts use drugs as object substitutes. Thus, by the 1970s, drug addiction was commonly seen either as a defensive strategy to deal with painful affects or a way of compensating for internal conflicts or self-esteem issues. Wurmser (1974) considers all habitual drug use an attempt at self-treatment. In speaking of the addict, he states, "The importance of the effect of the drug in the inner life of these patients can perhaps be best explained as an *artificial or surrogate defense against overwhelming affects* (original italics)" (p. 829). Similarly, Khantzian (2003) proposes that taking drugs is a means of self-medicating, viewing addiction as a way of soothing painful and upsetting psychological states. He proposes that substance users experience dysphoric emotions as intolerable and overwhelming, and that they cannot manage these emotional states on their own, using drugs to calm themselves. Interestingly, in writing about the nature of addiction, Kohut (1978) compares it to the digestive process. He writes:

> It is as if a person with a wide-open gastric fistula were trying to still his hunger through eating. He may obtain pleasurable taste sensations by his frantic ingestion of food, but, since the food does not enter the part of the digestive system that absorbs it into the organism, he continues to starve.
>
> (pp. 846–847)

The latter twentieth century brought an innovative idea about addiction proposed by Dodes (1990, 1995, 1996, 2002, 2003), who suggests that all addictions are motivated by the state of helplessness and powerlessness. He says that addictive behavior represents a displaced way of dealing with helplessness, as well as a means of expressing the anger engendered by that state of helplessness. He concludes that all addictions have the characteristics of compulsions. Dodes states:

> Rather than being a reflection of impulsivity or self-destructiveness, or a result of genetic or physical factors, addiction can be shown to be a psychological mechanism that is a subset of psychological compulsions in general. Addictive urges are never random, and when one understands the emotional factors that produce them, addiction can be mastered.
>
> (personal communication, Dodes, May 21, 2017)

Helplessness is an experience that most people find unbearable, as it is associated with vulnerability and may also bring up conflicts about dependency. Dodes believes that helplessness triggers an addictive behavior as a way of reversing the helplessness. Whatever the behavior, whether it is drinking alcohol, taking drugs, gambling, working too much, or excessive shopping, or bingeing, that becomes what we call the addiction: alcoholism, drug addiction, gambling, workaholism, shopping addiction, food addiction.

Inherent in the state of helplessness is an unconscious rage at the very state of being helpless. Dodes (1995) describes how addiction is a response to the narcissistic rage that the state of helplessness produces. Whatever the form of addiction, it provides "a sense of internal emotional control" (p. 133) sufficient to temporarily give a sense of mastery over one's helplessness. In a thorough explication of the analytic experience of helplessness, Hoffer and Buie (2016) point out that anger is an active state, whereas helplessness is passive. In my work with eating disorder patients, many of whom have binge-eating disorder, I have often been struck by the viciousness with which they attack themselves. Many become enraged with themselves for overeating, bingeing, or weighing too much, and castigate themselves in a notably vituperative manner. This can be understood as displaced anger to avoid the passivity of helplessness. Bingeing or any other addictive behavior is a way of undoing the passivity of helplessness, and the anger at one's helpless state can also be turned against the self.

Food addiction

Specifically with respect to food, the notion of addiction was first described by Glover (1925) in his exploration of the oral character. He observes that gratification in the form of overeating is often followed by some sort of physical pain, implying that bingeing implicitly provides the pleasure of indulgence and simultaneously gives the pain of self-punishment. Glover notes, "In more extreme addictions, the punishment system is rarely based on injurious effects alone and the necessity for assuaging guilt by the disapproval of actual objects is most marked. In the case of more larval indulgences, the addiction is to what is generally recognized as a food and the injury or individual consequences, e.g., a bilious attack, seem to meet the necessity for punishment" (pp. 148–149). In later writings (1932), Glover mentions what he refers to as an "ingestion compulsion" (p. 317) and gives an example of a patient who relieved boredom and depression by eating steak-pie, beer, and reading a newspaper.

Fenichel (1945) was the first psychoanalytic writer to use the term "food addiction." He writes (1946) that food addiction manifests for varying reasons, depending on the addict's level of development. For some, "no displacement has transformed the original object (food) of the strivings for simultaneous gratification of sexuality and self-esteem" (p. 381). Individuals attribute vastly different unconscious meanings to food and for some, eating is the only thing that connects a person to reality. This fits the experience of one of my patients who regularly binged to the point of being stuffed and uncomfortable. She mused that being so full was quite reassuring, as if by feeling her stomach press out against the confines of her skin, she could feel a sense of being there, as if, "my skin was hugging me."

Wulf (1932) describes several female patients who regularly experienced periods of intense overeating with those of fasting or normal behavior with food. All these women would eat "compulsively," and then be suffused with self-disgust. Wulf views this as a form of depression in which a person experiences a loss of love, followed by an eating addiction and then turns against the self. He sees the desperate eating as, "a regression phenomenon and attempt to restore object relations to the most primitive oral level" (p. 294). Eating is thus a way of unconsciously enacting a fantasy of incorporation, embedded in which is a simultaneous wish to exterminate the object; for others, eating symbolizes an erotic activity and a substitute for actual object relationships.

Linn (1953), in discussing orality and the mechanism of denial, suggests that some patients use food, and/or other substances, to induce a dreamlike, blank state, in which perception and memory are impaired, as a means of returning to the earlier, blissful state of infancy. He suggests that the satiety that an infant experienced is followed by a deep, pleasurable relaxation. "The pleasure which accompanies satiety in infant feeding is followed by relaxation, and a sleepiness which culminates finally in postprandial sleep. In this sleepy, contented state, old narcissistic hurts are forgotten. Bad memories are denied. Only good memories and affects hold sway" (p. 703). He proposes that adult patients use eating to create this post-feeding relaxation as a means of denying their trauma, and remaining in a state of "clouded consciousness" (p. 703), along the lines of Radó's (1926) "alimentary orgasm."

Other views of addictive behavior with food are similar to the mainstream psychoanalytic understanding of drug and alcohol addiction, which is that the behavior serves as a way of managing intense affects (McDougall, 1984). Wurmser and Zients (1982) propose that overeaters lack a compassionate superego, which ideally functions as protector, soother, and caregiver. Food takes the place of such an internal protective object, as does alcohol and/or drugs. When there is a prohibition against self-soothing, or an inability to give oneself comfort, food is experienced as an external object that provides care, much in the same way that drugs function as an object substitute (Krystal, 1982).

Binge-eating provides many functions, including serving as a means of self-soothing, filling a symbolic void, dissociating, converting emotional pain to physical pain, creating a symbolic reunion with objects, and providing a sense of mastery over an unpredictable world. When the reasons for their behavior with food are elucidated and the underlying conflicts worked through by the process of psychoanalysis or psychoanalytically informed therapy, patients are able to relinquish these problematic behaviors and cultivate a normal relationship to food.

Eating as a means of self-soothing and dissociation

As I have noted earlier, most self-reported food addicts believe they lack willpower and are biochemically addicted to food. In reality they are often struggling with a diagnosable condition known as "binge-eating disorder." "Binge-eating disorder" is the most common type of eating disorder, impacting an estimated eight million people in the United States (ANAD website) alone, and more worldwide. Many of those who fit the diagnostic criteria have no idea that their eating issues represent a symptom of an underlying disorder. Physically, binge-eating disorder patients may or may not be overweight, as the presence of obesity is not in itself an indication of binge-eating disorder. People become overweight or obese for various factors, including poor eating habits and heredity. They may not have the knowledge, ability, or financial resources to prepare nutritious food, or may not get enough exercise. These factors contribute to obesity but are not indications of an eating disorder.

Psychologically, despite differences in gender, age, ethnicity, or socioeconomic level, I find that all the patients I have treated for binge-eating disorder have deficits in self-soothing. From the earliest moments of life, the way we are spoken to, responded to, cared for, and touched form the basis of our relationships to ourselves. Drawing from Winnicott's (1953) conception of the "good enough" mother, when we have parents who are attuned to us, who try to understand our thoughts and emotions, and withstand our anger, we internalize those parental objects and develop a way of relating to ourselves that is optimally responsive. In the absence of the ability to identify with or internalize a loving, soothing presence, some people turn to the symbolic representation of comfort; namely, food. Alexander (cited in Portis, 1946) expresses it well when he writes, "The first relief from physical discomfort the child experiences is during nursing, and thus the satisfaction of hunger becomes deeply associated with the feeling of well-being and security" (p. 826).

In this way, food registers in our psyches as a symbolic representation of the soothing relationship between mother and baby. Notably, we use the same language to describe both food and relationships, describing each as "satisfying" and "fulfilling." Our cultural vernacular includes references that connect food to relationship, such as being "hungry for love" or "starving for attention." When people are unpredictable, unavailable, or unreliable, human connections and relationships can feel too dangerous, yet food is always predictable, available, and reliable. From a self-psychological perspective, "compulsive" eating is, according to Kohut (1984), "an attempt to replace the selfobject (and the transmuting internalization it provides) with food (and the activity of eating)" (p. 20). Sands (1989) discusses how disappointment in interactions with people causes some patients to turn away from human relationships and to turn toward food as a primary means of comfort. In this way, hunger for food essentially replaces hunger for love and connection.

In 1951, Hamburger wrote a paper titled "Emotional Aspects of Obesity" in which he presents four types of female patients who use food for the purpose of self-soothing. Of the 18 participants in Hamburger's study, all had "a history of some type of disturbed intrafamilial relationships in his or her home during the formative years" (p. 167). He describes one group who overeat to relieve nonspecific emotional tensions and a second group who use food as an automatic response to the tensions and frustrations of life. For a third group, overeating functions as a symptom of some underlying psychopathology, conflict, or depression. A fourth group, which he describes as "overeating as an addiction to food" (p. 166) reported uncontrollable cravings for food. Further investigation revealed that these patients used food as a substitute for love, affection, and security.

Turning to food for relief can be so automatic that many patients don't even realize that they are experiencing an emotional trigger or conflict. The activity of bingeing effectively distracts them from recognizing what they are feeling, thinking, needing, or wanting. Compulsive eating may facilitate a dissociative trancelike state that protects from painful or upsetting affects. As Tibon and Roth-schild (2009) put it, "Dissociation is thus considered as serving the patients with binge-eating symptoms, to narrowing thinking and perception of reality while being involved in the binge episode" (p. 70). This fits the description I hear from patients who say they are "in a zone" or "in a food fog" and report an absence of thought and emotion during episodes of compulsive eating. The world fades away, leaving only food and the act of eating, and a temporary sense of safety and protection from the intolerable exigencies of life.

Clinical vignette 2

Hannah, 30 years old, sought treatment for "food addiction" because she was 30 pounds overweight and miserable. She was single, employed in an upper management position at a national real estate firm, yet she felt like a failure because she just could not control her weight. She went on her first diet in early adolescence, after a gymnastics coach suggested she lose a few pounds, a comment she found deeply shaming, and she had been dieting for her entire adult life.

Food was all Hannah thought about, from the second she woke up until the minute her head hit the pillow. At breakfast, she was thinking about lunch. At lunch, she was thinking about dinner. At night, she was worried about what she would eat the next day. Hannah began one session by informing me that she could prove that she was a food addict, that there was nothing emotional or conflictual facilitating her binges. The previous night she had been watching television after work when suddenly, as she put it, "Ben and Jerry's was calling my name." "Calling my name!" she repeated, with emphasis. She told me that nothing was wrong, nothing was bothering her, and that her day had been perfectly fine and free of conflict. Since she was not eating for emotional reasons, she must be addicted to Ben and Jerry's ice cream.

I asked her what she'd been watching on TV, which turned out to be a show called *Charmed*. This was her favorite television program, and she was always happy when she got a chance to relax and watch this show. To Hannah, this was further proof that she was a food addict. She was happy to be relaxing and watching *Charmed*, so there was no reason other than addiction to explain her sudden craving for ice cream. When I asked for details about the episode, she said, "It's the one where the devil comes down and the sisters start fighting and everything gets really nasty, and …"

Her voice trailed. At that moment, Hannah realized that watching the episode of *Charmed* had activated painful thoughts and emotions about her sister, with whom she had a contentious relationship. Yet, before those thoughts and feelings could reach conscious awareness, she turned to Ben and Jerry's for comfort and distraction. Hannah was not turning to ice cream because her brain had formed a physical addiction. She craved Ben and Jerry's ice cream because her mind was looking for a way to escape the anger she felt toward her sister. If we had focused on her "addiction" to ice cream, we would have completely missed her conflict over feeling angry toward her sister, and her resistance to consciously recognizing that anger, along with a concurrent need for punishment for simply having those feelings. Guilt over feelings of hatred toward her sister was thus displaced into guilt for eating ice cream. By exploring the underlying hatred and normalizing her emotional responses and conflicts about her relationship with her sister, Hannah was able to make peace with food instead of using it as a way to dissociate from her affective experience.

Eating as an expression of somatic language

Psychoanalysis evolved from Freud's interest in understanding why, in some circumstances, there is a "mysterious leap" from mind to body. Many of his early patients suffered from hysteria, which was considered a somatic issue until the "talking cure" (Breuer and Freud, 1895) suggested that some kind of conversion was taking place, a shift from psychological to physical. Alexander later (1950) proposed a theory of psychosomatic medicine, which focused on the link between mind and body. Winnicott (1949) originally coined the term "psyche-soma" to propose the idea that the mind and body are not separate but are interrelated. The psyche refers to the mental structure of an individual and the soma refers to his or her physical body. When things go well in early development, infants develop a healthy sense of self and their minds and bodies are felt to be as one. When things do not go well, meaning that feeding leads to the internalization of a good object, the psyche and soma are not experienced as connected, leading to a mind-body split. When there is no unified "self" to provide support, comfort, and relief with words, people may turn to their bodies as a way of expressing their conflicts, needs, wants, and emotions.

Gedo (1997b) describes a developmental sequence in which somatization, the conversion of mental conflict into physical symptoms, serves as both an intrapsychic and interpersonal communication. Although his ideas center on physical symptoms and diseases, the notion of the body as a means of communication can be helpful when understanding people who eat to the point of pain, or whose physical bodies express some kind of fear or intention. Some patients believe their size protects them from sexual interest, and others feel more powerful because of their girth, needing to take up more space in order to feel visible and viable. There are a plethora of meanings embedded in the language of the body, and the size of the body, which must be understood and articulated verbally instead of somatically.

Many patients with eating disorders have great difficulty experiencing anything emotionally painful or depressing. McDougall (1974) notes that such patients often refuse to give in to psychic pain, anguish, or depression. She says, "This gives an impression of superhuman emotional control and is allied, I think, with a pathological ego ideal which refuses need and dependency" (p. 458). When people cannot allow themselves to trust in the basic experience of need and dependency, they may turn instead to food, which is the symbolic representation of nurturing. Others (Tibon and Rothschild, 2009; Target and Fonagy, 1996) suggest that when normal developmental processes do not go well, there is a failure in mentalization, defined as a failure to think about one's thoughts, or to experience mental states as representations. This failure in the ability to mentalize results in thoughts and emotions being experienced instead as physical distress. Eating, which can have a sedative effect, can therefore become a way of coping with anything distressful.

The inability to identify and express emotional states is called "alexythymia," and is common in patients who use food to numb and escape affects. Taylor and Bagby (2013) note that deficits in the ability to recognize and process emotions lead to focusing on the way the body responds to emotions, instead of an expression of those emotions. They also point to the tendency of alexithymic individuals to take physical action when they experience their emotions, such as smoking, binge-eating, or using alcohol and drugs. One patient would say, "I feel water coming into my eyes" but she struggled with the notion that she was emotionally upset.

One of the first psychoanalysts to write extensively about eating disorders, Hilda Bruch (1969), notes that when it comes to the state of hunger, it is important to distinguish between the physiological state of awareness that the body needs nutrition and other meanings, such as the understanding of hunger as "a symbolic expression of a state of need in general, or as a simile for want in other areas" (pp. 129–130). If hunger is a means of representing a state of emotional yearning, as in the common expressions, "hungry for love" and "starving for attention," then bingeing on food or overeating can be understood as an unconscious way of expressing the longing for relational experience. When people do not have access to language to describe what is going on internally, they communicate by other means, including using their bodies as a means of expressing conflict. Rose (2001) discusses several obese patients whose bodies expressed unconscious conflicts and wishes, and observes, "It is the body that 'thinks' out loud the 'feelings' that the mind cannot" (pp. 337–338).

Clinical vignette 3

Marta, 37, sought treatment because nearly every night she ate a family-sized bag of potato chips. She felt completely out of control when it came to chips. Yet, after a few weeks, she reported that she was not eating chips every night. She also was a model patient, showing up on time to every session, working hard to make sense of the concepts we discussed. She read about psychoanalytic principles, and diligently tracked her dreams, her emotions, thoughts, and interactions with others. Several months into the treatment, I went on vacation for a week. Upon my return, Marta shared that she had been upset with me for leaving. She immediately assured me that she was not angry with me and it was, "just the transference talking."

Marta reminded me of a student trying to please the teacher, instead of a patient undergoing analysis. Her parents had been authoritarian and inflexible, insisting that they knew what was best for their children and demanding compliance, rather than showing interest in their children's emotions and thoughts. Marta learned that acquiescence was the key to relational harmony. Only by perceiving what her parents wanted and then submitting, could she assure herself of their acceptance.

Unbeknownst to herself, Marta repeated this dynamic with me. It seemed that she was trying to please me instead of using our sessions to better understand herself. She also did not put herself in a position of vulnerability. Outwardly, she appeared to depend on me, but, actually, she was doing all the thinking and interpreting herself, excluding me in the process. She reported on her insights instead of talking about her feelings. She began to drop weight, losing a total of 80 pounds in just over six months. She considered this a miracle and attributed her success to me. "You're amazing, Dr. Nina," she exclaimed. "Nobody else has been able to help me until now. I'm so glad I found you."

I felt increasingly uneasy with her idealization, as well as with her notable weight loss. When I suggested that she was relating to me as she had her parents, and losing weight to please me, she quickly disagreed. "You're nothing like them," she assured me. I interpreted that her relentlessly positive attitude toward me might be hiding other emotions. I normalized anger, hostility, jealousy, and invited Marta to share these feelings, but she resisted the notion that her favorable feelings toward me represented idealization. She steadfastly held the position that her positive feelings toward me were simply that, positive feelings. She pointed out, "Even Freud said sometimes a cigar is just a cigar."

Shortly after she reached her goal weight, Marta began to binge again. At each session, she appeared to be visibly bigger, gaining weight in front of my eyes. She was no longer eating potato chips, but instead was "really into chocolate." I began feeling a palpable sense of helplessness, watching her gain weight at such a rapid pace. Marta bemoaned her loss of control, castigating herself and blaming herself. "I'm just a hopeless case," she told me, plaintively.

Her words were self-deprecating, her manner sorrowful, yet I found myself wanting to shake Marta for gaining weight, for rejecting our work together. I was frustrated with her for resisting the development of any true connection between us. I believed that Marta's ballooning weight was expressing what her mind could not; she was angry at me, since I represented an authority figure and she was also rebelling against my perceived authority over her. An overly obedient child, she never rebelled or differentiated herself from her parents. Now, by gaining weight, she was actively rebelling. She was also unconsciously creating in me the feelings of helplessness and anger that marked nearly every day of her childhood.

When Marta complained about the weight gain, I decided to be more transparent about my countertransference. I told her that I believed she was unconsciously letting me know how she had felt as a child, submitting to the expectations of her parents. At the beginning of our work together, she had related to me as she had to her parents, complying with the treatment and essentially losing weight. It was as if she did it for me, rather than for herself. Now, by gaining weight, leaving me unable to help her, she had effectively reversed roles, unconsciously making me the helpless, angry, and impotent one. I not only intellectually understood what she had lived through as a child, I now had a visceral sense of her experience.

Several minutes of silence followed. I had no idea what she was thinking or feeling. She left the session without saying another word, leaving me hanging (or so it felt). At the next session, she sat up on the couch and faced me, instead of reclining. With slow deliberation, she took a Toblerone chocolate bar out of her purse and unwrapped it. She looked at me as if daring me to react.

She placed the chocolate bar on the coffee table between us, as if throwing down a gauntlet. I considered it a moment before lifting my gaze to her watchful eyes.

"That looks yummy," I commented.

She looked startled. "You really don't care if I eat this or not?"

This rhetorical question was a first recognition that something had been playing out between us, a dynamic that needed to be better understood. Thus began a conversation about power, relationships, and, with it, a nascent form of true relating. When Marta was able to use words to express her anger at feeling controlled, and to talk about her wish to rebel against restrictions, she stopped utilizing food and her body to express those conflicts and wishes.

Eating as an expression of object hunger

Freud (1938) writes, "A child's first erotic object is the mother's breast that nourishes it; love has its origin in attachment to the satisfied need for nourishment" (p. 118). As infants, our experience of feeding is bound up with a sense of connection, safety, and love. In our psyches, food serves as a symbolic representation of mother, of mothering, and of love. The term "mother" is usually connected with the female parent, but for the purposes of this chapter, I wish to expand the definition of "mother" to refer to any primary parent or caregiver, regardless of gender.

Bingeing, with or without the resulting weight gain, may serve as a way of incorporating the maternal object, as a means of managing separation anxiety, or it may be a way of relating to or controlling internal objects. Jackson (1993) writes, "greedy eating attests to the power of the phantasy of oral incorporation of the mother" (p. 124). Since it seems to me that fathers are underrepresented in psychoanalytic literature, I propose that this oral incorporation can refer to any important object, whether mother, father, or another significant person. If food is unconsciously felt to represent people and relationship, then eating is a way of taking in and keeping these people internally, and of thus never being alone.

Savitt (1963) sees the impulse to use drugs as an indication of an "overwhelming psychic need for total fusion with the mother" (p. 48). This can also be true of the impulse to binge on food. Bychowski (1950) points out that such driven eating is a result of various forms of separation anxiety. He observes that after patients work through paternal transference, preoedipal attachments to the mother invariably occur, which he terms "an ultimate object of libidinal fixation and source of resistance" (p. 304). Overeating is a way of introjecting the mother, and may also betray a certain oral aggressiveness and rivalry with others. Incorporating the mother means having mother for oneself, which can be experienced as an oedipal victory, and/or victory over rival siblings. This explains the intense feelings of guilt that invariably follow the binges, guilt that is consciously about eating too much and unconsciously about the ravenous assimilation of the maternal object for oneself.

The notion of oral incorporation refers to the idea that bingeing is a way of taking in and holding the mother internally. Food functions as a symbolic representation of mother, and thus of mothering. Symbols are substitutes that represent the original object, and are often used to overcome loss. In times of stress, symbolic representation can unconsciously be felt as symbolic equation, meaning that the thing symbolized – in this case, food – is felt to be the same as the original object. This "food = mother" mental equation often underlies bingeing behavior, as is evidence in the following examples.

Clinical vignette 4

Arlene began treatment when she was in her late thirties, hoping to overcome her "doughnut addiction." Raised in a strict Catholic family, she was the oldest of eight children and during her childhood, she was expected to help her mother take care of the younger children. Her siblings were known as "the kids" and Arlene always felt her place in the family was as a second-class mother rather than a daughter or a sibling. Her mother proclaimed that leaning on, or depending on anyone else was a sign of weakness, yet she openly relied on Arlene's help for childcare, house-cleaning and more. Arlene found this "do as I say, not as I do" communication to be bewildering.

She was not close to her father, who died in a car accident when she was in high school. Prior to his death, he had been an amorphous figure, a businessman who came home and went straight to his study to relax and unwind. Every weekend, he left early for the golf course and returned home for supper. Arlene and her siblings were cautioned never to bother their father, and they had relatively little interaction with him. Her strongest memory of her father was that he constantly drank root beer, which he referred to as "mother's milk."

After his death, Arlene longed even more for her mother's unconditional love and acceptance, yet always sensed that she fell short of expectations. She interpreted this as meaning that she did not deserve her mother's love. The family focus was on achievement, and "negative" emotions such as anger, sadness, and disappointment were not tolerated. Arlene recalled that her mother became annoyed whenever anyone was sick. Illness appeared to be both an inconvenience and an indication of basic weakness. If Arlene had a fever and complained, her mother said, "Quit your bellyaching." No matter what Arlene did, it was never enough. If she brought home good grades, she was asked why they were not better. Why had she not done extra credit? Arlene recalled never feeling as if she were good enough, and also felt guilty about having any feelings about this lack of acknowledgment or love.

Arlene married young and immediately got pregnant. Shortly after she gave birth to her first child, she began having sudden cravings for doughnuts. She regularly bought a baker's dozen, and would sit in her car alone, stuffing doughnuts into her mouth, unable to stop, often with tears running down her cheeks. She was disgusted by her perceived lack of control, and, over the ensuing years, she managed this ego-weakness by going on a series of stringent diets. Inevitably, her willpower failed and she found herself driving to Krispy Kreme. Sometimes she bought only the doughnut holes, but they failed to satisfy her craving.

Arlene's identification with her mother was apparent from the beginning of our work, when she shared how ashamed she was for "bellyaching" about things that upset her. Becoming a mother had facilitated a deep hunger for mothering, which is when the "doughnut addiction" began. As we worked through many of these identifications, and wishes, the symbolism of the doughnuts became clear. Doughnuts have a missing piece at the center, representing the missing piece at the center of her mother. She had a mother but not a mommy. The sweet, sugary doughnuts were her way of incorporating a representation of her mother, complete with missing piece. By their very design, doughnuts conveyed the presence of an absence.

As the treatment progressed, so did the nature of Arlene's "addiction" to doughnuts. She developed a "thing" for creme-filled doughnuts, and only bought two at a time instead of the baker's dozen. One day, she bit into a cream-filled doughnut and to her dismay realized that the cream was missing. She became distraught and could not figure out why she was so upset and angry, but felt as if she had somehow been egregiously cheated.

She returned to the doughnut shop but they were out of white cream-filled doughnuts. "They had chocolate filled doughnuts but I didn't want those. I wanted the white cream. I just wanted that cream filling," she said, emphatically, holding her hands in front of her chest and moving them back and forth. "I really wanted it."

I was struck by the way her hands were cupped as if to form the shape of breasts. I suggested that the two cream filled doughnuts represented the full breasts of her mother, a version of "mother's milk" that she could actually take in. This resonated with Arlene, who reflected that she had shifted by symbolically focusing on what was not there, in the doughnuts, to craving something tangible and filling. Alas, just as there was no cream filling, there was no sweet maternal object to incorporate.

Clinical vignette 5

Jane, mid-twenties, grew up in a chaotic household dominated by a father who was prone to violent alcoholic rages and a mother who alternated verbal and physical hostility with expressions of concern. I have written elsewhere (Savelle-Rocklin, 2016) about Jane, who was overweight as a child and developed anorexia in her teens. She came to treatment when she was in her late twenties and living a thousand miles away from her family. Shortly after being fired from a job where she felt "like we were family" she started eating relentlessly. Losing the job facilitated an intense hunger for connection. She was starving for something relational, but turned to food instead of to people. She ate so much food that when she recounted the details of her binges, I felt physically sick. My counter-transference reaction doubtless revealed Jane's unconscious wish to be intrusive and sadistic with me, as well as convey the horror of her childhood.

Jane reported that her binges were comprised of foods that she did not actually like. She was "addicted to peanut butter" and mused that she actually hated peanut butter, although it was one of her mother's favorite foods. She often mentioned the calorie counts of various cookies, which were always 135 calories, or bemoaned the 135 grams of fat she ate one day. She mused that she would not stop bingeing until she gained 135 pounds. Not coincidentally, this was the exact weight of her mother. By gaining 135 pounds, Jane was recreating her mother in the ultimate merger, with her mother symbolized as a second skin of fat. This was her victory over the possibility of separation from her mother. Losing weight was akin to losing that maternal bond, and this was so terrifying to Jane that she could not stop eating, because to stop eating and lose weight meant losing that internal bond to her mother. Jane thus used food as a way of experiencing fusion with her mother, almost in a reverse pregnancy; instead of her mother carrying Jane in her body in preparation for birth, Jane symbolically carried her mother in her body, and never wanted to relinquish her.

For both Arlene and Jane, eating became a means by which they could express their deep hunger for relationship. They had unconsciously attempted to find in food what they could not find in their mothers. Only by working through the painful relationships of the past, and identifying how they had identified with their mothers and reenacted their traumas, did they begin to heal the wounds of the past.

Eating to express fear of objectification

Many individuals who struggle with their weight have a conscious desire to lose weight and an unconscious fear of being thinner or smaller. Bychowski (1950) describes the dream of a patient who had lost a considerable amount of weight in treatment. In the dream, she acted somewhat aggressive toward a man, when previously her manner toward him had always been maternal. Bychowski finds this a common theme in his patients, for whom their "adipose cushion served as a protection against masculine aggression and this in a double meaning of a literary protection. . . . On the other hand, it also helped to protect the patient from her own exhibitionism" (p. 313). Losing weight may put patients in touch with aggressive thoughts, feelings, and impulses, and that may be too threatening to bear.

Rubin (1973) elucidates several reasons why some people resist losing weight. "Thinness symbolically represents dislodgement from resignation, surrender of illusion, destruction of magic and confrontation with unrealistic expectations. It represents removal of a major cornerstone supporting an intricate neurotic defense system" (p. 40).

Clinical vignette 6

Willow, mid-twenties and overweight, had what she called the "pretty face" syndrome. Her grandmother would tell her that she had "such a pretty face" and if she would only lose weight, men would line up around the block to take her out. Willow knew that some men prefer curvy, voluptuous, plus-size women and it was possible for her to date at the size that she was, but she did not. Willow felt "like the cookie monster" from Sesame Street and regularly ate entire boxes of cookies at one time.

Willow had grown up watching her mother submit to her stepfather on every aspect of their daily life. Her stepfather decided what program to watch on television, where to visit on vacation, and what to have for dinner. Her mother was powerless to make even the most basic household decisions and had to justify all purchases, even the type of dishwashing detergent she bought, to her husband. Willow developed the idea that marriage meant being subsumed by the needs and wishes of the other person. As long as Willow remained heavy, her weight protected her from the kind of male attention that might lead to dating. She feared losing herself in a relationship and becoming just a "girlfriend" or "wife" and abdicating her sense of self. As Willow processed this fear in treatment, she began to date for the first time in her life. When her size no longer served the purpose of protecting her from conflict, she was able to stop bingeing on cookies and lose weight.

Clinical vignette 7

Many years ago, I treated Daisy, a 13-year-old girl who was morbidly obese. Her parents worried because Daisy had few friends and never wanted to go out on the weekends, preferring to stay home and eat, while reading or watching TV. She ordered pizza delivery and would eat the whole pizza by herself. Daisy seemed unperturbed by her lack of social interaction, and told me that she did not enjoy the activities that typical teenagers often enjoy, preferring her own company to that of others. As a result, her primary relationship was to food instead of to people. She told me, "Bad things don't happen to fat girls." She believed that all victims of rape and murder were skinny and attractive, never fat, and thus her size kept her safe, protecting her from the possibility of victimization. Additionally, she shared that she did not know who she should be if she were thin, fearing that any weight loss would render her "less huggable." Daisy's identity and perception of herself as huggable, which to her meant lovable, were tied to her size; losing weight was akin to losing her lovability and her identity.

Notably, she later shared fantasies of disemboweling her father, cutting off his penis, and leaving him to die a horribly painful death, leaving me to wonder about unconscious guilt as a motivation for fearing that "bad things" could happen to her. She could not articulate or consciously register this guilt. My hypothesis was that she feared that her aggressive and violent fantasies would be met by punishment from some nebulous threat outside the home.

Individuals who have painful experiences with intimacy, whether they received negative messages about closeness or were actually abused, often fear being objectified, treated as a body or a thing rather than as a person. For those who were sexually abused or molested as children, the danger of being objectified is more intense. Their weight often serves as a shield to protect them from the perceived dangers of human connection and relationship, which they have learned to mistrust. When children are mistreated as children, being small can be associated with powerlessness. Being physically big, taking up space and being a person of size can give the illusion of power and mastery over the exigencies of life.

Eating as a way of filling a void

Many binge-eating disorder patients describe a feeling of emptiness within their bodies, a chasm of nothingness, a hunger that no amount of food can fill. One patient described it as a "black hole" of oppressive nothingness, inescapable, and vast. Latzer and Gerzi (2000) describe the common experience of a "black hole" in eating disorder patients. They describe certain binge-eating individuals who have little frustration tolerance and find it "hard to be in a position of lack, of holes; they have to fill all the holes with food" (p. 35). The experience of emptiness is as terrifying as a black hole, and so unbearable that these patients turn to food and eat to fill their bodies, symbolically staving off that unbearable emptiness.

The notion of a black hole as a way of describing an individual's psychological conflict was first used by Bion (1970) to describe the experience of infants prematurely separated from their primary objects. Tustin (1972) introduced the idea of a black hole as a psychological void. Grotstein (1990) writes that the black hole "represents the place where the mother used to be, the place from which she has been prematurely ripped away" (p. 43). Patients who have suffered severe maternal deprivation or abandonment are vulnerable to this state, which goes beyond merely feeling empty, instead conveying a sense of being pulled inextricably toward a void.

Eshel (1998) describes patients who are either trapped in a world of maternal deadness or fear being pulled in. Rather than having a psychological space of deadness within, a void where mother should be, such patients are either trapped in a maternal black hole, or terrified of being drawn into that maternal deadness, resulting in deficits in relatedness. I propose that one solution to this impossible dilemma, a Scylla or Charybdis choice in which both alternatives are equally destructive, is to avoid connection with people. Unable to create bonds of closeness, love and intimacy with others, they instead have a primary relationship with food, which functions as a symbolic representation of mothering and nurturing. Thus, they not only fill the emptiness within their bodies, they create a self-sustaining relationship in which they protect themselves from the dangers of relating by having complete agency over their food, which functions as mother/nurturer.

Eating as a way of managing unpredictability

Those individuals who have experienced trauma often create elaborate strategies to prevent re-experiencing that trauma or feeling the effects associated with those traumatic events. This is true for those who have survived a single-event trauma and for those who endured an ongoing and protracted period of neglect, abuse, indifference, or other psychological pain. Shapiro (2012) notes that, "Emotional and physiological destabilization is likely to occur repeatedly during trauma treatment as implicit trauma memories become conscious, *because trauma memory is experienced in the here and now* rather than as narrative memory" (p. 55, italics in the original).

I have noticed how many survivors of emotional and/or physical trauma consciously believe that any positive, pleasurable, or good experiences are a setup for future disappointment. They avoid stepping onto the metaphorical rug of happiness, or do so cautiously, fearing that as soon as they are happy on that rug, it will be unceremoniously yanked out from beneath them. Inevitably, something bad happens and they ruefully point out the last good thing that happened, creating a pattern between the two events, as if somehow things had gotten "too good" and therefore it couldn't last. They perceive a causal relationship between positive and negative events and circumstances, and then find the evidence to support this causality.

One patient was devastated when she was fired from her corporate job, which occurred shortly after the company where she worked was acquired by a bigger corporation. She tearfully phoned her mother but was met with a less than comforting response. Her mother wasn't surprised by the turn of events, telling my patient that she had "climbed so far up in the world" that she was bound to fall sooner or later. Like Icarus, by daring to soar higher, my patient was left with the notion that she had brought her job termination upon herself and that she had only herself to blame. She turned to food to get the comfort she could not obtain from her mother or from herself, as she had not yet cultivated a different response from herself.

The fear is that if one dares to step into Paradise, it will eventually be taken away. The expectation of good leading to bad creates a compelling reason to be pessimistic or suspicious of anything good. This is a means of perpetuating an illusion of omniscience and omnipotence, since if someone "knows" that bad follows good, they can therefore avoid anything unpleasant or disappointing. One solution is to never allow life to feel too good, since an effective way to control the potential loss of well-being is to ensure that one never enters Paradise in the first place. As long as they do not enter Paradise, they cannot be cast out. Strategies to prevent the experience of well-being that will, in their minds, precede a fall, include feeling terrible about one's body, bemoaning one's relationship to food, and generally feeling terrible about oneself. This also facilitates a parallel experience of shame that may be temporarily assuaged with food, creating a vicious cycle of seeking happiness, fearing the loss of happiness, and using food in such a way as to destroy any sense of well-being or self-esteem.

Clinical vignette 8

Greg, 48 years old, owned a successful contracting business and built expensive homes in the most coveted neighborhoods of Los Angeles. His marriage was strong and his three kids were doing well in school, and were socially well-adjusted. Yet, the more successful he became, the more Greg focused on his "problem" with food. When he landed a huge contract for a Bel Air estate, his thoughts soon turned to his inability to control his weight. Greg responded to all positive events in his life by bemoaning his weight and helplessness over food, especially pasta.

His maternal grandmother was Italian and made homemade pasta every Friday night. He recalled going to a friend's house for a sleepover as a child, where he was served – to his horror – spaghetti with ketchup. The memory of this dinner made him visibly shudder, and he was still aghast at the memory. Greg realized how lucky he was to have his grandmother's cooking, which until then he had taken for granted, but which then took on more significance and pleasure.

Greg recalled an idyllic childhood, one he described as "absolutely perfect" until he was ten years old, when everything changed in what seemed like an instant. One moment life was good, and he was celebrating the fact that his soccer team had won a match. The next moment, or so it seemed, his parents were sitting him down with sober expressions and announcing their plans to divorce. Greg's life turned upside down in that instant. Greg felt himself suddenly and unwillingly cast from his perfect life.

Greg was an active child and played sports throughout his childhood and into college. He married his college girlfriend and they had a loving, strong relationship. His wife stayed at home and raised the boys while he built a lucrative business. He hired his father, who was also a contractor but had never achieved Greg's level of success. When Greg's oldest son was ten years old, Greg began overeating on a regular basis. He developed a habit of ordering pasta for lunch, along with bread and dessert, and gained weight for the first time in his life. He described feeling "like an addict" and could not stop thinking about eating Italian food. He quickly gained 30 pounds and was unable to lose it.

Greg was more financially successful than his father, yet the weight gain did not appear to be related to oedipal guilt. Greg started gaining weight when his son was ten years old, the same age that Greg had been when his parents announced their divorce. As a result of that seminal incident, he unconsciously developed a belief that happiness and success invariably lead to loss. When his son reached the age of ten, repressed fears of being cast from Paradise were reactivated during what might be thought of as an anniversary effect, and Greg began fearing that things were "too good to be true. It can't last." One way of ensuring that he never felt "too" happy was to always feel upset about his weight. As we worked through this underlying belief, Greg slowly began feeling more secure about his situation, and his fixation for Italian food, which he associated with childhood evenings with his Italian grandmother, slowly abated. He was eventually able to reach a healthy weight and his relationship to food normalized.

Concluding remarks

Although it is clear that there is little scientific basis for food addiction, many people are addicted to using food to alleviate distress or to express unconscious conflict. They often lack alternate means of self-soothing or comforting themselves, and have little ability to reflect about why they're eating. Also, when there is a fundamental distrust of relationships, it is often difficult to trust that a therapist will remain interested, attuned, and responsive. Therefore, a crucial aspect of treatment is to focus on the patient's experience, to find meaning in the eating behavior, rather than attempting to change that behavior. I hear from many individuals whose relationships with previous therapists devolved into power struggles. When the therapists tried to "get them" to eat differently, these patients resisted. Patients are often perplexed by this resistance, wondering why they will not change that which they actively and consciously wish to change. I ask them to think of their "addiction" to food as a kind of "frenemy," as it does something for them and in that case functions as a friend, and also hurts them, which makes it simultaneously an enemy. I tell them that I have no wish to take their eating disorder away from them or to force them to change their relationship to food. Instead, I want to help them to better understand their relationship to food, so that one day they may give up the disordered eating voluntarily. For some patients, this experience of the analytic relationship is the first time they are able to rely on another person's unconditional interest and genuine regard for them. When they internalize the goodness of the analyst, they relinquish their bad object identification. Eventually they learn turn to others for comfort, and to comfort themselves, instead of using food for that purpose.

Through the process of psychoanalysis, we discover why someone uses food to cope. Eating may provide a means of self-soothing, fill a symbolic void, allow for dissociation, convert emotional pain to physical pain, create a symbolic reunion with objects, and provide a sense of mastery over an unpredictable world. The key to healing from food issues is to identify what the behavior is expressing and to work through those original psychological wounds. By understanding how the past is repeated in the present, and translating the language of the body, we shed light on the hidden motivations that keep the symptomatic behavior in place. When people identify and work through what is eating "at" them, they stop using food or their bodies as a means of expressing their inner world.

Chapter 3

Sex addiction

Lawrence Jacobson

Compulsive sexuality seems to have become a more frequent phenomenon in clinical practices as well as in the general culture, reflected since the early 1990s in magazine and newspaper articles, the popular currency of the term "sex addiction," and in targeted 12-step programs. There is a fascinating confluence of the social and the clinical that has occurred along with shifting mores regarding sex. On the one hand, there has been something of a puritanical shift regarding sex in American culture, on the other an increasing toleration of sexual orientations and gender identifications, though the latter by no means evenly spread across the country. A continuing sexualization of the culture and comfort with using sexual imagery to power consumption, reflected in advertising and fashion, has accompanied a spread of popular cultural awareness of the place of power in sex, and of its use and abuse and its part in the subjugation of women. This time has been punctuated by periodic outbursts onto the public stage such as the Monica Lewinsky–Bill Clinton revelations and impeachment trial of the late 1990s, and the controversies about sexual harassment and assault in relation to Donald Trump and others with cultural and commercial power that continues to develop as I write.

The problem of definition

Regarding "sex addiction" itself, it seems to me that, as often is the case, old wine has been appearing in new bottles. People whom I understood as showing essentially perverse structures of desire, and as driven in their sexual appetites (sometimes very driven, sometimes less than was claimed), have been calling themselves and diagnosed as "sex addicts." Amidst the growing public conversation and often fraught controversies about the legitimate and illegitimate, the acceptable and the unacceptable, the reasonable and the outrageous, and the criminal in sexual behavior, addiction seems to have become – rather like trauma in recent years – an increasingly popular explanation for troubling goings on.

The thought that joins addiction and trauma may not be entirely random. Both terms locate cause and power outside oneself; a certain passivity and victim status accrues to the afflicted person. The word "addiction," according to the Oxford

English Dictionary, originally meant "a formal giving over or delivery by sentence of court," from which it came to mean "a surrender, or dedication of any one to a master." Thus, "addict" is by definition passive; "assigned, made over, bound" are its earliest synonyms. Compare "perversion," the root meaning of which is "thoroughly turned" – turned from the good, obviously, as its synonyms are "corrupt, incorrect, improper." Perversion is more active, and the ominous elements are in the person, not in some external master.

To suggest that sexual addiction may be seen as perversion is not to say that there is no addiction involved, any more than to wonder about the appeal of trauma as an explanation would be to deny that traumas occur. From a psychoanalytic perspective, addiction can be understood as a form of perversion (Glover, 1956; Keller, 1992; McDougall, 1985) or at least closely related (Bower et al., 2013). The *Dictionary* itself is suggestive: if addiction is surrender or dedication to a master, then, especially if it is sexual addiction we are talking about, the tinge of sadomasochism is unavoidable.

To speak of addiction or perversion, or even of seeking engagement, is to use terms that are highly socially constructed. With "nymphomania," which first emerged as a subject of medical study in the early eighteenth century, and "satyriasis," a term to be found in English at least since the Middle Ages, medicine at first borrowed from Greek myth to find a way to talk about excessive levels of sexual desire and activity. By the late nineteenth century, we find Krafft-Ebing (1886) differentiating florid acute cases that often lead to death, and which for contemporary clinicians may suggest severe psychotic or brain-damaged states, from milder chronic cases, which also are said to occur only in "psychically degenerated individuals" but have less dire consequences – although his Case 189 was ultimately sent to an insane asylum for the rest of her life even though "no other signs of mental anomaly could be detected in her" (Krafft-Ebing, 1886, p. 485). Ultimately, the nineteenth-century medical mixture of moral stricture and dispassionate sympathy gave way to the twentieth-century neutral observational stance of Kinsey's Reports (1948, 1953), which with scientific non-judgmentalness implied that whatever was found was acceptable, and which found much more sexual promiscuity than had been imagined. Hence, to the overtly extremely morally neutral – though perhaps it is acceptance and suppression of cultural mores that is more to the point – and not particularly elucidating return to Greek with the "paraphilic disorders" of DSM.

At any rate, it is a socially loaded question whether one is seen as addicted or perverse or seeking engagement. My focus here is on (1) what is the most useful rubric to work with clinically, yet clearly, (2) how the patient's social "framing" affects the clinical situation, and (3) how the clinician's understanding the patient (an issue sometimes confused with clinicians labeling patients) affects the clinical process. Some preference among clinicians for "addiction" over "perversion" arises from discomfort about the long-standing abuse of the term "perversion" in defining homosexuality. This area is particularly interesting for how the social plays out in the clinical in various ways and at different levels.

Three psychoanalytic viewpoints

What is the psychoanalytic notion of perversion? There are three major currents that overlap and intertwine, but that may be distinguished, broadly, as Freud's, object relations,' and Lacan's. This brief account of them necessarily passes over quite a few wrinkles.

In "Three Essays on the Theory of Sexuality," Freud (1905a) defines "perversion" as essentially overvaluation of pregenital sexuality. The good and proper that is being turned away from is genital union and reproduction, a normative development upon which, according to Freud, full psychosexual maturity depends. This notion has been used to support the destructive view of homosexuality as a perversion. I mention it but reject it. If genital union and the possibility of reproduction were the hallmark of proper sexuality, then addictive genital sexuality would appear on its face not to be perversion; however, in my view perversion has nothing to do with object choice per se, at least when the object is human.

But anyway, Freud's (1905a) larger point is not that human sexuality is properly limited to activity directed at genital union and reproduction, but to emphasize how little of it actually is so limited in its constitution and as an activity. If one begins with an idea of sex that is equivalent to the animal instinct to reproduce and then examines how it is constituted and developed in humans – who compared to other animals are born in a state of extraordinary immaturity and undergo a lengthy infantile dependency – and if one then considers the manifold and complex ways that sex appears in humans, one cannot help but see how thoroughly human sexuality has been turned from any such animal reproductive purpose. The point is that all human sexuality is at its core perverse. Though it makes no sense to claim that to have sex is in itself to be perverse, sex addiction is addiction to an activity that is at its core perverse.

In "Fetishism," Freud's (1927) emphasis shifts from the valuation of sexual activity in itself toward a splitting of the ego. The fetishist has been unable to acknowledge that the woman has no penis, thus denying what Freud termed the "reality" of castration. Effecting a "divided attitude," the fetish or fetishistic activity both re-evokes and disavows the penis as missing, and the substitute for something that was not there is compulsively sought. This is important to the psychoanalytic notion of perversion: something that is not there is compulsively sought. Freud traced that something to the mother's penis. The good that is turned from in this notion is not reproductive sexual activity but the acknowledgment of reality, whether that reality is castration in Freud's terms, or, as in more recent formulations, sexual and generational difference (Chasseguet-Smirgel, 1984; Kaplan, 2000).

The object-relations view of perversion is best exemplified by Masud Khan (1979). In his account, Freud's compact notion of "castration" for what could not be psychically processed is expanded to include experiences of humiliation, exclusion, inadequacy, and seduction into excitement. Unable to psychically work these experiences in transitional object relating – that is, unable to psychically sort them out into viable senses of self and other in the play of fantasy and reality that characterizes transitional object relating and underlies symbolization – transitional objects become warped into fetishistic enactments that compel into the external world dramas of damage and revenge that cannot be tolerated within. For Stoller (1975), revenge against a person who threatened the child's core gender identity through trauma or extreme frustration (such as what Khan called "cumulative trauma") is an especially important factor.

Thus, in the object relations view, perversion is emphasized as a failure in symbolization and a disorder of relating. A similar position was ultimately adopted by McDougall (1986) and the contemporary American relational view is essentially the same, though it is perversion as a disorder of relating that is emphasized and the failure in symbolization is more implicit (Celenza, 2014). The good that is turned away from is relating through the intermediate area, with its affective richness and its play of fantasy and reality and of self and other. Perverse sex lacks play; it is compelling the other into an externalized enactment of what cannot be psychically tolerated. Optimistically, the repetitive enactment embodies the possibility of finding some mastery of the earlier traumata, of translating it into experience that can be symbolically elaborated and psychically processed. In a more pessimistic view, what happens is merely necessary discharge of intolerable affect that inexorably builds or is evoked by particular situations (Wood, 2013).

Finally, in the Lacanian account (Lacan, 1998, 2007; Fink, 1997), "castration" is less like Freud's version than what American psychoanalysis called "separation." The infant – of whatever sex – must accept that the infant-mother pair is not self-sufficient, that the infant doesn't fully satisfy mother's desire. Mother lacks and desires something else than the infant; the infant lacks something the mother desires. What is lacking is the phallus. By phallus, Lacan does not mean the penis – though phallus and penis become associated – but that mysterious power that inheres in the adult world that underwrites not only sexual but symbolic exchange. It is what makes all that stuff that adults do – not just sex, but talking – important and real. To accept that you don't have it is a terrible blow, and to the degree that you don't accept it – to the degree that in Lacanian terms you believe you are mother's phallus – you don't enter the world of symbolic elaboration, the symbolic world in which you can psychically process your lack and gain compensatory satisfactions. And, it is only if one has accepted that one is not the phallus that one can begin to grasp that the phallus itself is illusory, that no such entity or power exists.

In this Lacanian account, perversion is less a circumscribed psychopathological entity than a basic structure of desire, of the order of melancholia or narcissism. The good that is turned away from is symbolic elaboration of separation and lack. Perversion refers to desire that in its lack of symbolic elaboration avoids concern with, indeed seeks to supersede the whole question of, dependency and relationship (cf. Kohon, 1987). Unable to psychically tolerate separation and lack, that which was not there has to be compulsively sought and re-sought to prove that one has it, in a mode of experience in which having it and being it are not really distinguished.

In the Lacanian view, it is the "paternal law" that makes the mother-infant separation happen. This paternal law – termed such even though it is a function that in the contemporary world may not be carried out by an actual father or even by a male – forces the infant from the experience of actually being the cause and fulfillment of mother's desire and forces the acceptance that mother desires something else too, that the infant and the mother lack. This means having to give up an area of "jouissance," which is a huge pleasure but a pleasure that in its very excess (its lack of lack) is also pain, and to accept symbolic satisfaction instead. This the paternal law forces, but also one may say, allows: symbolic satisfaction is otherwise not available, only the intense and awful driving excitement that is characteristic of perversion: intense sensation but deadened feeling (as also emphasized by Celenza, 2014).

This account of the failure of the paternal law to take effect and the consequent inrush of jouissance in lieu of the symbolic function and symbolic satisfaction that drives perverse enactments, grants the Lacanian view a similarly equivocal potential to the enactments as the object relations view. A certain staging or evoking of the paternal law is characteristic – although for Fink (1997) it is not merely characteristic but definitional – of perverse enactments, like a calling forth of the superego in its very transgression (in this way like Freud's "divided attitude" that evokes and disavows the nonexistent penis). Optimistically, this embodies a hope that ultimately the paternal law will effectively appear and so symbolic processing and satisfaction can occur. Less optimistically, what occurs is a continuing unchanging driven repetition.

Levels of conceptualization

From these currents can be distilled a psychoanalytic view of perversion from which an understanding of compulsive sexuality and addiction and their treatment emerges. In staking out this position, I want to keep two levels distinct: one of "underlying issue" and one of "secondary problems."[1]

The underlying issue is the inability to psychically process or symbolize experiences of lack. Psychic work and affective elaboration do not occur. Where sensations that could potentially become affectively and psychically symbolically elaborated threaten to emerge, what occur instead are driven need-loops of discharge, often associated with altered states of consciousness. Transitional objects are degraded to fetish objects; intermediate area play is degraded to compelled external dramas. Such dramas themselves vary in complexity and richness of articulation. Some perversions can display complex dramas of humiliation and revenge, genders and part objects. But their symbolic richness fails to carry therapeutic traction: the failure in symbolization accounts for the oft-observed failure of interpretation to have effect in treating perversion. In some substance abuse and eating disorders, the enactments seem to be hyper-compressed, sucked into a black hole from whose gravitational pull meaning is very hard to extract. These all constitute varieties of fetishistic addiction. They in turn become the further level of secondary problems.

At this level of secondary problems, the fetishistic addiction proliferates a host of psychological, interpersonal, and social consequences, which sustain the symptomatic behavior and bring the person to treatment, if they do come to treatment. They include all the ways that the activity has become interwoven into a life and consciously valued sense of self, and all the degrees of social support or condemnation of the symptomatic behavior. They include also the biological-chemical loops, perhaps through drug abuse or the chemistry of altered states of consciousness that can go with sexual arousal, that have often become well-established pleasures or anxiolytics.

To consider these two levels separately throws light on the issue of effective treatment and illuminates how the social is at work at both levels, but at work differently. The level of the secondary problems blocks access to the original issue. This partly works because the fetishistic activity is designed precisely to plug the hole of the unsymbolizable lack that is the original problem, to supersede it and render it as if it had never been. For a man to be repeatedly proving his sexual potency and capacity for excitement and giving and receiving pleasure renders dependency nonexistent, a nonissue requiring no psychic work. Similarly, compulsive masturbatory or virtual sexual experiences with no real person repudiate dependency implicit in an actual relationship. But the secondary problems also block access to the underlying problem because of the slew of secondary vulnerabilities, the further lacks and incapacities, that they create: the highs that cannot be done without, the rationalizations interwoven into the sense of self, the shame, the lack of relationships that might support dependency, and so on.

Clinical vignette I

Matt, a man in his late fifties, had organized his sexual compulsiveness into one compartment of his life, where it permitted what seemed a highly successful career and family life to emerge as hollow and false in major ways. To unravel the dynamics behind his sexual behavior requires acknowledging that his entire life-that-worked, in fact, did not. His long-term sexual hyperactivity had played such a large part in his life that to look at it took extraordinary courage. Matt engaged in brief sexual encounters that came in waves that peaked at two or three a day for a week or two, and then rapidly diminishing and none at all for up to a couple of months. His work often involved long work hours so his wife accepted his extended absences, and he was careful to minister to her needs and be a good father and be present for family occasions. Indeed, he was proud and satisfied with how well he had everything in control and how good was his family life at the same time as he was able to enjoy a large amount and variety of sex. Few men could manage that! It was only because he found he was developing uncomfortably complex feelings toward one of his paramours that he sought therapy.

Matt's father had died when he was very young and he, an only child, became an essential source of solace and satisfaction for his mother at a level of intense excitement well beyond what he was able to tolerate. Dependency and excitement became for him horribly interwoven but until coming to therapy, it had been dissociated from his home life and acted out in sexual encounters in a form that could never develop. One reason it could never develop is that he would never allow a single sexual partner to be around long enough until this one woman turned up so problematically. Dependency and excitement became a significant issue in the transference that was difficult to work, but as it was it became painfully clear to Matt how his relation with his wife and children had been so desiccated and emptied by it being kept elsewhere. What he had thought he had done so well at the secondary level in enabling himself to have both his sexual hyperactivity and his family had in fact been emptying out his capacity to love.

Therapeutic tasks

The "underlying problem," the need to symbolically elaborate experiences of lack (humiliation, exclusion, insufficiency), mostly cannot be approached, interpretively or via emotions or sensations that might emerge in the therapeutic relationship, without movement at the level of the secondary problems. The therapeutic task at this second level is largely strategic or instrumental. The truth – whatever one might mean by that – is not really an issue. What matters is getting through the secondary problems in order to work at the truth of lack and dependency and the truth of the awfulness of the pleasure, which is the underlying problem. The therapeutic aim is to get the patient to tolerate the sensations that the sexual activity short-circuits. It generally requires supporting some degree of delay or abstinence and achieving sufficient curiosity about the sensations for their psychic elaboration – the addressing of the underlying problem – to begin. A big difficulty is fear of the dependency that would accompany such support.

There are different strategies for dealing with this secondary level, and different degrees of therapeutic ambition. One might reasonably set no further therapeutic aim than alleviating problems at this level. Thus, one might substitute a less socially and physically debilitating substance or activity to plug the unsymbolizable lack, without any attempt at further psychic elaboration. Medication, for example, or God – "you gotta serve somebody," as Bob Dylan put it. The 12-step combination of group experience, higher power, and self-vigilance can be a powerful combination.

Always the unviability of this second level and its psychological, interpersonal, and socially problematic nature, is a crucial therapeutic ally. The "rock bottom," or the individual's need for something else, is beyond the therapeutic strategy. It is the given that provides traction for the therapeutic strategy, whatever it is, to work with. This is a crucial working of the social at this level: social labeling and shaming, legal and physical dangers, make a lot of difference, even create the problem as something calling for treatment. Successful perversion, on the other hand, gives no reason for treatment. A good example here is provided by Ryan's fascinating autobiography, *Secret Life* (1995), a memoir of a confessed sex addict. For some time, the bulk of Ryan's problems were expressed in addictions to sports, successively football, baseball, and bowling. For as long as his underlying problem (not that he sees it in these terms) had carried on in this realm, he would have been fetishistically addicted, but not with what generally would be known as an illness, and presenting no therapeutic traction.

So analytic engagement with sexual addiction often depends on making use of the social difficulties that the enactments create. At this interface of the two levels, the analyst nudges the evocation of the paternal law in its secondary level aspect of forbidding pleasure into a therapeutically effective place in which it motivates engagement with the underlying level. The analyst's relation to the social can thus become an important aspect of the transference, and equally, a piece of counter-transference to keep in mind. In the service of the analytic process, one is doing something manipulative or, as Freud might have put it, "tactful."

Let me interject here two ways in which understanding sex addiction as perversion may lead one astray. One is the possibility that what one is seeing is an obsessive sexual engagement that is neurotically driven, not perversion. A difference between them is precisely the complex relation to the social – the intense awareness of the transgression of social rules that thereby ensures that social rules are always a presence – that is so characteristic of perversion but is not, or not with anything like its intensity, to be found in obsessive sexuality. Moreover, when the behavior is obsessive there is some forbidden pleasure-danger that is foregone; the draw and fear of dependency, for example, may be quite palpable, and its interpretation is more likely to evoke analytic engagement, even if a hostile and negative one. In the perverse sexual addiction, it is most likely an emptiness, deadness, or profound lack that is quite close to consciousness, that is avoided and which, even though quite present, cannot be approached in speech for quite a long time. Finally, in obsessive sexuality the partner's own desire, where the partner is experienced as another subject, is more likely to figure in the sexual scene, whereas in perverse addiction sexual partners are little more than projective screens. In particular any suggestion that the other wants anything else than the perverse subject ruins the scene: partners may be unable to satisfy, their inhibitions and fears are okay, but not their desire for something else. In the real world, of course, the distinction cannot always be made quickly but in my experience, it is rarely a hard one.

The other is to be led astray by the high level of sexual activity, often in anonymous encounters, that is a not uncommon part of male gay life. Having made clear that perversion has nothing to do with sexual orientation, does seeing sex addiction as a form of perversion in conjunction with the frequency of anonymous sexual encounters among gay men risk a "re-perversifying" of the analytic view of homosexuality? In a word, no, but the issue touches on some interesting occurrences at the secondary level. One simple but not often noted (see Lewes, 2005) factor at work is that gay sex is all-men sex, and men, regardless of sexual orientation, don't associate sex with intimacy as much as women do. If straight women were generally as open to anonymous non-intimate sex as straight men then perhaps straight men would be having as many anonymous sexual encounters as gay men. There are a number of other factors at work in the intensity of a gay sexual life that arises amidst a history of homophobia, suppression, and liberation. These include a history of social obstacles to intimate relations, counters to shaming homophobia, idealization of transgression, and the development of non-heteronormative alternative ideas of intimacy. The effect is, in addiction terms, an enabling subculture. It can make sexual addiction harder to notice or distinguish but should not be confused with greater tendencies or even incidence of sex addiction or perversion. The social determines whether something is seen as problematic, and more subtly it forms the material for the complex perverse relationship with the social, but the question of perversion itself is formed at the underlying level.

The effect of gay subcultures might be compared to the role of the internet, which more than any actual subculture, in its facilitation of sexual activity in the absence of real people, its presentation of constant choice with no consequence, free of the vulnerable realities of dependence and physical limitations, fosters an aura of omnipotence that enables addictive engagement. Moreover, the internet appears with its constant pop-up drop-down inducements as part of a wider social phenomenon in which consumption and enjoyment are not only to be freely valued but are enjoined on one as part of full social membership. In play at this social level is perhaps a superego that, in effect, far from forbidding enjoyment, commands it (cf. Zizek, 1994). These effects create a complex situation at the secondary level where it can be denying rather than permitting oneself that becomes the perverse enactment, as in anorexia. But nevertheless, again, in this view it is not action at this secondary level that creates the perverse addiction nor effects underlying change.

Another aspect of the working of the social at the secondary level arises with the question of whether sexual addiction appears differently in women than in men. This is a part of the larger question of female perversion that, after many years of considering perversion to be a pretty much exclusively male domain, was opened up by Kaplan's (1991) book, *Female Perversions*, then by the film of the same name (1996) that was based on her book, and indeed by her own reflections (2000) on how the film moved beyond her book, and which continues as a theme today (see Celenza, 2014). Certainly sexual hyperactivity is generally more socially acceptable and less socially pathologized in men than in women, and females are conventionally more socialized to associate sex with intimacy. So sexual hyperactivity is more likely to evoke shame and risk social opprobrium at the secondary level. This makes shame a more conscious issue as experienced or warded off or embraced (shame and excitement making an intense combination) for sexually compulsive women.

The underlying issue – failing to symbolize and psychically process experiences of lack so that instead of psychic work and affective elaboration there are driven need-loops of discharge – is identical for men and women. There are, however, tendencies to differences in how they play out in action. In the attempt to ward off experiences of dependency or lack in sexual relations, men are likely to resort to objectifying the other. Women are more likely to objectify themselves (Celenza, 2014, also emphasizes this). Where men may get a rush of power at their performance of sexual potency that effectively disguises their enslavement to the compulsion, women may perform sexual submission that disguises the other's craven need in his excitement. One's own appearance has traditionally been more an area of women's fetishism than men's. But all these differences merely refer to tendencies that have become less prominent since gender and sexuality have been destabilized in recent decades and since the culture in general has become more narcissistic. The preceding observations may be better put in terms of versions of masculinity and versions of femininity than in terms of men and women, even more obviously so when it is sex between two men or two women or when one, other, or both are trans.

The social is also at work at the underlying level of the original problem of unsymbolizable lack. It has been at work, often obviously and problematically, through the family in the earliest relational experiences. But there is an important difference: whereas, at the secondary level, in the clinical context, the social figures most prominently as creating the problematic nature of what is going on, either by negative, forbidding, humiliating, etc., reactions or by amplifying or provoking it, at the underlying level the social emerges as normally fetishistic. What does this mean? Consider the fact of death, and the fact of the originary rupture of the human from the rest of nature that makes humans what we irretrievably are. These are irreducible and unsymbolizable originary lacks that we must reckon with and yet cannot reckon with. We instead have a "divided attitude" (Freud, 1927) toward them, acknowledging yet disavowing them, finding ourselves compulsively seeking that which is not there, a state of nonrupture.

Thus Ryan's use of sports. He threw himself into them fetishistically (or addictively, if one prefers), unable to tolerate any experience of lack within them. This should not be unfamiliar given the place of sports, working out, and other forms of exercise in contemporary American culture, or indeed, how some people throw themselves into making money, and are then presented as though models for us all. Consider the question, "What is the psychological function of nonreproductive sex anyway?" And, consider the French term for orgasm – *petit mort* (little death) – which suggests that with each orgasm, death is experienced, survived, overcome. It has been noticed that some people's interest in sex shoots up after a significant death.

It is hard to imagine a modern society in which fetishistic uses of activities or substances such as sex, consumption, and money are not at work. It is a realm of normality, of a form or structure of desire, rather than a pathological entity. Indeed, it is a realm that abuts areas of creativity. Both perversion and creativity involve elements of destructive interruption into the social symbolic realm, a realm to which clings a good deal of conventionality and inertia. There is considerable psychoanalytic literature on the relation between perversion and creativity (Chasseguet-Smirgel, 1984; McDougall, 1985; Whitebook, 1995). To understand perversion as like a creativity that has gone seriously awry provides, I think, a further reason to prefer the rubric of perversion to addiction, granting to "perversion" a therapeutic traction that I find "addiction" lacks. Leave aside the question of which word to use with patients, who generally provide the word themselves (some find the notion of 'perversion' intriguing, while others would be horrified at its being applied to them). At the secondary level of inducing the patient to tolerate sensations that he or she is short-circuiting through sexual activity, and of arousing curiosity about what may emerge in those sensations, I find that bearing in mind the normality of "perversion," its status as structure of desire, and its relation to creativity is more helpful than the externalization and passivity implicit in "addiction."

Note

1 Celenza (2014, p. 97) also writes of levels of perversion but what she is referring to is the degree to which perverse enactment may come to have a transitional function.

Chapter 4

Gambling addiction

Richard Rosenthal

Early analysts attempted to understand what was unique about gambling: the unpredictability, the excitement of risk, and the erotization of tension and fear (Laforgue, 1930; Von Hattingberg, 1914). They emphasized its competitive aspects and described the language of gambling in order to show its sexual and aggressive gratifications (Greenson, 1947; Stekel, 1924). Olmsted (1962) explored the psychodynamics of the games themselves while trying to understand their appeal for different individuals. Mostly, analysts attended to the various conscious and unconscious meanings associated with winning and losing.

Perhaps most important was the belief that to win at gambling meant one was special, in some way better than other people, and that the win was deserved. Lerner (1965) and Lerner and Miller (1978) referred to this as "the belief in a just world," and explained that, since the arbitrariness of the world was too frightening, people preferred to believe that even ostensibly random rewards and punishments must in fact reflect an underlying moral order. Gambling and divination have always been closely associated. The Old Testament was not against gambling, but against gambling done frivolously. Lots were cast to choose leaders, settle major disputes, determine guilt or innocence. The winning throw was thought to represent the "will of God."

Psychoanalytic literature contained a number of cases in which gambling was viewed as a way to answer important questions about what was permitted, about guilt or innocence, life or death, and about whether the gambler was loved and accepted by some all-important other. Such beliefs cross time and cultures. For example, among the early Romans, the winning toss of the dice was the "Venus throw"; it meant one was beloved by the goddess of love and beauty. Stekel (1924) was the first to view the gambler as continually challenging Fate. The game, he wrote, was an oracle for him. If the gambler won, his secret wish (for love or power) would be granted. This idea was frequently repeated in literature. Historically, oracles were portals through which the gods spoke to man. According to Fenichel (1942), the oracle was consulted to obtain advice about external situations, but especially with regard to inner conflicts: "whether what the individual had in mind was permissible or whether a punishment was to be expected. In such a case, the oracle was asked for permission that is for a divine decision, which might act as a counterweight against the twinges of conscience" (p. 18).

Freud (1928) was the first to suggest that the gambler may unconsciously want to lose. He believed this to be rooted in the young man's ambivalence toward his father: he loved his father but viewed him as a rival and therefore wanted to get rid of him. Losing was a way to punish himself, to expiate guilt about such feelings. Freud called this "moral masochism." He proposed a second kind of masochism, "feminine masochism," based on an identification with the mother; this was the negative or reverse Oedipus complex. Here, losing was thought of as a way to be loved and accepted by father (i.e., suffering = love). What linked the two types of masochism was the young man's urge to submit to the dictates of conscience on the one hand, and to a passive feminine relationship with father on the other.

Bergler (1936, 1943, 1958) picked up on Freud's idea that gambling was masochistic, but offered a different explanation. According to Bergler, the pathological gambler was in rebellion against the authority of the parents, and specifically, the reality principle they introduced. The ensuing guilt about such rebellion created the need for self-punishment. Behind the gambler's pseudo-aggression was a craving for defeat and rejection. Compulsive gamblers were involved in an adversarial relationship with the world. Their opponents at the poker table, the dealer in the casino, the roulette wheel or stock exchange, were unconsciously identified with the refusing mother or rejecting father.

Lindner (1950) presented his analysis of a compulsive gambler whose gambling started following the death of his father. Gambling was a repetitive questioning: did my omnipotent wishes kill my father? While Lindner emphasized aggressive and sexual conflicts in which winning had both positive and negative meanings and so did losing, the treatment's success may have had more to do with the uncovering of his patient's omnipotent fantasy. With the vast sums of money that he would win gambling, he would establish himself as a philanthropist and benefactor of mankind. While presented in the most beneficent terms, such fantasies often contain hidden hostility toward the parents, who are reduced to beggars when the tables are turned (Rosenthal, 1986, 1997; Simmel, 1920).

In the psychoanalytic literature on gambling, one finds unconscious guilt postulated as a force behind the pathological gambler's self-destructiveness but with multiple explanations to account for that guilt. A somewhat different etiology was described by Weissman (1963), who presented two analytic patients to illustrate how lifelong patterns of behavior, affecting every area of their lives, could be determined by the early interaction with their fathers, as revealed by their repetitive play. One patient, who was the son of a problem gambler, was programmed to seek out short-lived omnipotent victories followed by self-inflicted, annihilating defeats. As a child, the patient was permitted to greet his father by climbing all over him, pulling his hair, and punching him. Father's encouragement would alternate with pleas to stop, until he would suddenly detach himself from his son, scream at him, and force him to stand unbearably still. This pattern, which repeated what the patient's father had learned from his father, was the basis for their later interactions. As an adult, the patient's masochistic behavior elaborated on the sequence.

Weissman's examples demonstrated the role of early trauma in patients who compulsively reenacted their experience of intrusive parenting, overstimulation, and forced helplessness. Wurmser (1980) and others have noted the role of gambling as an attempt to turn passive into active, to defend against helplessness, and take magical, omnipotent control over frightening and uncontrollable situations.

In summary, the early psychoanalytic literature presented different masochistic formulations but also a number of positive, non-masochistic motives and explanations. Contemporary psychodynamic perspectives (Rosenthal, 2008; Rosenthal and Rugle, 1994) have borrowed from the treatment of substance abuse while addressing what is unique about gambling (e.g., the psychology of chasing, being in action, starting over). That pathological gamblers want to escape from problems, and use gambling to self-medicate intolerable affect, is considered so central that it was made one of the diagnostic criteria (APA, 1994). Gambling lends itself to various substitutions and simplifications aimed at making problems seem manageable. Thus, gamblers may substitute an arbitrary test (e.g., the ability to predict the outcome of an event) for their dependence on others; may reduce all problems to a single financial solution; or prefer the clear rules and immediate, all-or-nothing feedback of a game, to the complexities and messiness of life.

Problems with the concept of masochism

There are some who believe that all self-destructive behavior is masochistic. For example, according to Forrest (1984):

> Alcoholism is a form of masochism. Alcoholics inflict pain upon themselves via fights, physical injuries, automobile accidents, divorces, arrests, job losses, suicide, emotional problems, and family problems. Alcohol-induced liver disease, neurologic impairments, gastrointestinal problems, and other bodily system disorders are excellent examples of masochism and self-destruction.
>
> (p. 16)

Forrest had confused the result of a behavior with its intent, thereby extending the meaning of masochism to include all self-destructive behavior. But *all* neurotic and mentally disordered behavior is self-defeating. Are we to infer that all our patients are masochists? This is one way in which the concept has been expanded to the point of meaninglessness.

Equally troublesome is the notion of *normal masochism*. Childbirth and altruism are two frequently cited examples. Kernberg (1988) regarded the student studying for exams, the athlete in training, the executive who diets and exercises regularly, as all engaging in masochistic behavior. De Monchy (1950) viewed as normal masochism the desire to be useful, to serve a doctrine or social cause, to sacrifice oneself or subordinate to a higher authority, to be dependent in early life on one's parents, or to need to be part of a larger unit. Others have evoked the concept to explain such culturally diverse initiation rituals as scarification, circumcision, fraternity hazing, and ear piercing. Unfortunately, there is no precise or agreed-upon definition of masochism. The term is used in a variety of situations and has multiple meanings and explanations. Maleson (1984) noted: "The term is used with little consistency and at varied levels of abstraction. . . . It is not always explicit which meaning is intended or what inferences, if any, are meant to be drawn" (p. 354).

Masochism originally described a specific sexual perversion. The term was coined by Krafft-Ebing (1886), who named it after Leopold von Sacher-Masoch, a popular novelist whose best-known work, *Venus in Furs* (1870; see Lenzer, 1975), depicted the hero's subjugation and torture at the hands of a voluptuous but icy woman. The history of research on masochism paralleled, and was shaped by, the development of psychoanalysis. Over a 20-year period, Freud wrote a series of papers in which he kept coming back to it. In 1905, he began by noting Krafft-Ebing's observation that "pleasure in pain," in the sense of physical pain, was less essential than subjugation and humiliation in conjunction with sexual excitement occurring at the hands of an idealized love object or authority. As Freud's concept of masochism evolved, the relationship between the partners became the model for a relationship between intrapsychic agencies, in that the superego became identified with the sadistic, dominant, or active partner, the ego with the masochistic, subservient, or passive one. This, in itself, was not confusing as it was still based on masochistic perversion.

The problem may be traced back to two changes in Freud's thinking. From 1905 to 1920, the prototype for mental life was the perversion; his famous (1905a) formulation: "neuroses are the negative of perversions" (p. 165). The new post-1920 prototype was the behavior of children. This is what led to the search for normal forms of masochism as a developmental stage of childhood and in adulthood. The second change was the introduction of Freud's (1924a) concept of "moral masochism," in which there is a need for punishment in response to an unconscious sense of guilt. The form it takes is displaced, disguised, the punishing parent abstracted into "Fate, destiny or God" (Fenichel, 1945, p. 145). To elicit punishment, "the masochist must do what is inexpedient, must act against his own interests, must ruin the prospects which open out to him in the real world" (Freud, 1924a, p. 169). As Grossman (1986) has emphasized, Freud discarded the requirement of a conscious link with sexuality, as well as the requirement that suffering should come from a love object. This formulation, more than any other, radically altered the concept of masochism that Freud inherited from Krafft-Ebing and Sacher-Masoch.

Masochism was freed of its link to perversion and, particularly with the emphasis on *unconscious* guilt, the concept cast an ever-widening net until it included all self-destructive behaviors. The term was used indiscriminately amid growing uncertainty as to its clinical value. There were some, like Schafer (1984, 1988) and Grossman (1986), who insisted on the most narrow, rigorous definition where for a behavior to be characterized as masochistic, there had to be a dominant orga-nizing fantasy modeled on masochistic perversion. Others expanded the definition and, as noted earlier, went so far as to include most forms of self-destructiveness and even normal development.

Types of masochistic behavior

Sexual masochism

This is what masochism originally meant. There is a restrictive, obligatory enact-ment of masochistic behavior to achieve sexual excitement and orgasm (Laplanche and Pontalis, 1973). The behavior typically includes pain, humiliation, and a giv-ing up of control (passivity, subjugation, bondage). There is always a partner or love object, even if only in fantasy. Kernberg (1988) made a useful distinction between sexual masochism as found in a neurotic individual from what one would see in someone with borderline personality organization. In the former, there is typically a scenario that is highly specific, that the masochist wants his or her partner to follow. There is safety within the script and agreed-upon limits and boundaries. Kernberg noted that the scenario has an "as-if" quality to it, a qual-ity of play-acting, and that the repetitive aspects of it help provide reassurance against unconscious anxiety and guilt. With the borderline personality masochist, on the other hand, situations are open-ended, risk-taking and actual danger may be present, the individual can get seriously hurt.

Nonsexual masochism (masochistic character or personality disorder, moral masochism, relational masochism)

The *masochistic character* or *personality disorder* is defined by a lifelong pattern of unconsciously arranged difficulties and failures in multiple areas of function-ing. When success is achieved, it is at great expense and at a level far below what might be expected. More often the outcome is what Reik (1941) called a "victory through defeat." In treatment, these patients may provoke the therapist to abuse them with cruel comments, excessive criticism, or premature and non-empathic interpretations.

While historically, authors regarded masochistic character as synonymous with *moral masochism*, others have viewed the former as more pervasive, and the latter as more internalized and discrete (e.g., specific inhibitions, lack of satisfaction, fears of success). The defining feature of moral masochism is unconscious guilt.

Another type of masochistic symptomatology is based on the need for a "bad enough" object (Rosen, 1993, 2007). In *relational masochism*, one's "relationship is unconsciously believed to be dependent on one's suffering or victimization. Existence outside of one's current relationship, however abusive it may be, may seem unimaginable" (PDM, 2006, p. 44). Berliner (1947, 1958) described the masochist's need to be loved by a "hating love object." Masochism may also be in the service of revenge; spitefully depriving the parents of pleasure in their child's success, while simultaneously eliciting their concern (Berliner, 1947, 1958; Gabbard, 2000, 2012).

Unless distressed and questioning ego-dystonic symptoms, the individual is unlikely to seek treatment. Individuals with sexual masochism may be otherwise successful (Baumeister, 1988; Krueger, 2010); the perversion remains encapsulated (Asch, 1988). However, some analysts have noted an inter-relationship between the two types of masochism. Kernberg (1992) described how patients with depressive-masochistic personalities will, as treatment is successful, introduce sadomasochistic sexual fantasies, play, and interaction, which facilitate the analysis of the underlying conflictual object relations. As their sexual masochism becomes more overt, he observed, there is a coincidental reduction of their masochistic character defenses.

Other analysts, however, have found sexual masochism coexisting with characterological masochism. Berliner (1958) thought they invariably did so, and finds evidence of this in the life of Sacher-Masoch and in his fictional characters. Glick and Meyers (1988) and Ornstein (2012) note the lack of a sharp delineation between the different types of masochism and conclude that they occur on a continuum.

Motives for seeking pain and suffering

Many explanations have been offered for why people might seek out pain and "unpleasure" (Bach, 1994; Grossman, 1991; Wurmser, 2007). There is agreement that the pain and suffering are not the goal or source of gratification in and of itself, but is a necessary condition for one or more of the following: (1) to expiate guilt, and symbolically allow gratification; (2) to avoid some greater pain, for example, the pain of suffering is thought preferable to the pain of loss; (3) to manipulate and control a more powerful person, or otherwise maintain magical control; (4) to please a parent; (5) to reenact a traumatic situation, and turn passive into active; (6) to protect love objects from destruction; (7) to inflict suffering on others.

Some authors have focused on the parents of masochists. Wurmser (2007) emphasized the role of multiple severe traumatization in childhood and attributed special importance to the squashing of individuality by a systematic, chronic disregard for the emotional needs, expression, and autonomy of the child. Studies have involved direct observation of mother-child interactions, the treatment of children who grow up to become masochists, and the treatment of masochistic adults (Glickauf-Hughes and Wells, 1991; Lebe, 1997; Markson, 1993; Novick and Novick, 1987, 1991; Shainess, 1997). Mothers of these infants derive little pleasure from their babies; they are unpredictable as parents; they externalize hated, devalued parts of themselves onto their children; and they are less able to contain their children's aggression. In fact, they often intensify aggression by their intrusiveness, their constraint of normal moves toward independence and autonomy, and their interference with the child's pleasure.

Self-defeating personality disorder

An alternative to the term *masochism*, aimed at getting away from its historical usage and connotations of sexual perversion, is *self-defeating personality disorder*. The newer term was adopted in response to feminist opposition to masochistic personality disorder, which was thought to have a gender bias and would be used against victims of rape and spousal abuse (Caplan, 1985; Fiester, 1996; Kass et al., 1989; Rosewater, 1987; Walker, 1987). The results of a letter writing campaign are found in Robert Spitzer's donated papers in the DSM-III and III-R Archives at APA headquarters.

Self-defeating personality disorder (SDPD) appeared in the appendix of *DSM-III-R* to encourage research and further debate (APA, 1987). However, it was not included in *DSM-IV* (APA, 1994). Some studies argued for reconsideration (Cruz et al., 2000), while others failed to support its validity as a separate disorder, largely on the basis of comorbidity with borderline, avoidant, or dependent personality disorder or with depression (Huprick et al., 2006; Skodol et al., 1994). Stone (2012) noted that this was true for many of the patients accepted into psychoanalytic treatment; that is, that they meet partial criteria for several personality disorders. Personality disorders overlap far more than they exist `pure;` thus, the frequent reliance on such terms as "subthreshold," "comorbid," and "not otherwise specified (NOS)."

According to Cooper (2009, p. 904), "it is long past time to acknowledge the existence of the masochistic personality disorder" (see also Gabbard, 2012, p. 104). It was not considered for inclusion in DSM-V. However, DSM-V has adopted the procedure used in the International Classification of Diseases, and has replaced the NOS category for personality disorders with Other Specified (301.89) and Unspecified Personality Disorder (301.9). ICD-9 (Centers for Disease Control, 2013) lists masochistic personality disorder as an example of "Other," (F310.89). ICD-9 was the official diagnostic coding system used in the United States, and remained so until October 2014, when it was replaced by ICD-10 (Centers for Disease Control, 2014). Masochistic personality disorder has been replaced by self-defeating personality disorder (F60.89).

Masochistic pathological gamblers

Sexual masochism

As part of the first genetic study of pathological gambling (Comings et al., 1996), a Human Behavior Questionnaire (HBQ) designed to provide a symptom review for 32 different diagnoses was administered. One question asked: "Have you ever had a period, lasting for at least six months, when you had recurrent intense sexual urges or arousing fantasies involving being humiliated, beaten, bound or otherwise made to suffer?" This was the *DSM-IV* criterion for masochistic perversion. Out of 140 pathological gamblers (110 male, 30 female), 9.4% answered in the affirmative. In Comings' previously published (1994) control group, none of the respondents answered yes to this question. He noted that follow-up interviews consistently validated responses to the questionnaire.

Among Comings et al.'s other findings, 16.5% of the pathological gamblers acknowledged an aversion to being touched (sexually or affectionately); 22.5% had an aversion to any kind of sexual contact with a partner. Yet of the males, 33.3% described themselves as having a greater than average sex drive; 18.4% answered that they had more recurrent thoughts about sex than others their age.

In our attempt to understand the relationship between masochism and gambling, it may be easier if we begin with some of the more extreme examples in which sexual masochism coexists with a masochistic character. These are individuals who not only act out their perversion but have severe inhibitions about success-oriented behavior. It is important they not pursue their desired goal, but if it should happen serendipitously, it may be permitted. One patient said that the only time he could allow himself to be treated lovingly or be taken care of was when he was sick or suffering. However, it had to happen accidentally. "That's the only time I feel I have a *right* to be taken care of because it's not of my own doing." By leaving things to chance, gambling allowed such accidents. Patients like the one just quoted may flip a coin, play computer games, or engage in various forms of *covert gambling* (Rosenthal, 1987, 2005) to determine whether they can pursue some desirable activity such as asking a woman for a date. They may make "mind bets" about the occurrence of some random or arbitrary event. Winning is interpreted as permission, with the individual then free to act.

A second explanation for the relationship between perversion and gambling has to do with the excitement common to both. In his book on perversion, Stoller (1975) stated, "To create the greatest excitement, the perversion must also portray itself as an act of *risk taking*" (p. 4). He observed that the greater the danger, the greater the excitement.

Clinical vignette I

Mr. M is a 40-year-old pathological gambler with co-occurring sexual masochism and a masochistic character. He has been playing poker for 26 years and works as a dealer, primarily in underground Chinese clubs. While growing up, he was teased and mistreated by his older sister. He was also beaten up regularly at school, where he was the only Jew and stood out because of his dark complexion. He has always identified with minorities, especially Asians. He felt unwanted by his parents. No one in the family ever showed affection. "If I told my father that I loved him, it would somehow be used against me."

The patient's father had lived in the shadow of a famous mother and a successful, preferred older brother. "Everything went to the brother," said Mr. M.

"The family treated my father like garbage." Mr. M strongly identified with his father. He pursued the same career as his father and paternal grandmother. Like his father, he failed at it, although he appears to have had the talent to succeed. Failure was safe and familiar; he has never felt comfortable with success. Mr. M is passively suicidal: "I have tried all my life to get myself killed." This is substantiated by accounts of his travels through the Middle East, his experiences working for a criminal organization, talking back to thugs, and provoking fights with strangers.

His early sexual experiences were failures – he was impotent until he learned to focus on masochistic fantasies. His partners have not been dominatrices or prostitutes, but girlfriends. His preferred relationships are with women who enjoy inflicting pain. He wants the woman to be dominant and cruel. If she is not, he will fantasize that she is. When not in a relationship, he will masturbate compulsively until he has dry orgasms and his penis is bloody.

With regard to his gambling, Mr. M did not have an early winning phase. He could not stand winning, and would hyperventilate whenever he did. More memorable were his losses. After a big loss, he would come home and have "incredible" sex, accompanied by particularly vivid masochistic imagery. According to Mr. M, he has often been sexually aroused and had orgasms while gambling.

The preceding vignette was of a masochistic individual with a borderline as opposed to a neurotic personality organization (see Kernberg, 1988). His masochistic fantasies are not specific scenarios acted out with a safe partner; they are open ended. Comparable behavior in his everyday life has led to his getting beaten up, and someday may result in his getting killed. His behavior is to be contrasted with that of the more neurotic sexual masochist.

For the neurotic masochist who is fearful of intimacy, the scenario acted out with a dominatrix or prostitute is a way to master a frightening situation. Just the fact of paying for sex may be sufficient to ease their anxiety about how much of themselves they will have to give. Having a scenario to act out relieves them of fearful expectations and pressure to perform. Gambling is similarly viewed as a way to control an uncontrollable and frightening situation. One patient said that the only thing he loved more than sexual masochism was gambling. When asked what it was he loved about it, he replied: "I guess it's the feeling of control. I get to decide what table I play at and whether to stay in a hand and how much to bet."

Masochistic gamblers, particularly those who combine sexual masochism with a masochistic character, may not have had an early winning phase or a history of a "big win," but may instead describe a particularly memorable "big loss." One young man attributed his getting hooked on gambling to the time when, in the course of an afternoon spent flipping baseball cards, he lost his entire collection. He was devastated, but remembers it as the first time he realized that he had the power to punish himself. He was eight or nine years old at that time.

Winning, as in the case of Mr. M, may be uncomfortable. One masochistic gambler said that when he lost everything, he felt relief. It was the only time he slept well and had a normal appetite. Another said: "If I won I felt guilty, and if I lost I felt guilty. But the guilt of losing was easier to tolerate." This is not just late in the gambling progression. The masochistic gambler may say that he never enjoyed gambling.

Masochistic gamblers may put themselves at a disadvantage by introducing additional obstacles for them to overcome. They may take unnecessary risks or try to win "the hard way." Since they may feel uncomfortable when they are ahead, an ideal situation would be one in which they are losing until the very end, but manage to avert defeat. For some gamblers, it isn't winning that is all important, but not losing (Rosenthal and Rugle, 1994). They "live on the edge," and flirt with the possibility of falling off. It is the risk of getting hurt or of losing everything that is exciting for them. These kinds of situations may be sexualized.

Nonsexual masochism

As part of the progression in the pathological gambler's career, we see not only an increase in the preoccupation with gambling, and in amounts wagered and lost, but an increase in shame, guilt, and depression (Lesieur and Rosenthal, 1991). Shame is a prominent response to being out of control. Feelings of disgust and self-hatred lead to a wish for punishment. Gambling then becomes a means for self-punishment. In these later phases of the disorder (Lesieur and Rosenthal, 1991), gamblers may feel exhausted but unable to stop. Wanting it to be over, they cannot get rid of their money fast enough. This is a wish that is often verbalized. While the gambler in these later stages *appears* masochistic, what we are seeing is a consequence of the gambling, and not something reflecting character pathology.

A better example of masochistic behavior is provided by those gamblers who live from crisis to crisis, digging themselves out of one hole only to put themselves into another. They have a fear of success ("success neurosis" – Freud, 1916) and work hard at sabotaging themselves. There are multiple explanations but, clearly, they seem more comfortable being in debt. These gamblers are most vulnerable to relapse when they have finally paid off what they owe and are just starting to have something for themselves.

Clinical vignette 2

Ms. N says that she has never enjoyed gambling but thinks of it as a means to an end. Once she has created a financial crisis, she has a purpose and feels alive. She will work three jobs in order to avoid being evicted and to keep her phone and utilities from being shut off. During this time, she has tremendous energy and motivation. She loves the feeling of getting herself out of a jam, even or perhaps especially one she created. At other times, she does not know what to do with herself and feels dead.

She first went to Gamblers Anonymous five years ago, not for herself, but because she met someone at a casino and, recognizing *his* need, took him to a meeting. She stayed and has become active. She volunteers for phone duty, serves on committees, sponsors people. When not gambling, she spends money compulsively, buying presents for others. The recipients usually feel guilty since she lets them know of her self-sacrifice. She thinks the solution to her problems is to feel more needed. The reason for her seeking therapy is that she is currently in her first healthy relationship, the man wants to take care of her, and this makes her extremely uncomfortable.

A frequent dynamic involves a power struggle between the action-seeking, competitive male gambler and his father. In this battle between the generations, money is the weapon of parental control. The gambler believes that his father wants him to fail, so that he will remain dependent on him and the family. He has mixed feelings of love and hatred and his ambivalence leads him to vacillate between loyalty and rebellion. Both sides of the conflict are expressed through gambling.

Clinical vignette 3

Mr. P is aware that he consciously tries to hurt his father by spending his father's money, and by "messing up." At the same time, he thinks of himself as the "good son" who is giving his father what he wants. It would be disloyal to grow up, he explains, and to want his own family and career. He believes that his father wants him to remain an emotional cripple. Being helpless and irresponsible is the way to get his father to show him love. "If I'm a loser, my father will love and take care of me." There appears to be some validity to this. Mr. P's father continued to bail him out until therapy showed early signs of success, at which point he abruptly withdrew his support, and bribed the patient into leaving the state.

The gambler may be angry at his father for not loving him the way he wants to be loved. He wants to punish his father, to make him suffer, but cannot do so without hurting himself. Sometimes the intent is not directly self-destructive, but to hurt his father's son, to make the father a failure as a parent. When the gambler loses, he wins, and vice versa. There are other cases in which the father is already considered a failure, most often in comparison with another family member. Mr. M's father was the "black sheep" of the family. In such situations, success for the patient is invariably believed to come at the expense of another. The gambler feels trapped in a situation he cannot win.

Clinical vignette 4

Mr. Q described the disparity in the family between his uncle, a wealthy and successful surgeon whom everyone looked up to, and his father, a college dropout and failed businessman. When his uncle would take them for expensive dinners or vacations, the patient found them exciting but was aware of how humiliating they were for his father. He identified with his father's pain. "We were the poor relations," he said. "I felt ashamed." At the same time, he felt guilty about wanting to be like his uncle, and for resenting his "loser" father. Complicating it further, his father was always putting him down, taking out his own frustrations by making the patient feel he would never amount to anything. Mr. Q, however, grew up to be extremely successful, far surpassing his uncle. He has never felt comfortable with this success. After each professional triumph, he goes on a gambling binge. There is shame and guilt, perhaps especially when he wins, and he is adept at punishing himself.

In this last example, the humiliated parent made himself feel better at his son's expense. The patient, in turn, both identified with his father and felt victimized by him. In some cases where the gambler's father is viewed as a failure, the mother may turn against her husband and try to put their son in his place. The patient feels not only suffocated by real and imagined expectations, but is sensitive to mother's rejection of the father. In each of these situations, pain and pleasure intermingle; winning and losing get confused.

Treatment of a masochistic pathological gambler

Ms. K is a 45-year-old chemical dependency counselor, with over 15 years of abstinence from alcohol and drugs. She began gambling just two years ago. At the time of admission to an inpatient gambling program, her gambling was out of control; she was severely depressed and actively suicidal.

Gambling history

Two years ago, she purchased a scratch-off lottery ticket and won a thousand dollars. This occurred on her way to an AA meeting, and when she got to the meeting and shared her "good fortune," everybody applauded. She felt rewarded, blessed, and high. At the time, she was working as a CD counselor, was going to at least two AA meetings a week, talking with her sponsor regularly, and working the steps. She thought she was "living the program." But she resented "having to be good all the time." She felt something was missing from her life. She wanted to be rebellious, and gambling presented her with what she thought of as a "safe way to be bad." So she bought more lottery tickets, and then went to Las Vegas.

The first time she set foot in a casino, her heart started racing, her breath became shallow, she started sweating, and her hands got sticky. This was before she placed her first bet. She felt she was in a place that was out of control, where there were no rules or boundaries, where "anything goes." When she started playing a nickel slot machine, she felt anticipation, hope, and fear. Her response was partly related to a belief that anything intensely pleasurable is necessarily associated with pain.

"You always have to pay for feeling good with pain." She described gambling as simultaneously offering both sets of sensations: "It's exhilarating, titillating. Kind of painful." A moment later: "It's exciting in a negative way," and "It's very uncomfortable."

She was confused as to whether gambling was bad or good. But, also, gambling was used to sort out her confusion as to whether *she* was bad or good, and whether she *should* be bad or good. "When I win, it's like God saying "I love you and you're a good girl." When I lose, which is most of the time, it reinforces how bad I am. Losing is a punishment, and if I'm punished, I must be bad."

Her machine was chosen carefully, and she believed she could influence it by concentrating very hard and controlling the energy flowing through her into the machine. Not only was it an extremely personal, important relationship for her, but her gambling was sexualized. While at the slot machine, she would become sexually aroused. She felt a great deal of shame and was embarrassed talking about it. Three months prior to her admission, she began masturbating with the fantasy of being in front of a slot machine that was paying off. While returning from her most recent trip to Las Vegas, she was flooded with memories of incest with her father. She had never forgotten the experience, but had not previously remembered it with such clarity and affective intensity. Shortly afterward she was admitted to the hospital.

Past and family history

Ms. K's parents were alcoholics who separated when she was a year old but who continued to fight over custody and child support. They would threaten each other, and the patient's father would threaten to kill his brother who had subsequently married the mother. Once, her father put a loaded gun to her head. Starting when she was an infant, he sexually abused her. This involved oral copulation and partial penetration. He would never physically hurt her but would call her his princess and tell her he loved her. She says those were the only times either parent expressed love for her. She remembers being regularly aroused during those weekends with her father. When she returned home, she'd be confronted by mother's anger at father's refusal to pay child support.

Her mother never acknowledged awareness of the sexual abuse, which continued until she was 11 or 12 years old. Instead, she berated the patient for being a burden. The patient described her mother as an angry, rejecting person. If she asked her mother for something, her mother's reply would be, "Why should you have that? I never did." She never experienced a loving relationship with her, and was surprised that she felt depressed when her mother died seven years ago.

The patient views her stepfather as her true father, and since he stopped drinking, he has been the one good parental figure in her life. Approximately 13 years ago, she broke off all contact with her biological father. Several years ago, he sought her out, and wrote her a series of letters expressing his interest in a romantic relationship with her.

Because of her need to please others, to be the "good girl," she did well in school, although she felt restless while there, and would stare out the window, mostly worrying about what she would find when she got home. Two of her three siblings also became alcoholics. She has been married twice, and did not feel she got close to either of them. Her first husband died from alcoholism. They had two sons who are now in their twenties. They turned out well, she says, and speaks of their upbringing as her proudest accomplishment. Her second marriage ended in divorce after six years. She currently has a fiancé, whom she describes as nurturing. The relationship is the first healthy one in her life. When he asked her to marry him, and she accepted, both the gambling and her depression were exacerbated.

Treatment

The patient had been seeing a female therapist for three months prior to her admission, but admits that she did not mention either her gambling or the sexual abuse. These two areas became the focus of treatment during her hospitalization.

I often had the feeling that I was treating not a gambler but a repetitive self-mutilator. She did, in fact, have obsessional thoughts of train wrecks or of her children and others whom she cared about being mutilated. The dynamics were similar to those of many habitual cutters (Rosenthal, 1988) in that, if she wanted or needed something, and reached out to someone for it, if she didn't get it she would blame herself and feel wrong for having wanted it. She believed that her neediness made her "bad," and would attack and punish herself for it. This was conceptualized in treatment as a sadistic mother chiding her, "Why should you have that? I never did," and then tearing her to pieces.

It was clear that marrying her fiancé meant leaving her dysfunctional family. She was aware of wanting to be taken care of by him. Yet becoming healthy was scary. "My life has been out of control for a long time. It's not comfortable, but it's familiar." When things are peaceful and quiet, she feels something is wrong. During her years of sobriety, she always felt that something was missing. "I found it again in the gambling, and I'm not sure I want to give it up. Gambling recreates the chaos, terror, panic, rewards, and punishment."

During the latter part of treatment, she focused most intently on her pain, which she referred to as "the glue that holds me together." By pain, she meant both emotional and physical pain. She estimated that she had headaches, backaches, or stomach pains 70% of the time. These had been present since childhood. Gambling was associated with intense physical discomfort, and exacerbated all her physical symptoms. However, it was those times when she was not in pain that troubled her. "To just relax, to let go, is scary. It means not being on guard, not being prepared." She clenched her fists and tightened the muscles in her arms and shoulders to show me. I was reminded of Reich's (1949) *muscular armor*, and the hypervigilance of those who have been traumatized.

Gambling was a way to feel connected. "The excitement, the intensity, and the pain were all there. I feel *myself* while I'm gambling. My body is humming and I feel alive. And even though it hurt . . . well, that's what alive meant to me." The opposite feeling, one of disconnection, which she called "floating in space," related to the dissociation from her feelings when exposed to intense overstimulation as a child and also to the experience of feeling cut off from her mother and abandoned by her. Pain protected her, held her together, and had multiple meanings, which had to be addressed before she could begin to let go.

Follow-up

In addition to illustrating a number of masochistic dynamics, the case illustrates the kind of intensive therapy that can perhaps be best conducted or at least begun in a residential or inpatient setting where the patient can feel safe and be seen frequently. Following discharge, Ms. K had two brief slips with regard to gambling. She took her father to court and pursued a judgment against him. It is now more than five years since her hospitalization. She is happily married to her fiancé, working in the chemical dependency field, and abstinent from alcohol, drugs, and gambling.

Concluding remarks

Gambling offers an escape from problems and serves to self-medicate intolerable affect. There are compensatory fantasies. A "big win" may prove one is loved or be the "spectacular success" that demonstrates one's worth to others. Individuals assign their own meanings to winning and losing; they play with risk and uncertainty, set up arbitrary tests, provoke responses; the immediate, all-or-nothing outcome may be used to determine where the gambler stands in relation to whatever is most important. In addition to "positive" motives for gambling, the activity may serve a masochistic agenda in which pain, loss, suffering, or humiliation are thought essential to expiate guilt; to gain control over traumatic helplessness; or to obtain love, attachment, power, and validation.

I presented clinical vignettes and a more extended treatment account to re-establish the legitimacy of the masochistic gambler and to demonstrate some distinguishing features. These may include a reversal of normal attitudes about winning or losing, the absence of an early winning phase, perhaps a memorable early loss. Masochistic gamblers may sabotage opportunities for success or create unnecessary obstacles for themselves. Losing may be more comfortable than winning or may be overtly sexualized. Instead of a slowly progressive course, they may become "hooked" with their first bet and progress rapidly.

In the presented case material, the masochism of the gamblers was not difficult to recognize. However, a couple of suggestions may help with the evaluation of similar patients. When gamblers are asked why they gamble and what they like about it, many will respond by mentioning the excitement or "action." Rosenthal and Rugle (1994) and Khantzian (1997) emphasize the importance of repeating and rephrasing the question until one gets a more personally meaningful answer.

They note that one person's "action" is not another's; it is necessary to pin down what is meant. With regard to the use of assessment instruments, I routinely use the Gambler's Self-Report Inventory (GSRI), a slightly updated version of the questionnaire used to develop the DSM-IV criteria (Lesieur and Rosenthal, 1998) and to study various physical and emotional responses (Rosenthal and Lesieur, 1992). It includes questions about sexual arousal.

Recognition of the masochistic gambler has important treatment implications. These are the gamblers for whom psychoanalysis may be most appropriate. Without some form of psychodynamic psychotherapy, they do not do well (Rosenthal, 2008; Rosenthal and Rugle, 1994). They may stop gambling but find that abstinence does not bring relief. They become more aware of their other problems and a sense of futility leads to relapse. Masochistic pathological gamblers may be among the chronic, frequent relapsers who never seem to put together more than short periods of abstinence. They may switch or substitute addictions and wind up attending multiple 12-step programs.

Conversely, they may never really connect with or feel comfortable in Gamblers Anonymous. This may be particularly true for single males, who are acutely aware that the majority of GA members are married. They cannot discuss their sexual masochism, and even the way they gamble, perhaps especially their attitude about winning and losing, causes them to feel different from other people in the program. They feel a strong sense of shame and self-identify as "sicker" than the others.

Masochistic pathology is underdiagnosed in gambling treatment programs. These patients "fall through the cracks" because they will not discuss their fantasies or behavior, in group or even with their individual therapists, unless they are made to feel comfortable and have reason to believe it will help. Medication may be useful in making negative affects more tolerable. However, they will require psychodynamic therapy to understand the purpose and meaning of their behavior.

Chapter 5

Shopping addiction

Ricardo Rieppi and Jean Petrucelli

Aside from sex and food, perhaps, money is the most emotionally charged subject in contemporary life and in the psychoanalytic consultation room. To be sure, the power of money over human kind is unsurpassed as either a reinforcer or universal narcotic (Rendon, 1991). Seen as having both symbolic meaning and quantifiable value, money is a carrier of conscious and unconscious feelings, significance, and strivings (Aron and Hirsch, 1992; Dimen, 1994; Krueger, 1986). While money can be defined as a unit of agreed-upon value exchanged for goods and services, its meaning is also suffused with conscious and unconscious associations to power, status, security, self-worth, love, happiness, freedom, control, greed, dirtiness, etc. (Fenichel, 1938). Cultural background, family values, developmental experiences, and emotional needs, in turn, influence our symbolic representations and perceptions of money and have a tremendous impact on our money-oriented beliefs and behaviors (Stone, 1972, 1979; Wahl, 1974). Because these meanings may remain outside of our awareness, unconscious motivations may clash with our conscious intents and, subsequently, create problematic money symptoms. Compulsive shopping[1] is one particular manifestation that illustrates the process and content of money symptoms gone awry.

We define "compulsive shopping" as a maladaptive preoccupation with shopping or buying that either (1) is experienced as overpowering, intrusive, and with irresistible urges or (2) frequently leads to spending more money or buying more items than intended, buying unnecessary items, and/or spending more time shopping than intended. Compulsive shoppers tend to buy items impulsively and in a pattern of shopping binges, and they inevitably experience significant social, occupational, or financial distress because of their shopping and buying behavior. Chronic compulsive shopping is not to be equated to the occasional shopping "spree," as the latter is not an attempt to regulate affect, release inner bodily tension, or to self-medicate depression and emptiness. Moreover, the addictive process of compulsive shopping can be differentiated from other, related problems associated with money, such as revenge spending, money addiction, the inability to enjoy money or acquire money consistent with one's potential (Krueger, 1988). From the perspective of action symptoms, compulsive shopping or buying is considered an attempt to amend a missed or derailed developmental need. This form of pathological shopping is seen as having both multi-determined defensive and compensatory features with the intention of temporarily regulating affect and tension states, creating the illusion of meeting a fundamental need, and serving a self-object function (Krueger, 1986, 1988, 2000).

Compulsive shopping, as a disorder, can be linked to emotional deprivations in childhood and it is seen as a way to fill internal voids and meet needs, which include seeking excitement, an inability to tolerate negative feelings, perfectionism, approval seeking, excessive dependency, impulsivity, compulsiveness, hoarding, and the need to gain control (DeSarbo and Edwards, 1996). Addictive compulsive tendencies toward consumption and the extent to which an individual perceives the experience of shopping and purchasing has an effect on their perceived feelings of desirability in the world at large. So, in that sense, the search for self and one's identity may be wrapped up in compulsive shopping and buying, and may target the vulnerability in those whose identity is rooted in a non-stable sense of self that results in a self-medication of sorts.

Compulsive shopping, as a presenting problem in the consultation room, might occur through referrals from legal or financial catastrophes. However, more often than not, compulsive shopping reveals itself through the course of an ongoing treatment in various ways. Sometimes, patients begin to speak directly about their relationship with money; at other times, we experience their relationship to money indirectly – through the relational enactments of behaviors such as wearing new outfits each session, arriving with loads of shopping bags, repeated compulsive gift giving to others, attempts to give many gifts to the therapist, or consistent lateness in paying therapy bills. When a patient jokes, "I'm a bit of a shopaholic, you know" or uses the expression "I shop until I drop," we may be offered unwitting glimpses into the needed exploration into the darker side of their relationship to money.

Unfortunately, the psychoanalytic study of compulsive shopping and buying has attracted relatively little attention throughout most of the twentieth century, with the exception of a few psychoanalysts (e.g., Krueger, 1988; Lawrence, 1990; Winestine, 1985) and independent research groups who presented case studies (e.g., Christenson et al., 1994; McElroy et al., 1994; Schlosser et al., 1994). Furthermore, despite the ubiquity and profound emotional and motivational impact of money, *the* vehicle that drives compulsive shopping, it too has consistently remained under-examined and, some would say (e.g., Krugeer, 1986), a psychological taboo topic in the literature and within our consultation rooms. While psychoanalysis has identified itself as a discipline that confronts disowned parts of the self, studies powerful emotional forces, and prioritizes the importance of gaining deep, personal understanding, it has consistently neglected a comprehensive understanding of the real, symbolic, and personal meanings of money (Krueger, 1991). This omission is unfortunate because a comprehensive and extensive exploration of taboo material associated with money and how patients regard and handle money can teach us a great deal about them. Not only does it help us reveal, understand, and resolve our patients' most powerfully influential attitudes, beliefs, and feelings, but it also provides us with an opportunity to potentially explore deeper issues of developmental arrest and psychic conflict (Krueger, 1986).

Our contribution will discuss historical and contemporary psychoanalytic perspectives on money and its use, with a primary focus on central themes that underlie our clinical understanding and treatment of compulsive shopping and buying. We feel that in order to understand the psychoanalytic meaning, clinical process, and treatment of compulsive shopping and buying, it is imperative to include substantive discussion of how money is perceived and understood in the psychoanalytic literature. Given that compulsive shopping is conceptualized as an action symptom involving money and its associated conflicts, we need to include a broad and thorough understanding of the relationship one has with money as it also reflects other ways of relating in relationship to others. Moreover, the inclusion of money is necessary when you consider that, unlike other compulsive and behavioral addiction disorders, compulsive shopping and buying is a sociocultural phenomenon that is greatly facilitated by financial forces, such as disposable income, marketing strategies, shopping opportunities, and consumerism (Faber and O'Guinn, 1992; Elliot, 1994). Although many psychoanalytic writers have begun addressing this "money taboo" (Krueger, 1991), it remains "as mysterious as sex, as steeped in ritual as religion and as volatile as politics" (Yablonsky, 1991, p. 66). It commonly evokes a deep, potent sense of greed, fear, shame, and disgust, which stems from an internal economy ruled by both unconscious fantasies of wish fulfillment and unorganized primitive experience (Carrington, 2015). Money also carries a deep relational meaning in that it represents a "microcosm of all social relationships and the vehicle for the individual's "realization" in our society" (Rendon, 1991, p. 160). Because money is located on the boundary between the concrete and the symbolic domains, it provides the means for managing our many anxieties by moderating unconscious libidinal and destructive desires while simultaneously facilitating rational, conscious, and economic transactions. It allows us to negotiate the complex oedipal configurations, including its key anxieties of absence and presence, by denying dependency, bypassing the fear of losing one's potency or the pain of not being the chosen one, and channeling the aggression that results from unmet needs (Carrington, 2015). Our chapter is organized into four sections: (1) psychoanalytic perspectives on money; (2) contemporary psychoanalytic perspectives on compulsive shopping and buying; (3) treatment of compulsive shopping; and (4) clinical material that illustrates issues related to the treatment of compulsive shopping.

Our discussion will include both the intrapsychic and the interpersonal/relational domains, but maintain that both inner and outer world, fantasy and reality, etc., inform us about the complex and personal stories that are evidenced by the symptoms of compulsive shopping. This will entail understanding the sufferer's relationship not only to money and buying but also to their caretakers on whom they depend, and who, to some degree, failed to meet their developmental needs. Like eating disorders and other various substance and behavioral addictions such as alcoholism, compulsive gambling, or even hoarding, compulsive shopping has overlapping dynamic issues to be considered. For example, shopping compulsions could also be thought of as "disorders of desire in which wanting, longing, hunger, and the vulnerability of reaching with one's appetite toward the 'world of others' has been subverted" (Petrucelli, 2015a, p. 14).

In order to fully understand and successfully treat compulsive shopping – like most other complex compulsive conditions and impulse disorders – we must also consider the sociocultural context while simultaneously holding in mind the various psychological determinants. Culture expressed by the advertising industry can be particularly influential with the promise of "buying this product and you can become whatever idealized self you aspire to be; and if you don't buy, you join the ranks of the outcasts" (Benson et al., 2010, p. 25). We will show how the symptoms of compulsive shopping are seen as both expressive and defensive in nature, and how these symptoms articulate, via behavioral enactments, what cannot be metabolized and expressed through the mind (Stolorow and Atwood, 1991). We will integrate a broad range of ideas from relational psychoanalysis – e.g., affect regulation, multiple self-states, body-states, dissociation, unformulated experience, mutuality, and intersubjectivity – in order to understand the unspoken bargains our patients make to protect their selfs.

Psychoanalytic perspectives on money

Despite the powerful and ubiquitous influence of money, psychoanalysts have written in rather emotionally distant and technical ways, suggesting a universal presence of deep and potent fear, shame and disgust (Carrington, 2015). Early psychoanalytic theorists were significantly keen on discussing instinctual components of money as well as prescribed techniques for handling money matters with patients. Freud (1908), for example, listed stinginess as a major trait of obsessional personality and traced its etiology to the pleasure felt by the anal phase child in retaining feces. Using illustrations from mythology, fairy tales, language, and dreams, Freud argued that money and feces were both domains of repressed mental life and he linked money with the unconscious psychological conflicts that led to anal character traits and symptoms (e.g., miserliness and greed). Freud's equation can still be found in contemporary language, with phrases such as "filthy rich" and "money grubbing" (Geistwhite, 2000). He viewed bowel movements during the anal phase as a child's original gift to others, proposed that this offering transforms to a wish to give or have a baby as the child enters genital organization, and considered gifts of monetary value as symbolic of procreative wish during adulthood. The developmental pathway becomes pathological if any factor of instinct or experience is too extreme, as can be seen in cases where excessive suppression leads to obsessive-compulsive symptoms (Freud, 1917b). Freud's (1909) famous case of the Rat Man suggested that a patient's monetary obsessions represented a way for him to bind hostile and erotic urges. In other clinical case material, he wrote about the relationship between preoccupations with money and defecation, and he claimed that he cured a patient's constipation by confronting and analyzing his patient's money complex (Freud, 1897a).

When it came to recommending techniques for handling finances, Freud (1913) famously observed that "money matters are treated by civilized people in the same way as sexual matters – with the same inconsistency, prudishness and hypocrisy" (p. 131). Furthermore, he recommended that money "is to be regarded in the first instance as a medium for self-preservation and for obtaining power" because "powerful sexual factors are involved in the value set upon it" (p. 131). Despite his observations and recommendations, Freud's case histories generally focused on intrapsychic meanings of money and rarely discussed his own money issues and how they might have affected the transference (Aron and Hirsch, 1992).

Freud's proposals were subsequently supported and elaborated by his early disciples (Ferenczi, 1916; Jones, 1918; Abraham, 1923; Fenichel, 1938) and the feces – money equation became an established psychoanalytic maxim (Akhtar, 2009). Ferenczi (1916) took a more developmental perspective and explored the gradual sublimation process that accompanies the progression and diversification of interest in money. He viewed our "capitalistic instinct" and interest in money as having a rational as well as an anal erotic component that included pleasure in both defecation and retention.

Jones (1918) described the vicissitudes of anal eroticism in adults, and highlighted a child's pleasure in withholding feces to intensify the pleasure of release and how this was related to procrastination, persistence, and narcissistic belief in one's perfection. He also elaborated on anal erotic drives and the problems associated with giving drives too free a reign, and argued that allowing these drives unrestrained expression could lead to unbridled generosity and a tendency to overspend. Abraham (1923) extended Freud's view of fecal matter being gifts, and saw fecal presents as babies given to or produced in identification with the mother. Therefore, the money spent on gifts can represent anal or genital interests, but the acts that are symptomatic of the anal stage can be due, in fact, to issues of the genital stage. For example, excessive cheapness and stinginess are not due to a fixation on the anal stage, but instead can result from a *regression* to an anal level because of genital conflicts.

Fenichel (1938) connected "the drive to amass wealth" with "the will to power" and "the will to possession." He described the former as narcissistic, rooted in the gain and loss of regard, and as a way for the adult to regain the feeling of infantile omnipotence. He stated that to regain that feeling, the ego needs a narcissistic supply from the environment. Fenichel believed that money was a primary source of supply and stated, "The original instinctual aim is not for riches, but to enjoy power and respect whether it be among one's fellow men or within himself. It is a society in which power and respect are based upon the possession of money, that makes all of this need for power and respect a need for riches" (p 79). Fenichel sharply distinguished "the will to possession" from "the will to power," as the latter extends one's ego and protects it from the threat of diminished boundaries. He viewed the desire for many possessions as a symbolic effort to protect against "ego shrinkage."

New conceptualizations of money began appearing as psychoanalytic theory shifted from its instinctual foundations to object relational and self-psychological approaches. For example, Klein (1935, 1937) theorized that greed originated in oral frustration and aimed to angrily devour the withholding breast. In Klein's model, money came to symbolize this elusive source of security later in life. In Kernberg's (1975, 1988) portrayal of narcissistic personality, he illustrated the fervor with which some narcissists pursue wealth and discussed the simultaneous role of money in creating omnipotence and dissolving the risks of attachment and dependence. In more recent Kohutian self-theory, money became a universal self-object. For example, Krueger's (1986) self-psychological perspective on money emphasized the exhibitionistic aspects of wealth aspirations, as well as how affluence was a way of finding affirmation, positive self-image, vitality, and coherence in an otherwise fragile self. Others have hypothesized about the psychological meanings of aspirations to acquire large sums of money, such as phallic competitiveness with one's rivals and sadistic wishes to triumph over one's "enemies" (Blanton, 1976; Fuqua, 1986; Kaufman, 1976).

As a counterpoint to psychoanalysis' early biological slant on human nature, a number of psychoanalysts from the ideological left began to look more deeply into social issues and institutions, and provided a critique of capitalism and its money fetishism (Rendon, 1991). These analysts – most notably Alfred Adler, Wilhelm Reich, and Erich Fromm – branched out from tradition and created a sociological and anthropological branch of psychoanalytic psychology. They were all influenced by Freud and Marx, and stressed socioeconomic issues, the role of money as an object of social relationships, and the relationally destructive and alienating nature of capitalistic societies. Adler focused on childhood experiences and the human need to compensate for weakness, and theorized that a striving for superiority develops to compensate for excessive feelings of inferiority and leaves the individual with an unattainable self-ideal. Reich criticized psychoanalysis for being paternalistic, patriarchal, authoritarian, and overly accepting of bourgeois morality, and openly questioned the existence of oedipal repression (Rendon, 1991). Fromm (1947), strongly influenced by Freudian ideologies, wrote about selfishness and altruism as two basic character orientations that are relevant in the discussion about the various meanings of money. He felt that drives are the result of faulty socialization and that people relate to the world through productive and unproductive assimilation and socialization. Fromm speculated that a number of productive and unproductive character orientations can result. A productive orientation refers to a person who accepts his/her biological and social nature while simultaneously striving for freedom and taking responsibility for his/her actions. Unproductive character orientations relate to aspects of compulsive shopping or buying. For example, someone with a receptive orientation receives satisfaction from the outside world, yet passively waits for others to fulfill their needs. Exploitative-oriented people, on the other hand, aggressively take what they want. Those with a hoarding orientation save what they already have obtained, be it their opinions, feelings, and material possessions. Marketing-orientated people are essentially empty and see themselves as commodities. Their self-worth and value are dependent on their ability to sell themselves.

Some of the more contemporary views have also focused on how our unique developmental experiences help form our identifications with money. We may have a positive identification with a successful parent, develop a self-definition (Scott, 1974) or ego ideal that is comfortable with success, and subsequently feel that work and material acquisition are possible (Hennig, 1974). On the other hand, we could identify with a parent who is unsuccessful, limited, or frustrated in the work arena, subsequently feel the invisible shackles of limited potential, and develop conflicts and fears around autonomy, achievement, and money management or acquisition (Krueger, 1986). For example, an individual who struggles with autonomy may manifest difficulties around money by retreating from matters of financial responsibility, wishing for someone to take over and make financial decisions, maintaining financial dependence on someone else, or creating financial crises that require rescue. Financial dependence may be emotionally equated with being loved and cared for, while financial independence and skill may be closely linked with losing love and nurturance. Other manifestations of autonomy struggles can be seen in people who distance themselves from dependency needs or who deny financial or emotional needs, such that they obsessively avoid any financial responsibility or demands that restricts independence (Goldberg, 1978), focus on acquiring money for its promise of freedom, or reject money because they believe its pursuits will encroach on freedom.

Clinical vignette 1

John, a 23-year-old male software designer and computer programmer with an Ivy school graduate degree finds himself in a new city with a new job and the promise of a "millennial" west coast ideal work/life balance. After seven months at this new job, feeling flat, bored, unfulfilled, and empty, he decides to give away his expensive bed purchased by his parents, and now sleep on the floor. By his account, "feeling the hardness of the floor" was an attempt to deny his physical needs, using his body to inform him and "feel" the lack of comfort. He explains this would be his body-to-mind reminder of his dissatisfaction with his current work situation, which remains acknowledged but unexamined in a frozen freeze frame state. However, John's experience on the floor is short-lived as he begins the flipside of a reckless cycle where he goes on a shopping spree that spins out of control. Feeling entitled, deserving, and re-energized from feelings of stress and deprivation, he now impulsively buys enough furniture for a small house and charges it on his parent's credit card. They gladly pay, because "they just want him launched and off the floor." John's urge to splurge in one fell swoop alters his mood state, gives him the opportunity to say "f – ck you" to his parents for using money as their emotional currency, and continues to keep him removed from facing the challenges and disappointments of a job lacking the passion and creativity he yearns for.

Struggles with relationships; parental dependency; fear of autonomy; "attempts" at individuation; feelings of anger, depression, isolation, and anxiety; and the subsequent relationship to compulsive buying all get enacted, in this example, on and off the bed. In the case of those who suffer from an addiction to money acquisition, we generally find an absence of a stable internal self-image and the chronic use of external sources to supplement deficient internal regulation (Kohut, 1977). They rely on others and possession of objects for esteem, and attempt to internalize these external sources through their lust for acquisition. They tend to relentlessly idealize what is greedily desired but unavailable (e.g., money, expensive items, admiration, fame, power, etc.) and equate financial worth with internal value, so their unending acquisition and insatiable desire provides narcissistic gratification and renewable pleasures. Money acquisition not only serves as a validation of worth but also reverses the chronic envy this person feels toward others (Stolorow, 1975). As the charm of the acquisition quickly diminishes, however, the goal is devaluated and the individual is left feeling disappointed, bored, and in need of an escape into new pursuits. In the consultation room, they often express vague complaints without clear psychological content. For example, they might not report problematic symptomatic behaviors but may instead complain about feeling empty, unmotivated, dissatisfied, and burned out.

Psychoanalytic perspectives on compulsive shopping

Pathological shopping has been recognized as an entity since the great descriptive psychiatrists like Kraepelin (1915) and Bleuler (1930). Bleuler wrote, "As a last category, Kraepelin mentions the buying maniacs (oniomaniacs) in whom even buying is compulsive and leads to senseless contraction of debts with continuous delay of payment until a catastrophe clears the situation a little – a little bit never altogether because they never admit to their debts" (p. 540). Bleuler described compulsive buying as an example of a "reactive impulse," or "impulsive insanity," which he grouped alongside kleptomania and pyromania. The study of compulsive buying went largely ignored for the next 60 years, and continues to be in relative infancy compared to other types of substance and behavioral addictions, such as alcoholism, drug abuse, and eating disorders (Benson, 2000).

Although still poorly understood, there is a rising consensus that psychological and biological parallels exist between compulsive shopping and addictions. Some consider compulsive shopping to be an addictive disorder (Glatt and Cook, 1987), and have grouped it with alcohol and drug use disorders. Others consider it falling on the spectrum of obsessive-compulsive disorders (Hollander et al., 1996) or mood disorders (Lejoyeux et al., 1996). Most recently, compulsive shopping is seen as sharing features and similarities with substance use disorders (Holden, 2001; Potenza, 2006; Shaffer, 1999). These similarities are also echoed in proposed core elements of addiction (Shaffer, 1999). For example, both involve (1) continued engagement in a behavior despite adverse consequences, (2) an appetitive urge or craving state prior to engagement in the behavior, (3) compulsive engagement in the behavior, and (4) diminished or lost control.

According to Dodes (1996), although compulsions and addictions are similar to each other, they have always been treated as quite separate and different entities. Moreover, he argued that there has not been an attempt to integrate them as diagnostic categories in the analytic literature. He proposed that "addictions are always compulsions, while compulsions frequently take on the characteristics of addictions and in these cases may be more usefully thought of as addictions" (p. 815). In fact, Dodes (2003) argues that addictions are psychologically indistinguishable from compulsions, which have always been understood as displacements of a forbidden drive. His view suggests the treatability of many addictions by psychoanalytic approaches that have focused on compulsions. For example, while compulsions are routinely consciously experienced as ego-dystonic, the unconscious elements in conflict that they express (the compromised nature of compulsions) can be discovered through psychoanalysis and resolved effectively.

Further supporting the notion that compulsive behaviors can be conceptualized as an addiction is the observation that compulsive shoppers' attitude toward their purchased goods is in some ways similar to the substance addict's stance toward their substance of choice. Their urge to buy items is usually expressed in a pattern of shopping binges and is frequently experienced as frantic and irresistible. The purchased items are not of intrinsic value or inherently desirable, are often useless and go unused, and are typically obtained in order to fill a subjective sense of internal emptiness. This compulsive shopping binge typically occurs in response to strong, negative feelings, in hopes of suppressing the emotional intensity and finding relief or euphoria. Moreover, compulsive shoppers are more prone to episodes of uncontrollable buying when they experience anger, loneliness, frustration, or irritability. They may also experience withdrawal-like symptoms, especially in situations where they miss "the one-and-only" opportunity to buy an item (Lejoyeux et al., 1999).

The behavioral act of buying often leads to intoxicating feelings of a "high," "buzz," or "rush" and works as the key emotional regulator. To the compulsive buyer's dismay, these positive feelings of pleasure or excitement are merely momentary and fleeting. Upon realizing that the purchases failed to fill their emptiness, compulsive shoppers often experience depression, disillusionment, shame, and guilt, and subsequently self-punish (Faber and Christenson, 1996; Krueger, 1988).

Clinical vignette 2

With Laura, age 34, there is no planned buying, there is only impulse buying, from external objects to food. If she sees something in a store she likes or while browsing on the internet, she must have it and cannot stop herself. Often it is expensive designer bags, or trendy clothes in a size 10, a size she desires to be, and once was, but doesn't quite fit into now. Shopping is her excuse to leave the apartment and it boosts her mood for a few hours. When she is home, she does not try on the clothes or use her designer pocketbook but hides them in the closet for fear that her husband will find out her "dirty little secrets." Riddled with feelings of guilt and shame in the aftermath, she feels complicit in driving her family into the financial debt they face. She believes, with conviction and contempt, that it is all her fault for the current predicament they are in. Laura's overspending began after the birth of their twins about seven years ago, and while at the time, she felt she got "two for the price of one." She also feels like she has lost herself. Never having money of her own, she applied for credit cards, racking up $22,000 in debt and then attempting to take out a bank loan, which she did. It ultimately ended up costing her almost double the amount owed. Laura's experience, while not a financially extreme example compared to some, is a typical and common occurrence that supports the psychological need for compulsive buying to be better understood as a maladaptive attempt to solve deeper-rooted issues – a way for Laura to come out of her closet – the place where her buried feelings reside.

Psychoanalytic treatment of compulsive shopping

There are several psychoanalytic viewpoints of addiction and their interventions that are relevant to our understanding and treatment of compulsive shopping. Each view offers a unique perspective, yet also overlaps with the other ideas to some degree. They can be roughly categorized into the following four areas that help us understand and treat shopping compulsions: (1) affect regulation and management; (2) the somatization of affect and psychosomatic illness; (3) limited access to fantasy, play, and symbolization; and (4) unique characteristics of the transference-countertransference in treatment. In regard to a therapeutic stance or attitude, the analyst needs to consider that compulsive shoppers tend to be action-oriented and therefore may need an approach that actively and meaningfully engages patients and incorporates their dynamics. In addition to exploring the intrapsychic variables that involve compulsive shopping, analysts need to utilize the transference-countertransference issues arising in treatment and collaboratively arrive at a better understanding of how the compulsive shopping expresses conflicting relational needs, as well as help the patient find new forms of relating that will undo old, destructive patterns (Bollas, 1987; Mitchell, 1988).

Affect regulation and management

In regard to affect disturbance, we find that those with problematic addictions demonstrate an inability to identify affects and to differentiate between affective states (Krystal, 1982), which Sifneos (1973, 1975) has coined "alexithymia." We find an underlying deficit in regulating, managing, tolerating, and processing the vast array of emotions, and this problem is compounded by the poorly developed ability to effectively use language in the management and processing of feelings (Barth, 2000). They also show an inability to use affects as signals to one's self, coupled with a general lack of reflective awareness (Krystal, 1974; McDougall, 1985). This is why the initial phase of treatment must directly name and address feelings manifesting in bodily symptoms or compulsively driven action behaviors such as compulsive shopping and buying, as it helps patients improve their emotional awareness and functioning. Patients with alexithymia tend to experience bodily sensations as opposed to feelings, such that anxiety and depression are experienced as somatic and not psychological states (Krystal and Raskin, 1970). For example, a person who compulsively shops can be more invested in the act of shopping, especially the feelings associated with shopping, than in the purchased item. When the act itself becomes the necessary action, the consequence of the act may be secondary. This leads to duplicate purchases of the same item because the individual has no memory of purchasing the item in the first place – a shopping "black out" resulting in a feeling of exhaustion or burn out that is a kind of altered state or as Bromberg (2010) has written about, a self-state that contains the creative use of dissociation. The mind selects the self-state configuration that is most adaptive at a given moment without compromising affective safety. In other words, whatever unbearable feeling the person may be having, the act of compulsively shopping serves to keep that state of mind out of awareness, thus avoiding the conflict which would create affective instability. The bodily manifestation after a shopping "binge" is one of short-lived euphoria often followed by guilt, shame, and intense bodily fatigue.

Several authors have pointed out a relatively higher incidence of compulsive shoppers who also present with eating disorders (e.g., Christenson et al., 1994; McElroy et al., 1995; Schlosser et al., 1994; Petrucelli, 2004). One explanation of this consistent finding is that individuals who exhibit binge-eating and those with shopping compulsions experience serious difficulties in regulating impulses and managing feelings. It is also noted that both use rituals (eating and shopping) to relieve tension and ameliorate affective disturbance. For example, preparing or eating food, just like looking for and buying items, can serve as attempts to soothe, relax, and energize. Naturally, these activities become highly problematic when used repetitively, compulsively, and as undifferentiated responses to a range of different feelings. In both cases, the individual is unable to process or manage feelings that include both psychological feeling-states and body-states that are unlinked to their eating and shopping behavior (Barth, 2000). As noted previously, a primary therapeutic intervention educates the patient about their attempts to cope, to label and differentiate the psychological and physiological feeling-states, and to identify the emotional triggers and links associated with the impulsive and compulsive eating and shopping behaviors.

Somatization of affect and psychosomatic illness

Drawing from early object relations literature (i.e., Klein and Winnicott), McDougall (1974) referred to addictions as "action disorders" (p. 449); in addictions, painful psychic states are dispersed and evacuated through action rather than through feeling and talking. McDougall (2001) later suggested that the repetitive behaviors typical of addiction are caused by perpetual and circular states of satiation/starvation fantasies. Moreover, she argues that this is not a masochistic attempt to cause self-harm, but rather a misguided attempt to address an early source of deep psychic pain. Stuart (2001), speaking from an interpersonal psychoanalytic perspective, agrees with McDougall but adds that addiction patterns are also a way to manage complex and problematic interpersonal problems. In addition to exploring the internal experience and emphasizing the intrapsychic aspects of addiction, Stuart considers it essential to explore very carefully the patient-therapist relationship and focus on the transference-countertransference. Through these methods, she adds, we gain more access to a patient's early history and to their deepest domains of needs and psychic pain.

Addictions are also seen as ways to regulate (Khantzian, 1985), defend against (Wurmser, 1974), and contain (McDougall, 1985) overwhelming affect. This has led Khantzian (1985) to introduce the "self-medication" hypothesis of addiction. Similar to other compulsions and behavioral addictions, we also find disowned and dissociated self-states and body-states that accompany compulsive shopping (Petrucelli, 2015a). In their attempt to maintain "self-continuity and self-organization" (Bromberg, 1998, p. 206), they rely on symptoms of compulsive behaviors, such as shopping, buying, etc. The communication through bodily actions, such as compulsive shopping, point to a clinical population that is heavily overrepresented in the realm of alexithymia (Barth, 2000; Krueger, 2000) and unformulated experience (Stern, 1997).

Krueger (1989) argues that the developmental deficit associated with pathological action symptoms involves the arrested development of the body self as well as the psychological self. He notes that the deficit of body self includes a distorted or incomplete body image, as well as an overreliance on the perception of others. Among patients who exhibit significant arrest in their self-development, disturbances in differentiating self and other inevitably influence their ability to symbolize their body self and the affective self. Therefore, their distinctions between the symbol and the object symbolized are incomplete, which leads to concretized thinking about the self and a poor capacity for abstraction or representation of the body and its contents. Without a basic distinction between symbols and objects symbolized (other, self, feelings, etc.), the compulsive buyer must rely upon the immediate experience within the body to elicit a self-representation. However, the representation of self can only take place through the body of experience and cannot be achieved symbolically. Krueger (2000) states that therapeutic interventions need focus on integrating the distorted and dysfunctional body self and psychological self, thereby helping the patient develop a more cohesive self and internal point of reference. He believes that empathic attunement plays a central role in treatment, as the therapist is able to gather information by placing him/herself inside the patient's entire experience, the patient has earlier empathic failures addressed by a therapist who attends to and acknowledges internal experience, and the therapeutic process helps the patient develop self-empathy, self-structure, and self-regulatory capacities.

In situations where there has been an empathic rupture in a self-object bond, or the unavailability of a necessary self-object, the compulsive buyer attempts to fill the emptiness and restore the bond. Krueger (1989) argues that compulsive shopping and spending can be seen as an attempt at external enhancement of body attractiveness and desirability, hoping to address loneliness and emptiness by engaging others to validate their worth and desirability. Because no consolidation of a distinct and complete image of either the body self or the psychological self has taken place, the compulsive buyer is functioning at a concrete, non-symbolic level of operation and is unable to allow for the required psychological distance for movement beyond a transitional object. Symbolic equations replace true symbols (Segal, 1978), and the individual sees and experiences the purchased items as original objects rather than as substitutes. There is no "as-if" quality, and the individual must engage in specific, concrete, body-oriented stimulation or another form of action (i.e., compulsive shopping) in order to achieve a representation of the sought-after object.

An individual with a defective or poorly developed body self (and, by extension, psychological self) will be motivated to complete and repair that basic defect (Krueger, 1989). When the self-object experiences have not been met accurately and consistently enough over developmental time and not fully internalized, an individual will find alternative means to seek self-organization, cohesion, tension relief, and vitality. The symptomatic use of money, for example, is a way to soothe, calm, revitalize, establish, or restore an affective experience because it provides a sense of control and immediate and tangible effectiveness. Going forward, future threats to an individual's sense of cohesion will likely lead to the same pattern of using money or of shopping to restore self-cohesion (Krueger, 1991).

Limited access to fantasy, play, and symbolization

Patients with shopping addictions tend to exhibit a remarkable absence of a fantasy life, such that they lack a capacity to utilize their imagination in the service of self-soothing (Krystal, 1995). There is a failure in symbolic functioning (Wurmser, 1974; McDougall, 1985) that results in a lack of awareness and reflection, as well as an absence of dream and fantasy material. Addicted individuals are unable to self-soothe due to the lack of an internal representation of the mother as a caretaking introject (McDougall, 1989). McDougall (1984) also noted "a psychic gap between emotions and their mental representations" (p. 388).

The process of helping a patient to symbolize by focusing on their ability to make significant connections between their internal experience and behaviors is not a straightforward or simple task. This is true even when working with intelligent, articulate, and seeming insightful patients, who may still lack access to inner processes, have trouble conceptualizing emotional cause and effect, struggle to symbolize thinking, and lack a sense of personal agency (Barth, 1998, 2000). Thus, they typically have problems moving beyond the concrete level of subjective experience and often suffer from what Benjamin (1992) calls "foreclosure of symbolic space" (p. 56) and what Ogden (1986) describes as a collapse of the "space between symbol and symbolized" (p. 213). Given that compulsive shoppers utilize action to communicate unsymbolized experience, we need to look directly *at* their concrete actions in order to just begin to outline their conflicts. It is therefore common to observe that they remain unaffected by well-intentioned complex interpretations, but instead benefit from a gradual understanding of how their behavior is purposeful and meaningful. We find that patients will benefit most – i.e., develop an internal structure, trust in others, ability to observe themselves, and an ability to tolerate affect – from a therapist who communicates genuine interest in the patient's areas of interest and who patiently explores the experience-near details (Tolpin, 1983), including the concrete details related to their eating and shopping behavior.

Transference and countertransference in treatment

In considering transference and countertransference issues in the treatment of compulsive shopping, we invariably need to consider the role of enactments in analytic practice (Ellman and Moskowitz, 1998). In interpersonal and relational theory, enactments are regarded as both unavoidable and, yet, *the* central medium of treatment. Through enactments, the analytic dyad can jointly experience and revive old relational patterns, and can use them to observe, understand, and work toward change within the analytic relationship (Mitchell, 1988). By placing enactments at the heart of analytic work, practitioners can widen the door of psychoanalysis to compulsive shoppers because it provides them with a mode of communication that is action-oriented and preferred by compulsive and addicted patients. They also provide a bridge between action and meaning, purchased item and object, act of shopping and underlying relational needs.

As we know, various affect disturbances and problems with symbolizing experience can easily result in pronounced impairment in the patient's ability to free-associate, dream, and engage in fantasy and play. Clearly, these are all difficulties that profoundly impact the therapeutic relationship. Take, for example, Krystal's (1995) experience with patients who present with compulsions and addictions: "On first impression, the patients strike observers as especially practical (they like to think of themselves as 'action people'). In actuality, they have a 'thing' orientation as opposed to a people (and self) orientation" (p. 69).

Krystal noted that when working with alexithymic patients, analysts commonly feel misled by what appears to be superb adjustment to reality. Underneath this pseudo-appearance, however, the patients struggle to empathize and feel emotionally involved or connected with others. Consequently, the transference relationship may present as "dull" or "dead" and the analyst may feel increasingly helpless, frustrated, tired, bored or guilty. Not surprisingly, poor patient engagement is one of the major factors that leads to addictions treatment failure.

Krystal (1995) has noted that signs of trauma or posttraumatic stress are routinely encountered in addicted individuals. Given the established relationship between trauma and dissociation, this may also explain the presence of dissociation in shopping compulsions. In addition to alexithymia and affect intolerance, there are often problematic inhibitions in self-care (Khantzian, 1985; Krystal, 1995) and a pervasive distrust of people and, more importantly, the analyst. Khantzian (1978) and Wurmser (1985, 1995) also wrote about the remarkable challenges of working with the contradictory and alternating sides or attitudes of these patients. Khantzian (1978) referenced Kernberg's (1975) writing on splitting and primitive dissociation usually present in narcissistic disorders, in which apparently opposite and extreme attitudes may coexist in alternating patterns, as a way to explain why addicted individuals exhibit these ways of relating.

Wurmser (1985) observed the presence of "split identities" amongst patients with addictions, a phenomenon that is highly consistent with others' observations of dissociative processes (Bromberg, 1998; Davies and Frawley, 1994). Wurmser describes how rapidly and unexpectedly these patients can shift from one self-state to another self-state that sometimes contradict each other (Bromberg, 1993; Davies, 1996a). He asserts that these part-identities are in conflict with each other, but he suggests that the individual may also be alternating between dissociated states that are impermeable and thus unknown to each other (Bromberg, 1993; Davies, 1996b). For patients to experience and reflect on their experience of conflict, they would need to have simultaneous access to and contact with more than one self-state, which would be considered a major therapeutic achievement and signal greater fluidity between self-states (Bromberg, 1993). The following case material illustrates how the issue of compulsive shopping, a symptom contained in a self-state, served as a continuation of a patient's battle with symptom substitution in her struggle with addictive behaviors, internal emptiness, and identity.

A detailed clinical illustration

Tina was 25 when we started working together. I (JP) was surprised by how unkempt and disheveled her appearance was. Aside from her long, greasy, unwashed hair, ripped and surprisingly not-so-fashionable grubby jeans, she had holes in her sneakers, food stains on her shirt, and a flat vacant expression on her otherwise exquisitely beautiful face. I remember my first thought and it was startling, relatively unkind or maybe just filled with utter confusion: "She had sounded so put together on the phone . . . is this the same woman I spoke with?" What I didn't know then is that Tina would and could physically look and dress like a different person almost every time she entered my office. I grew to expect the unexpected, be it pink hair, blonde hair, red hair, brunette, punk clothes, Goth, the little black dress, business suit, summer floral dress, trendy downtown New Yorker, Prada, Gucci, Chanel, Versace, or Ralph Lauren designs. Today, I was getting one of her "fuck it" days, she explained. She started with an apology, probably in response to the look on my face, which was a mixture of surprise, curiosity, and apprehension: "I'm in the worst part of my cycle now. If I could hide in the woods, even the wolves would run away, so don't be afraid or alarmed."

I'm not an easy sell but her charming way of disarming me now had my full attention. After all, this was a consultation, nothing had to be decided immediately. But I wondered, who was this person who could show up at an office for the first time, pay full fee, dress like a bag-lady and be so perceptive and unabashed to call herself out with her opening line while recognizing the need or having the feeling that she might also need to reassure me? Her opening anxious comments served to deflect and confuse – hiding what might really be of import with an expectation to not be understood. Her enigmatic expression could be flat with deliberate indifference and confusing unawareness, switching into a smile with thirsty eyes – all of which seemed to serve as part defense and part offense. Over time, I came to understand that the presence of another part of her behind the scenes, a more vulnerable part, felt that the only way it could enter the treatment room was by literally "dressing the part." I began to wonder what role dissociation played in her psychic structure, holding the awareness that her hypervigilance was, on some level, serving to protect her against affective dysregulation.

Although Tina's husband initiated the process of her entering treatment, after a year and a half of weekly psychotherapy, she requested to come to treatment three times a week because: "she knew I was a psychoanalyst," "more was always better," and since her husband was traveling so much and never home, "therapy could be *her* distraction." Feeling unvalued was a predominant theme in Tina's life, which often translated into her purchasing valuable things, and I wondered if therapy was now her new "purchase" and I was to be likened to the "salesperson" giving her the devoted attention she craved and received while shopping. Would she be trying things on for size, buying and returning, wearing things for show, or storing unused items in her closet, collecting items of value to ensure constancy countering historical feelings of low self-worth and emotional impermanence? What I did know is that this would be an extended shopping spree and we were in for the long haul.

Money for Tina was also once removed and "could feel like play money" as it all came from her husband's earnings. Would the treatment have a "once-removed" distance inherently protecting her from calling it something of her own? What role would money have in our relationship? Money was allowing her the possibility of a genuinely new experience in the analysis, in addition to remembering, repeating, and working through her issues from the past – including the knowledge that Tina would never have had the opportunity to do treatment if it were not provided for her. While understanding the realities of her situation, I also had to confront the monetary bind that in order to be paid, I had to hold the discomfort that in her not paying for her own treatment, I would be, like her "husband" colluding in her lack of agency. Dimen (1994) has written about how money inherently makes the analysis itself a commodity for both the analyst and the patient that influences the transference and countertransference field. The symptoms that brought Tina into treatment varied in intensity over time but ran the gamut from depression, anxiety, a history of cutting, to substance abuse with cocaine, pot, alcohol, opiates, and cigarettes; to anorexia, bulimia, bulimarexia, and compulsive buying and shopping. She saved the compulsive shopping part to tell me last, which was of note at the time, and in the interest of this chapter, will be the issue I will focus on. It was also the symptom that endured.

A brief mention of Tina's early history growing up in chaos and confusion includes her struggles with feelings of abandonment, insecure attachments, self and affect regulation issues, living in a non-stable body, and a co-dependent relationship with her depressed, alcoholic, often un-properly medicated mother. Tina's father left her mother when Tina was a year old and was intermittently involved in her life in her early years. Her father remarried when she was six, then disappeared completely from her life with his newly created family. Tina's mother, a raging alcoholic and factory worker, raised her as a single mom; possessions became a sense of security for Tina and her mother, very early on. In terms of possessions, her mother was a hoarder, buying items from the dollar store. Twice they were forced to vacate apartments due to the fire safety and health hazards created by the amount of physical stuff her mother accumulated. Tina grew up in the Midwest and for a brief period of time, they lived in a trailer. She was exposed to her mother's everchanging boyfriends as "strange men who would be making coffee in the morning" and then come and go. Sitting down to do homework, if done at all, usually took place at the local bar, waiting for mom.

Tina was a shy, quiet kid, always afraid to ask questions in class. She had enuresis until she was 11 years old, never went to doctors; her mother forged all her medical records for school. Tina moved out at the age of 17, came to NYC with a boyfriend, and began modeling. She had a modicum of success, landing a few jobs that took her to Japan – where she also became anorexic, bulimic, and then addicted to cocaine. At 19, she met a successful, wealthy, workaholic older man, got pregnant, and they quickly married at City Hall.

Money was no longer a concern; with two nannies and plenty of time on her hands, shopping became her daily activity to fill the void. Money also became the psychic economy to "buy her entourage" – "friends" were people that worked for her or people she gave money to as they inevitably took advantage of her. This included family members. When Tina's mother asked her for money for her third cosmetic surgery, Tina finally set a boundary and distanced herself from the relationship. After Tina said no more money, her mother was never in touch with her again. In the years that followed, Tina, still estranged from her mother, came to understand that this relationship was a complex toxic and disorganized attachment only fueled by her supply and her mother's demand. Out of sight, out of mind, was the only way she knew how to deal or "soothe" herself from the unbearable feelings of yearning, loss, disappointment, anger, and rage. Her experience of talking about these painful feelings would involve intensely reliving it with me, and we did. The more real the experience felt with me, the more its existence threatened to betray her mother, who had hurt her, and betray the parts of Tina that also identified with her mother. It took years for this to become a co-created known and felt experience between us. The pattern that she kept repeating involved getting into relationships with people who didn't care about her, while simultaneously using a substance or engaging in a compulsive behavior, which varied over time. Regardless of which substance she was using and working on to stop using, the consistent symptom that remained unchanged was her compulsive shopping – her "secret weapon" to protect herself from the excruciating feelings she didn't want to name or know.

During the initial phase of treatment, each outfit Tina wore to sessions depicted a different part of her which served as the headline representing a feeling or self-state that would distract while her more conflicted parts or unruly feelings could remain dissociated – out of her awareness. They were often in direct contradiction: if she felt insecure and needy, she wore her black Gucci business suit with stiletto heels; if she was feeling "don't mess with me," she wore Goth; if annoyed with me she fluctuated between imitating my style and wearing a similar "one of a kind" vintage jacket (that we both happen to own) and extra jewelry; when her aggression was more dissociated, she would dress in dirty ripped grunge clothes that would have me wondering if a towel was necessary for her to sit on; if in "trouble" she wore floral dresses and Prada shoes. A part of Tina would be "talking" through her costumes, conveying things that served various relational needs, while always living in fear of the anticipated disappointment of the other, which inevitable happened between us. She kept me in the dark and I stayed there – not knowing what it was I *didn't* know. Sometimes, she felt I was showing a preference for her to "be a certain way" and she would raise topics she perceived I might want to hear about – sometimes accurate and sometimes not. And while this occurred, we came to understand that another part of Tina would remain hidden and focused on keeping her emotionally safe. Due to the dissociated trauma of her past, no matter how safe a given situation might seem to most, trusting in an Other would be dangerous to Tina's sense of stability and selfhood. Words had failed her, the trust in human relatedness had been broken and Tina needed to rely on a dissociative mental structure in order to "feel safe." In comparison, shopping for clothes, shoes, and bags and spending money felt "safe." As mentioned in the first part of this chapter, compulsive shopping and buying provides the means for managing one's anxieties by moderating unconscious urges and destructive desires. This may have helped Tina also negotiate other issues – e.g., feeling secure by denying dependency, bypassing the fear of losing one's potency or the pain of not being the chosen one, and channeling the aggression that results from frustrated needs.

For alexithymic patients who are compulsive buyers, the buying deadens, stimulates, and comforts simultaneously (Barth, 2000). When Tina compulsively shopped, she was avoiding getting in touch with any inner thought processes; initially, she did not have the ability to conceptualize emotional cause-and-effect, could not identify triggers leading to impulsive behaviors, or have any desire with agency to be the captain of her ship. She found it safest to withdraw from others as much as possible, upping the ante by responding vehemently with a louder binge and purge cycle, increasing the frequency of alcoholic black outs or syncope occurrences, or the random $20,000 shopping spree. In order to build the kind of internal structure Tina needed, I had to communicate genuine interest and curiosity about the most specific and concrete details of what was most important to her – clothes, shoes, and handbags – and to be honest, it was not too difficult to do. While I never understand the handbag phenomenon, I did share a penchant for clothes and shoes. In addition to addressing the more pressing symptoms of her addictive personality and her eating disorder, which we did over the course of this seven-year treatment, we also addressed the symptom that remained over time – her compulsive shopping and buying.

In the course of our work, we dissected every moment of her actual shopping behavior, understanding that her compulsive buying is serving some "maladaptive" purpose to be unearthed but respected and understood. She has paid focused mindful attention to her experience in an attempt to understand the self-state she enters that embodies her shopping urges . . . pre, during, and post. She has looked at shopping binges as a way to act out her anger, feelings of envy, jealousy, deprivation, loneliness, fears of being judged or rejected, feelings of low self-worth, neediness, or her efforts to win approval, loyalty, love at any cost. She has unpacked her "bulimic spending," a way to keep her bank account always broke, psychically empty and evacuated, as soon as money enters. However, the "bulimic spending" also ensured, albeit superficially, "attention" from her husband whose only response would be to quickly tell the accountant to replenish her account – never getting angry at her about it. Tina recognized that her husband treated her more like a mistress than a wife, never asking where her new things come from and often not even noticing. Tina felt entitled to engage in whatever behaviors suited her; the cyclical pattern remains. While we kept looking to try to understand Tina's relationship to the thing itself (the shopping and merchandise), I wondered perhaps if feeling bad, in and of itself, was what Tina was driven to seek.

What we came to understand over time was that Tina was a woman who felt neither liked nor wanted, unloved and unlovable, never feeling secure in the world, and had always felt inferior, unsure of herself, and aware of her "limitations." She was disengaged from people and being alone was safe and comforting in a lonely kind of way. Her lack of curiosity was palpable; she was a woman who did not ask questions and did not seek answers. Lost like an outsider in a world she does not understand and does not seek to understand, she only came to treatment at her husband's request or rather "demand" in an effort to "please" him. And so, for much of her early treatment, she was uncomfortable with herself and afraid to find out who she is. In treatment, she presented her "false" self (Winnicott, 1960) to protect the vulnerable parts of her in search of a home. Her clothes, shoes, and pocketbooks were her costumes, her decorations, and her armor. To reiterate something mentioned in the first part of this chapter, "symptoms of compulsive shopping and buying are seen as both expressive and defensive in nature, and how these symptoms articulate, via behavioral enactments, what cannot be metabolized and expressed through the mind" (Stolorow and Atwood, 1991, p. 181). And money, the vehicle that enables compulsive shopping and buying, can evoke a deep, potent sense of greed, fear, shame, and disgust, which stems from an internal economy that is ruled by both unconscious fantasies of wish fulfillment and unorganized primitive experience (Carrington, 2015).

Gradually, over time, she became curious about herself and her steady stream of symptom substitutions, which started to puzzle her. With every symptom, she had to hit a dramatic rock bottom before she, and she alone, and on her own would decide SHE had finally had enough. This growing curiosity was reflected in her presentation of and willingness to work on dreams. Dreams felt safe to her and she could muse out loud with me while feeling like she could still protect her vulnerable parts. Dreams became her pathway to knowing herself and the various parts of herself. References to dream themes and the unconscious meanings of her creative, symbolic imagery were central throughout our work. And in all her dreams the one thing she could always remember was what she was wearing.

In her dreams, themes emerged that represented conflicted feelings around aliveness, attachment, and often contradictory behavior: Tina seemed playful but didn't know how to play; Tina showed up for sessions but sometimes to the wrong office and when that happened, she was upset and worried if I would be upset, too; Tina would dream that she almost had "slips" of self-destructive acts and would feel relieved when she woke up. More recently, she would dream of returning clothes and not remember buying them and/or not have access to her favorite shops. For example, in one dream – *"Barneys was closed down. The lights were gone. I thought, where am I going to get my grilled cheese? The ceiling was painted white. I was wearing my red stiletto high heeled shoes but they didn't match my dress."*

Her associations were to her feeling state of being in shock – "Why did "you" close?" she asked, and then laughed at her "slip." "I meant *it* not *you* but are you my Barneys?," she giggled, "That's my most important shop." If shopping at Barneys was her "go to" place of shopping addiction, if it were out of sight, out of mind, shut down, then she "couldn't" shop. We were approaching a summer break, but what did "being Barneys" mean to her. Was she worried she would shut down? Be symptomatic? Be relieved that she had a break and didn't have to "work" on herself? But, am I also "Barneys" in the sense of holding the attachment – she keeps a place – through having symptoms? Was she ambivalent about feeling more connected, wanting it while needing to push it away? Her "slip" of referencing me reminded us of her need to hold on to our connection via having a symptom. In her mind, was she worried she would have to give up treatment if she stopped "shopping?" Where was the line of healthy dependency versus an unhealthy attachment? I needed to stay mindful of not "feeding her" while helping her learn how to "feed herself." Tina was surprised that it wasn't missing the buying of clothes that she was most upset about: it was the grilled cheese – her comfort food – which was the one food she fondly remembers her father lovingly making for her in the early days. We explored together why the ceiling in her dream was "white" – she thought a reference to a clean start? I considered the reference might also be to the White Institute (again related to her connection with me). I wondered if the red stiletto shoes represented her longing and desire and its dangerousness or "mismatch" to other parts of her, as she was getting stronger in her resolve to find her own voice with agency and integrity without using a symptom.

Symptoms maintain a state of mind, full of fantasies of possibilities of a moment or a life, without what "*feels*" unbearable (Petrucelli, 2004, 2010, 2015a). Can Tina begin to genuinely know what it feels like to be alive, feeling longing and desire? Her compulsion to buy became a hyperaware 'solution' to avoid the consequences of living a life that felt empty while imagining others having something that she *does not* and *cannot* know what that experience is. The resulting hyper-deadness (anesthetization) that followed from shopping, buying, and returning forced her to focus on nothing but her symptoms even if she would *prefer* not to. It allowed her to believe she was "getting away with something" (Phillips, 2010). In reality, Tina had protracted the torture, deferring the moment of punitive truth of accepting imperfection. In the illusion of pseudo desire, appetites and their wants could *seem* bearable.

"I can have all the designer clothes I want and never face the idea of the thing not chosen. I can keep everything in my closet and no one can hurt me." Tina felt enslaved by her inability to contain desire as regulatable affect. It is, rather, experienced as an overwhelming state in which she wished and hoped to have everything all the time – commonly known as "greed." Particularly regarding human contact, greed overwhelms the patient who therefore attempts to control "appetite." Trying to eliminate the potential for traumatic rupture in human relatedness, one replaces relationships with objects, a self-contained solution not subject to others' betrayal (Bromberg, 1998). The desire to have it all runs into pressure and the need to choose. This necessity creates either a refusal (no more wants and frustration) or, if one chooses, one must contend with the loss of the thing not chosen. External indifference and non-recognition that this is a loss leads to dissociative "indifference" and making sure that loss becomes impossible by foreclosing desire (Bromberg, personal communication, 2016).

To make meaningful choices, one must feel meaningfully related to others. That requires giving up omnipotent fantasies of having it all (or, alternatively, depriving oneself of all), and dealing with the losses that reality – real dependency needs and the pleasures and pains of real relationships – entails. So, what was Tina really desiring? A nurturing loving mother she never had; a supportive, consistent, available parent with boundaries; a father; a way to not feel hurt by her mother's narcissism, abandonment of her, and toxicity? Was staying "bad" (to use her words) a symptomatic way to keep her mother alive in her or elicit a good mother to attend to her, and accept all the different aspects of herself? If money was the thing that "broke" the relationship, money would be the arena she would have to play out her attachment struggles on. Staying "bad," i.e., symptomatic, also kept her in treatment with me. In fantasy, her mother lives on in her – a place to express her anger and contempt and reverse her envy – "see how much money I can spend on me, not you." A way to stay feeling unworthy (she never earned the money she was able to spend); it all came from the loveless marriage – another price she was willing to pay dearly for. How does she imagine I feel when I see her in a new outfit every session; is she dressing up for me and to what end? Questions we have now begun to explore. Her intentions may imply a desire, a wish to relate and connect while feeling lost in the world and alone. When she remains afraid of genuinely interacting with others in the world around her, she engages in acts that leave her feeling inconsequential. I have come to understand how important her hiding has been and how she has needed her psychic retreat where substances and things serve as her "safe companions."

In this treatment, there were many years of symptom substitution where each symptom represented a relational demand involving enactments, challenges, crises, and "rock bottom" moments before Tina would "decide" the "drug of choice" no longer served its function; be it to anesthetize, inhibit, soothe, bury anger, envy, dependency, loneliness, abandonment, and other unbridled feelings and needs. We repeatedly explored how her conflicted feelings found concrete expression in characteristic acts of various drug use that served to perpetuate her internal conflicts through the combined effects of reinforcement and disguise. As we uncovered the components of the relational binds (Director, 2002) that were embedded in her relationship to the substances or the food, we were able to reformulate these forces in symbolic terms, and revisit them in the dynamics of the transference in the hopes of opening up new pathways for opportunities of exchange.

Overall, this was a complicated treatment where each symptom played a role in keeping parts of the self safe and sequestered in their own silo. She remains sober in recovery for alcohol, cocaine, anorexia, bulimia, opiates, and pot, and has stopped smoking cigarettes. She went to a prestigious college, received a graduate degree in poetry, studies Greek and Russian classical literature with a tutor on her own, and took up swimming and dance. However, her urge to shop, although not compulsively, remains as her closets continue to expand. In moments of opportunity, we get glimpses of her conflicted feelings of having agency with the occasional outbursts of, "Well, can't I keep this issue??? (shopping) . . . the rest have all gone! *You* have even taken away *my* dissociation!" I tell her, "I want to hear from both parts of her – the part that feels she will lose her connection to me if she doesn't keep a problem to continue to be working on, and the part that feels stronger, more hopeful and has agency but is afraid she won't be able to protect herself when the rug gets pulled out from under her again when she least expects it. Maybe this conflict feels too loud in your head and you want to be sure that I know you want to embrace feeling stronger even though you are scared." With a twinkle in her eye, she playfully and nervously joked, "So I shop till *you* drop?"

Tina has been making room for a fuller self to emerge with a greater connection to all her parts, which means giving herself license to have her voice without restriction and maybe even with passion and liberation. I welcome her feistiness.

Conclusion

While we live in an era where our culture supports abundance and wealth, we are faced with financial crises, an ever-increasing income gap between the well-off and the poor, and a diminishing middle class. We are simultaneously bombarded with advertisements through television, texts, the internet, and social media. Immediate gratification has become the norm and runs counter to mindful living and being. As we work harder, longer hours, and make more money, we risk the cost of feeling alienated from ourselves and each other. Given that inner poverty – consequences of emotional and relational starvation – are at the core of most compulsive shopping and buying behaviors, we need to find better ways to help people build other forms of gratification through genuine, meaningful relatedness with others. We hope our contribution adds to the currency of your understanding of compulsive shopping and extends hope for those suffering in isolation, guilt, and shame.

Note

1 We acknowledge both the overlap and the distinction between compulsive shopping and compulsive buying, but for the sake of clarity, for this chapter, we are using the term "compulsive shopping" to imply both the search and purchase of items. Although the term "compulsive shopping" is used interchangeably with compulsive buying and compulsive spending, these are related but distinct behaviors (Nataraajan and Goff, 1992). For example, one can buy items without shopping, just as one can shop without buying items. Contemporary views of compulsive buying disorder focus on the relatively narrow act of taking possession of something and differentiate that from the broader act of shopping and spending. For example, shopping behaviors may include searching for items and gathering information, a recreational activity, and a way to satisfy non-purchase motives (Nataraajan and Goff, 1992). Spending is considered an activity that relinquishes funds, and may occur without even shopping or buying.

Chapter 6

Internet addiction

Charles Wisniewski, Stanley Kletkewicz, and April Fallon

In 2009, while a South Korean couple was caring for a "a cooing and cherubic mini-avatar" virtual child in an online game for six to twelve hours at a time, their three-month-old baby Sarong (translated to mean "love") starved to death due to their negligence (Salmon, 2010). This was the first known fatality from internet gaming. In March 2014, a 19-year-old British male was hospitalized resulting from an overdose suicide attempt after failing to capture the perfect "selfie." He had lost almost 30 pounds, dropped out of school, and remained in his house for six months where he spent ten hours daily obsessively taking selfies (Grossman, 2014). A shared dependence of the online experience offers a glamorous representation of one's ideal alternate reality, but can also have devastating consequences.

Unlike some of the other addictions presented in this book, "internet addiction" is a relatively new and evolving phenomenon that has burgeoned with the infusion of technology into our everyday life. It is also very unique, in that it is widely utilized for both social and business purposes and incorporates many aspects of life into its core structure. In this chapter, we give a brief history of internet use and define contemporary use and abuse. We then offer a multidimensional examination of the phenomenon, including sociocultural, intrapsychic, and neurobiological aspects and theory of its etiology, with case examples.

Our cyberworld

As a result of military communication issues discovered during the Korean conflict, in the early 1950s, the United States Air Force began development of a network of connected computers that comprised the SAGE air defense system (Winkler and Webster, 1997). SAGE combined disparate sources of computerized data which were designed to alert the United States of a Russian nuclear missile attack. At the same time, in the academic and research world, users started "time-sharing," where they would log on to a mainframe computer at another remote site in order to access data stored only on that computer (Campbell-Kelly and Garcia-Swartz, 2013). By the mid 1960s, demand for access to these large mainframe computers extended to commercial entities, specifically engineering and financial firms, organizations that at the time could not afford the cost of a mainframe computer but needed the advanced computer power available through time-shared access (GE Information Services, 1985). Demand for access to these original networks continued to grow through the 1970s from a myriad of organizations, such as the phone company, airlines, and banks.

Increasing demand through the 1970s and 1980s led to an explosion of technological developments that helped to make access to the mainframe computers more efficient and much less costly. The most significant of these new technologies was the introduction of the personal desktop computer, which led to the consumer sector demanding access to networked computers. Although CompuServe was the first access point for consumers in 1980, by the early 1990s America Online (AOL) dominated the market, due to their user-friendly interface and enhanced features such as "chat rooms." From 1980 to 1995, America Online, CompuServe, and Prodigy introduced networked computers – the internet – to millions of subscribers who primarily used it for email. During that time period, the number of subscribers measured by individual households increased from a total of 8,200 to 6,951,000, with the majority of those subscribers coming online between 1990 (852,000 subscribers) and 1995 (Campbell-Kelly and Garcia-Swartz, 2013).

Cost reduction for sending an email message played an important role in the development of consumer demand. In 1988, CompuServe charged an annual subscription rate of $39.95 and then an additional $6 to $12 per hour of service. Today, with a Wi-Fi-enabled device and a Gmail account, sending an email can be absolutely free. Increasing demand for access led to lucrative capital venture investments in "searching" technology. Eventual growth in searching capability and the development of an easy-to-use graphical user interface led to the launch of the World Wide Web – a series of connected databases that made finding information a simple point-and-click. Although Google was not the first search engine, it transformed the first search engine, Gopher, to searching from title to within text, which was a tectonic shift. Motivated by economic opportunity, those humble beginnings have evolved into the ability to access unlimited sources of data through a pocket-sized device that also takes pictures, texts, and places phone calls.

Contemporary internet use

The internet today has expanded into every aspect of contemporary life. It is a portal into a world of commerce where one can receive all goods needed without leaving your home. Reporting $178 billion sales for 2017, Amazon estimated shipping is approximately 1.6 million packages per day (Perlman, 2016). Think of something you want today in the morning and Amazon can deliver it later in the day. The web is used to acquire historical and contemporary information about our world. Google is used to search for information 3.5 billion times per day (Collins, 2018). It is evolving into a major source of entertainment. Five billion videos are watched daily on YouTube alone (Flahive, 2017). Video games are played by 49% of all Americans, split relatively equally between men and women (Duggan, 2017). It is the vehicle for much personal and industrial communication. Most larger companies house information about human resources, payroll, and policies on an online platform. A "face-to-face" meeting can occur with individuals from Japan, China, and India, who never leave the home offices of their respective countries, on one of the many conference platforms such as ZOOM. The web has broadened ways of social connection as siblings, separated by continents, Snapchat pictures of food to each other. Extended families spanning the globe stay connected and plan holidays in real time with group chats. Forty-five billion active users log on to Facebook daily (Facebook Inc., 2018). Through Facebook, people post news and activities and find others who are like-minded. Political leaders across the world send messages to each other and their constituents with up to a 160 character "tweet." Through the web, one can even turn on your home lights in Pennsylvania while vacationing in Hong Kong. The desire for connectivity, the initial purpose of the cold war development for defense purposes, has fueled the development of the internet, as the vehicle, into a ubiquitous method for almost anyone to reach out and connect with an entire world of goods, services, and people.

Demographics of use

In 2012, there were almost 2 billion individual users of the internet. Today, that number has swelled to 7.6 billion users worldwide (Miniwatts Marketing Group, 2018). In terms of percentage of users of the total population in the representative countries, North America and Europe stand out at 95% and 85.2%, respectively, while developing nations represented by Latin America (67%), Middle East (64.5%), Asia (48.1%), and Africa (35.2%) experience a lower level of total population usage, as indicated (Miniwatts Marketing Group, 2018). Populations with higher income populations, and countries with advanced economies report greater use of social media, however, this number has plateaued in the past three years. Among 19 emerging and developing countries surveyed in January 2018, there was an approximate 20% increase in internet use, ownership of smartphone, and use of online social networking sites from five years prior. For example, 64% of Vietnamese and 42% of Nigerians use the internet or own a smartphone (Poushter et al., 2018). This is corroborated by two of our authors who sloughed off their cultural biases after living in small villages in Africa and witnessing a seemingly rudimentary tech-savvy culture liberally incorporate smartphones, even when they did not have enough food or a physical abode for their families to reside in.

The infrastructure for the desktop computers developed over many years in wealthier nations. In developing countries, the cost of desktop or laptop computer was prohibitive and the infrastructure was not available for the average person. The decreasing costs of mobile devices has made the internet available to more diverse income groups. Thus individuals in developing nations have more access to the internet through mobile devices. For instance, 57% of the German population accesses the internet through mobile devices while a full 90% of the Indonesian population uses mobile devices (comScore, 2017).

In the United States, approximately 9 of 10 residents are online (Pew Research Center, 2018). Over 97% of the 18- to 49-year-olds are using the internet, while 87% of the 50- to 64-year-olds are active on the internet (Pew Research Center, 2018). The growth of the 65+ category has been dramatic over the past 18 years, increasing from 14% in 2000 to 66% in 2018 (Pew Research Center, 2018). When examining race and gender, there is no difference in internet usage in the United States (Pew Research Center, 2018).[1] Across income, the United States mirrors the trend among countries; 81% of those earning less than $30,000 per year compared to 98% of those making $75,000 or more per year are using the internet (Pew Research Center, 2018). Similarly, higher levels of education correlate to higher usage rates ranging from 65% of those with less than a high school degree compared to 97% of college graduates (Pew Research Center, 2018). Even in the United States, the desktop computer is quickly becoming a dinosaur. According to research conducted by the Pew Research Center (2016), 20% of all Americans use their smartphones to access the internet foregoing any other method of connection, even in their own homes. That number has grown from 8% just five years ago. The lower cost of a smartphone compared to a computer in combination with ease of access through phone carriers has enabled many who in the past could not afford the combined cost of a computer and a monthly internet access fee to have a connection to the web. Income disparity determines the method of access; 31% of adults making less than $30,000 per year use their smartphone alone to access the internet, while only 9% of those making $75,000 or more per year do so (Pew Research Center, 2018).

In contrast to this American difference in use with disparity of income, a study in India, found no significant demographic differences between the Indian internet users when testing for age, education, income, or gender (Ahmed et al., 2015). Access to and use of the internet is becoming commonplace among a wide demographic, worldwide with cell phone technology that allows for ease of connection at an affordable price.

The demographics of who is accessing the internet, how they are accessing the internet, and what they are doing once they have accessed the internet are in constant flux due to the exponential growth in worldwide users and the creativity of entrepreneurs. Recent events in the United States presidential elections in 2016 are an indicator of the value of information about who is online. A targeted message tailored to either a small niche or larger mass market can have significant impact answering the needs of that messenger, whether it be a political party attempting to influence one's vote or a publisher promoting a new book about the latest psychotherapy theory (Ahmed et al., 2015). The value of this knowledge drives a plethora of academic, commercial, and governmental institutions to gather and analyze this data.

Due to the nature of method of access, apps are used as a method to access the internet. With no variance due to age, over 96% of the worldwide population who accesses the internet on their mobile devices, do it through their top 10 favorite apps exclusively (comScore, 2017). Age does impact which apps are used.

Younger users (18- to 24-year-olds) spend more time on Snapchat than on Facebook, while those over 55 years of age spend significantly more time on Facebook than Snapchat (UKOM Insights, 2016).

The evolution of social interaction is becoming more complex with increased use of mobile devices. Leisa Reichelt, formerly Head of Service Design at the Digital Transformation Agency of the Australian Government, and the Head of User Research for the Government Digital Service (GDS) in the UK Government, coined the term "ambient intimacy," which speaks to the idea that people can intimately keep in touch regularly using social media despite being separated by time and space. Social media allows you to see what friends are doing and expressing in their life without actually being there. We can speculate that perhaps people feel less alone or enjoy a medium that "feels" intimate, but is not necessarily intimate in the traditional sense of a physical or psychological connection. Contact through social media, texts, and email can enable some people to feel less alone, but it also has the potential to exacerbate loneliness, as it often appears to those that are already lonely that others are leading exciting, fun, and sociable lives.

The use of mobile devices is fast becoming a priority in many people's lives – 55% of those surveyed stated they would forego dining out for 12 months instead of giving up their mobile devices and almost a third would give up sex for a year in order to keep their mobile device (comScore, 2017). It has also transformed into a platform for a generation of pop-culture and trend-focused individuals to express seemingly narcissistic sentiments often multiple times daily. This has had far reaching implications compelling tourist destinations, such as the city of Mumbai, to impose no selfie zones due to the risk individuals put themselves in when using social media/taking a selfie and ignoring dangers in their immediate environment. Although many states have laws that prohibit texting while driving, it often neglects to include the taking of selfies while driving. A survey conducted by AT&T and Braun Research including 2,067 people ages 16 to 65 concluded that about 17% of drivers admitted to taking selfies while driving (Matyszczyk, 2015). This is certainly as dangerous as texting while driving.

From internet use to internet abuse

With the increasing infusion of the internet into a multitude of everyday activities, some might argue that it has become an essential element in successful functioning from middle school through senescence. Problematic internet use might manifest as fear in using it or engaging excessively in it. The research and clinical literature does not yet appear to have a consensus on the possible criteria of "normalcy" in this realm. Such norms are evolving rapidly.[2] Defining an addiction to the internet, or various internet-based media such as social media (including social networking sites, gaming, and pornography), blogging, chatting, shopping, or emailing can be very challenging. Is checking email 15 times per day a necessity for work, an uncontrolled desire for connectivity, or a fear of missing or being left out?

Defining abuse

In extreme cases, most would agree that the following news report would qualify as an internet addiction: in New Delhi, two unmarried brothers, 19 and 22 years old, lived at home and played multiplayer games with their online friends all over the world. Within months of starting their gaming patterns, their gaming spiraled out of control to their devoting almost every waking hour to their habit. They did not change their clothes or bathe for days, and often skipped meals. They cut communications with school friends and family members, often refusing to answer phones. Their concept of reality became so altered that their home was robbed twice during their game play; they began urinating and defecating in their clothes. The young men lost interest in all social interactions, their grades plummeted, and a pattern of avolition and anhedonic behavior persisted, with exception to gaming (Naskar, 2016).

As the internet permeates almost every aspect of our lives, it becomes more important to define where pathological behaviors emerge. The DSM-V only briefly mentions that "gaming disorder" is worthy of future study and it was only recently, in June 2018, that the World Health Organization classified "Gaming Addiction" as a mental health condition in ICD-11 (American Psychiatric Association, 2013; World Health Organization, 2018). Criteria requires at least 12 months of "impaired control over gaming, increasing priority given to gaming to the extent that gaming takes precedence over other life interests and daily activities and continuation or escalation of gaming despite the occurrence of negative consequences" as well as significant impairment in functioning (World Health Organization, 2018). Andreassen and Pallesen (2014) define social networking site addiction as "being overly concerned about social networking sites, to be driven by a strong motivation to log on to or use social networking sites and to devote so much time and effort to them that it impairs other social activities, education/job, interpersonal relationships, and/or psychological health and well-being" (p. 4054). When denied internet use, the "internet addict" may engage in uncharacteristic behavior, such as lying, using aggressive words/behaviors, and illegal activities. Essig (2012) explains that impairment may go beyond behaviors. Individuals may not be able to meet crucial life milestones such as being able to regulate emotions, form an identity, establish independence, build confidence in self, and perfect social skills. Internet addiction can even go so far as to impair physical health! In the preceding example, an extreme one, the boys demonstrated impairment in social, educational, and interpersonal functioning. Had their addiction not been treated, developmental tasks such as identity development, self-regulation, and independence may not have happened. However, there are other examples that may be less clear. There have been reports of Chinese adolescents who urinate in diapers in order to prevent pausing their video games (Brown, 2016). Although we might view this behavior as regressive, if this behavior was limited only to weekends, we would not necessarily label this as addiction. Behaviors that may interfere with functioning for one individual may not be problematic for another based on their tolerances. Time spent online might not necessarily indicate a person is abusing the internet as many of our daily work, school, and recreational activities have moved to a web-based platform. Tolerance in internet addiction can be modeled after the structure of substance use disorders in the DSM-V. It would then be defined as "a need for markedly increased amounts of [internet] to achieve intoxication or desired effect" or "markedly diminished effect with continued use of the same amount of [internet]" (American Psychiatric Association, 2013). Through understanding how an individual's tolerance increases with internet use, we can better understand if the person meets criterion for tolerance. Unfortunately, a comparison of 68 studies before 2014 primarily utilized cross-sectional data, making it difficult to appreciate change in internet use over time (Kuss et al., 2014). In addition, there are a number of scales that have promising validity and reliability in the literature that can assist in the diagnosis of internet addiction. However, there is a lack of consensus within the field in terms of a universal assessment.[3] Many scales utilized to make a diagnosis of internet addiction are not necessarily validated in the same cultural context; college students and adolescents are overrepresented in many of these studies (Huang et al., 2007; Osada, 2013).

Correlates of problematic internet use

There is no consensus about where the divisions between peer-appropriate internet use, problematic, and addicted use lie on the spectrum of "internet use." Currently, about 1.5 to 8.2% of adult Americans and anywhere from 4 to 25% of college-aged Americans may struggle with internet addiction (Williams et al., 2011; Mihajlov and Vejmelka, 2017). Similarly, approximately 4.4% of the European population may be involved in problematic internet usage (Durkee et al., 2012). Psychological correlates remain difficulty to categorize. Age remains a controversial correlate as use of the internet is dramatically increased in youth; however, this does not necessarily indicate pathology (Durkee et al., 2012). Contrastingly, less time spent online has actually been found to have a relationship with higher degree attainment. Two studies named factors associated with internet addiction in both adults and adolescents: sociodemographic variables, how one uses the internet, psychosocial factors, and comorbid symptoms (Kuss et al., 2014; Gentile, 2009). Male gender is the most common sociodemographic variable in internet addiction, with males 5.2% and 3.8% females affected in Europe, which is a trend that appears to be consistent in the United States; however, the association may be mediated by confounding factors (Durkee, 2012; Kuss and Lopez-Fernandez, 2016).

It is difficult to find specific data about how many patients present specifically for treatment of internet addiction. It appears clear that individuals with comorbid psychological disorders such as mood disorders, OCD, PTSD, ADHD, and anxiety (most commonly social anxiety and social phobia) encompass a large portion of the affected population (Kuss and Lopez-Fernandez, 2016). Psychological and social factors can affect individuals' preferences of media use. Personality disorders with high harm-avoidance, novelty seeking, reward dependence, and low cooperativeness were positively correlated with internet addiction in adolescents (Ha et al., 2007; June et al., 2007; Mottram and Fleming, 2009). Impulsivity traits and neuroticism (because of its inherent feelings of anxiety, anger, loneliness, and envy) both appear to put individuals at risk for internet addiction as well (Kuss et al., 2014; Blackwell et al., 2017).

In 2016, Wegmann and Brand suggested that individual characteristics and internet-use expectancies can predict online communication applications use disorders. Brand et al. (2016) proposed a model called the "Interaction of Person-Affect-Cognition-Execution (I-PACE) model for specific Internet-use disorders." They suggested that an individual's addiction to specific internet applications or sites can be explained, in part, by neurobiological and psychological characteristics, responses to environmental triggers, coping styles, and internet-related cognitive biases. For example, a 30-year-old patient, with history of anxiety and interpersonal struggles, reports constantly checking of his "Farmville" mobile app game (Zynga Inc., 2014). The game appears inconsequential to the rest of his life decisions; however, he wakes up many times throughout the night anxious that he will miss the time to harvest his crops or that he will not be able to enjoy the victory of expanding his farm. What is unique to the internet is that one may develop an "addiction" specifically to Farmville, while other internet-related behaviors remain inconsequential. In this way, factors such as online duration, type of web application, and psychological symptoms like anxiety and loneliness can play a role (Kuss et al., 2014).

Other researchers have focused on the relationship between adolescents and caregivers to best explain risk of developing "IA." Xiuqin et al. (2010) stated that early weak parental bonds and poor quality of mother-offspring emotional and social reciprocity may predispose people to negative relations to others, poor social skills, self-perceived loneliness, interpersonal incompetence, sadness and anxiety, which may lead to one preferring online interactions to face-to-face experiences. Family conflicts and poor academic achievement may drive adolescents to develop dysfunctional online coping mechanisms. Instead of facing problematic issues and communication barriers with parents, the children of these families may turn to the internet. They can continue the process of separating from their parents and constructing their own identity in the virtual world. Disconnected families, especially those experiencing adverse environmental/living conditions may be more at risk to these behaviors (Suissa, 2014).

Excessive/problematic use of the internet may be a learned behavior to cope with depression or PTSD. Stressful or traumatic experiences may have a role in the onset of internet addiction among adolescents (Tang 2014a, 2014b). In this way, the internet may become a tool or an avoidance mechanism to cope with adverse life events or preexisting psychopathology (Kardefelt-Winther, 2014; Schimmenti and Caretti, 2010). This raises the question as to whether researchers are limiting their view of repeated internet use behavior by assigning an addiction criteria to it. By classifying a behavior as an addiction, we may be ignoring the rich subtleties that drive one to seek refuge in a virtual world (Kardefelt-Winther, 2017; Schimmenti and Caretti, 2010).

Theories of internet addiction

While the internet has enhanced our lives in so many ways, with this tantalizing and instantly gratifying resource comes the possibility of over-involvement and abuse. The initial understanding of the etiology and maintenance of misuse and abuse have been the application of other kinds of addictions to this unique one. Goldberg (1995) was the first to suggest that the same processes that mediate substance abuse characterize internet addiction. Around the same time, Kimberly Young, founder of the Center for Internet Addiction Recovery, came to see internet addiction in a similar light. In her publications, she posited a link between excessive internet use and pathological gambling, a disorder of impulse control in the DSM IV (Young, 1998, 2004). She adapted the DSM IV criteria to relate to internet use when she developed the Internet Addiction Test (IAT). She further delineated internet addictions into categories: cyber-sexual addiction, cyber-relationship addiction, net compulsions, information overload, and computer addiction (Young, 1998, 2004). In this section, we review theories on neurobiology, attachment, and self-psychology that have been used as a framework to understand the development and maintenance of internet addiction.

Neurobiology

The brain's reward system, or mesolimbic dopaminergic pathway, has been identified as a major component that facilitates behavioral, substance, and gaming/internet addictions (Greenfield, 2010). Many different brain circuits are implicated in the phenomenon of internet addiction that are similar to those that contribute to substance abuse disorders. The variable reinforcement ratio[4] of the internet affects brain physiology by leading to rapid, persistent responses and addictive-quality behaviors (Kuss, 2013; Choi, 2017). As digital technology evolves to be more immediately gratifying and more sophisticated with faster internet speeds, there is a higher risk of addictive properties that may accumulate.

Dopamine is the neurotransmitter that plays a major role in reward-motivated behavior, incentive salience (unconsciously or consciously craving a rewarding stimulus) and reinforcement, as well as playing a role in mediating executive functioning, motor control, and arousal. A reward, such as an addictive drug, increases dopamine release in the mesolimbic pathway (also known as the "reward pathway"), which spans from an area in the brainstem to the nucleus accumbens[5] (Wanat et al., 2010). Prolonged exposure to immediate rewards can blunt the ability of neurotransmitters to be taken up by dopamine and glutamate receptors in the nucleus accumbens. A person may begin to form tolerance, withdrawal symptoms, and a decreased physiologic responsiveness from activities not internet-related (Sussman, 2018; Kuss, 2013; Choi, 2017). This would explain why a casual involvement in gaming such as the Indian brothers or the Korean couple may start out as appropriate recreational activity and quickly evolve into an ever increasing time commitment.

Sussman describes a model for the neurobiological mechanism of addiction as a disruption of the "go" network and "stop" network of the brain (Sussman, 2018). The "go" network is able to recognize specific stimuli that may predict a reward. A more robust "go network" overpowers the "stop network" in addictive behaviors, substance use, and ADHD, as well as in adolescent brains (Sussman, 2018). The size of the nucleus accumbens and caudate nucleus (the aforementioned basal ganglia structures) are increased in the "go network" of internet addiction and internet gaming addiction. However, they are more responsive to the addictive behavior and less responsive to natural rewards that occur regularly, such as anticipating eating your favorite meal or taking care of a real infant (Sussman, 2018). Many companies have capitalized on this unique brain function by creating YouTube videos that feature eggs and various other gifts that are unwrapped to reveal a gift. This intoxicating build up and reward attracts many young child viewers through "kids youtube" (AWESMR, 2014). In addition to the reward pathway, decreased gray matter has been identified in the anterior cingulate cortex, posterior cingulate cortex, prefrontal cortex, orbitofrontal cortex, and insula, regions involved in cognitive planning of complex behaviors and impulse control (Yuan, 2013; Zhou et al., 2011). With absence of input from these structures to guide and inform parts of the brain involved in procedural memory, patterns of behavior become more fixed. In other words, there will be a loss of variation in the neural network that works to automatically perform complex behaviors (e.g., riding a bike) unconsciously through repetition. It is understandable then that complex activities such as reading to and cuddling a child may be abandoned in favor of the gratification of mindless viewing of egg openings in the presence of a child. Lastly, the insula, which is responsible for evaluation of interoceptive awareness (e.g., visceral and somatic bodily sensations), may contribute to an enhanced rewarding experience in internet addiction and motivate one to continue use (Cerniglia, 2017).

The "stop network" plays a role in our ability to curb our desire to give in to impulses. The prefrontal cortex has been found to be reduced in adolescents with internet gaming addiction, suggesting impaired executive functioning ability and decreased mature cognitive mechanisms for efficient inhibitory control (Sussman, 2018; Hong et al., 2013). Impairment in this system can cause a person to be more motivated by short-term goals opposed to delaying gratification. Functional magnetic resonance imaging while gaming and results of neuropsychological testing have illustrated the decrease in executive functioning and ability to regulate impulses (Dong, 2017; Wang et al., 2017; Jorgenson et al., 2016).

Social connection

While neurobiological explanations are applicable to aspects of addiction and tolerance in internet gaming, not all vulnerable individuals (such as those with ADHD) become addicted to internet games. In addition, other forms of internet misuse seem less applicable to a neurobiological etiology. The following example illustrates this:

For graduation, parents of a college graduate offer her a month of international travel to visit overseas relatives and experience a safari as well as other exotic locations to give her the treat of a lifetime. However, while abroad she finds herself constantly checking her friends' Facebook/Instagram, and wishing she could have gone to a friend's monthly get together for drinks. Had she been given the chance to choose again, she would change her decision to travel. She expresses anxiety about missing out on what her friends are doing and being part of their interactions. This anxiety was not alleviated by posting her own exotic photos to the social media platforms that her friends would see.

This fear of missing out would have effectively interfered with her ability to enjoy *any* event. This phenomenon has been labeled FOMO (fear of missing out) and is not necessarily exclusively related to internet addiction. It has been defined as "a pervasive apprehension that others might be having rewarding experiences from which one is absent" (Przybylski et al., 2013, p. 1842), and is often exacerbated by one's uncertainty in belonging to a social group (Rifkin et al., 2015). As in the case of the preceding example, one may feel that they should be engaged with their social group instead of another activity in order to ensure their group does not permanently evolve without them (Rifkin, 2015). It is not the rush of "gaming" that engages the individual to be compulsively checking friends' social profiles or emails, but rather the fear or apprehension that they may be left behind in despair.

Inadequate psychological needs may be linked to social media engagement through FOMO, as many adolescents with issues such as anxiety and depression are at higher risk of FOMO because of perceived social deficits. Lack of connectedness with others, general mood, and life satisfaction may also be linked to this intense social media engagement (Casale, 2018). Heavy internet and mobile app use, compulsive checking behaviors, and excessive engagement with media such as Instagram/Facebook can lead to worse addiction profiles (Oberst et al., 2017).

The root of this issue may lie in the early parent-child connection. In the absence of environmental catastrophes or biological deficits, when a child is parented in a functional, secure and "good enough" (Bettelheim, 1987) manner, the outcome is typically an adolescent who is oriented toward a world outside themselves, ensconced in healthy interpersonal and intrapersonal relationships. Alternatively, dysfunctional parenting results in an adolescent turning from the outside world inward, compensating with internal, made-up connections (internal object relations) as a source of comfort from the loss of outward relationships (Winnicott, 1968).

Attachment and object relatedness

Multiple research efforts have shown that insecure attachment is one of the strongest predictors of internet addiction (Cerniglia et al., 2017). In repeated studies, those experiencing insecure/anxious attachments with primary caregivers associated with feelings of loneliness, anger, detachment from parents (Ballarotto et al., 2018), social incompetence (Cerniglia et al., 2017) are shown to fulfill the need for connection through a readily available cyberworld where they experience community and belonging (Jia and Jia, 2016). Interestingly, not all attachment problems lead to problematic internet use. One study found that anxious attachment predicted problematic internet use while attachment avoidance did not (Jia and Jia, 2016). Those with anxious attachment use hyperactivating strategies to foster and promote their intimate connections. These activities typically include a focus on attaining, "proximity, support, and love" (Mikulincer and Shaver, 2005, p. 151). For example, when trying to foster and maintain intimate connections, they demand more intense and frequent contact with those they consider intimate. Email, Snapchat, Instagram, and texting offer stellar platforms to quell anxieties concerning connectedness. Texts such as "Whuz up?" have the potential to engage and function as a "coping skill" to reduce experiencing unpleasant emotions generated by attachment insecurities (Ballarotto et al., 2018). They also allow those more with an avoidant attachment style to maintain a connection without an intimacy. However, FOMO is a better predictor of higher internet use than is insecure attachment (Blackwell et al., 2017).

Self psychology

The self is an "organised and organising center of human experience which constitutes our identity and very sense of being" (van Schoor, 1992, p. 206). Individuals with internet addiction may seek a connection because there is a basic drive to connect with others in order to maintain intersubjective orientation and a cohesive psyche in what Stern (2004) calls "intersubjective motivation." This person may need the approval/validation from others to form and hold themselves together. In a narcissistic fashion, the other person becomes an extension of the self. This serves as a support for a delicate sense of self. In the online world, the "like" button on Facebook or heart-shaped emoji on Instagram endorses and rewards a shamed and insecure self.

The internet offers not only connection to others but also connection to information – information that can support one's narcissistic view of oneself and the development of self-objects. In this instance, narcissism is not necessarily a pathological issue but rather a part of normal development. Disruption or absence of the opportunity for mirroring, ideation, and twinship leaves a void and results in the lifelong search for individuals to serve as self-objects (Kohut, 1977). These self-objects can be found through adventures in the cyberworld. Whether through connections with others or through seeking information that is used for self-validation in a real or "cyber" sense, the internet is akin to a self-object shopping mall open 24 hours, offering whatever one desires, frequently at no actual financial cost.

While many use the internet to maintain connectedness with real objects, many use the internet not to connect but to replace connection and lack of real life gratification with fantasized identities and relationships. For example:

A socially awkward engineering male college graduate from a religious family took a job after college in a new state. Without friends, he began recreationally spending time developing avatars on Second Life Platform. At first, he enjoyed creating a new identity, filling out his profile, and physique as a thin athletic male. As he continued, he developed identities of a rock star and actor. He then became more intensely focused on utilizing avatars of a young boy, a gay male, and a gay female, all of whom he did not acknowledge as having an affinity toward. As he became more involved, he neglected his work, and gave up all efforts to make social connections in the city where he had relocated after college. He was referred to therapy by the company EAP for depression. In therapy, he also revealed that the only significant relationship he had had during his adolescence was an entirely online intense sadistic relationship. He expressed a desire for an intimate relationship and friends but was very critical and disappointed with the imperfections that occurred for him in his relationships.

With more moderate engagement, role players may use virtual spaces as creative outlets and socialization (Williams et al., 2011). This young man, lonely in a new environment and uncomfortable with his own self-image, needs role playing for more than a creative outlet; he begins to replace the real life experience with a more desirable fantasized identities. The constructed avatars are vibrant identities that temporarily augment his impoverished self-image. He actively engages with other two-dimensional visual and auditory avatars in real time that is perhaps more substantial than he might risk in everyday life. Religious affiliation, fear of his parents' disapproval, and his own harsh critical review of himself prevents him from openly acknowledging and exploring issues of identity, sexual orientation, and attraction. His adoption of the various avatar identities allows him to retreat into fantasy without ever acknowledging his wishes and thus he is temporarily gratified by this escape from the caldron of conflicts within him. Fantasy becomes better than reality and the boundary of reality and fantasy begin to blur. Yet the "as-if" nature of identity leaves one with an unreal and empty connection.

Khantzian's (1997) "Self Medication Hypothesis" posited that addicted individuals are continuously trying to regulate their emotions, affect, their sense of self, their relationship with others, as well as their behaviors. In the absence of substances as a means to cope, such individuals are repeatedly troubled and/or overwhelmed by their emotions, self-image, relationships, and behaviors (Khantzian, 1997). He noted that patients seek out drugs due to suffering and pain, not pleasure seeking. Aggression, rage, and depression long precede their use of any illegal drugs, but inadequate ego mechanisms for properly controlling and directing aggression lead to use of opiates as a means of coping. Disordered emotions and poor self-care are inherent to someone with drug-dependence and disordered self-esteem and problematic relationships are contributory (Khantzian, 2003). Khantzian's framework can be meaningfully applied to internet abuse. The internet provides a convenient channel of self-object experiences that can soothe its users. Social media and internet applications are less confronting and more controllable than that of real world social interactions, which makes them ideal outlets to be used defensively. Compared to substance-addicted individuals, those engaged in excessive online social networking are less likely to struggle with basic self-care as they are to deal with loneliness, low self-esteem, and interpersonal relationships (Casale, 2018). For some individuals, this is more preferable than the pain and risks involved in genuine real-world relationships as is the case in the preceding clinical example. Social media may allow one to bring back some semblance of familiarity in an environment where someone feels alone or out of place. However, this may come at a cost, as persistent excessive internet use can lead to further loss of self-regulatory skills, psychological strength and ability to overcome personal hardships (Khantzian, 2003). This theory is further corroborated by a preliminary study by McNicol and Thorsteinsson (2017) that suggests internet addiction is associated with increased avoidance and maladaptive coping and decreased "adaptive problem-focused coping responses" in both adolescents and adults.

Treatment

A myriad of kinds of internet addiction and a range of severity allows for many kinds of treatments that may be effective depending upon the particular case. We offer two different examples that vary in severity and kind of addiction.

Clinical vignette 1

A couple in psychotherapy feels hopeless about their 14-year-old son's future. The couple has had to restrict their son's gaming: he was not completing homework and household chores because of the amount of time he was playing online games. At first, he was told not to go online, but he would simply close his bedroom door and continue playing. One evening while his parents were asleep, he took his mother's credit card from her purse and used it to buy hundreds of dollars' worth of downloadable gaming content. When his parents realized what he had done, his father decided to remove the gaming system from his bedroom. The child became physically aggressive toward his father while he was removing the gaming system. The child then refused to attend school for weeks afterward. He was sent to an intensive in-patient program for addictions as his parents described the following days as "watching someone detoxing."

When addiction reaches this level of intensity, a residential treatment may be required. A period of abstinence (or detox) from internet-related activities is sometimes necessary to allow an individual to initiate the treatment model. From a neurobiological point of view, the treatment helps break neural pathways associated with their maladaptive use pattern. All addictions involve both disruptions of the mesolimbic reward circuitry as well as ritualistic behavioral patterns. With new brain pathways developed through treatment, the quantity of dopamine receptors will begin to normalize (Weinstein and Lejoyeux, 2015). A 2016 systematic literature review of treatment modalities in 46 empirical studies found that psychopharmacology treatment and therapy modalities with most efficacy focused on combination treatments using psychotherapy and medications such as SSRIs, SNRIs, bupropion, antipsychotics, methylphenidate, strattera, and nal-trexone. Psychopharmaceutical interventions are often aimed at trying to regulate mood and behaviors and minimizing the elated feeling the addiction evokes by regulating the imbalanced dopamine system (Kuss and Lopez-Fernandez, 2016).

Short-term treatment goals are focused on disrupting problematic coping behaviors, thoughts, self-medicating behaviors, and identifying triggers. Common triggers are the ease of access, boredom, anxiety (particularly social anxiety), and academic/work avoidance (Brand, 2016). The most commonly utilized therapy to implement these goals is CBT and a preliminary meta-analysis states it is the most effective therapy-based treatment, however, the literature is limited (Young and Brand, 2017; Williams et al., 2011).

Group therapy appeared to have a greater advantage over individual therapy, due to its ability to establish a supportive network of people with similar issues. Multimodal school-based groups, MFGT, family therapy, and multi-level intervention model appears beneficial for young patients. In addition to the psychiatric maladies that internet addiction appears to influence, treatment has started to focus on some of the medical comorbidities that plague many individuals with problematic overuse. Dr. Jo Begent, a pediatrician practicing in the University College London hospital, states that originally her team was faced with physical complaints such as sleep deprivation and obesity; however, she states many adolescents are facing imbalances in hormones due to lack of sleep, which can affect pubertal development. She was faced with an even more inconceivable case in June 2018 when a ten-year-old boy presented with a dilated bowel after restricting himself from toileting so he could continue his game without interruption (Cambridge, 2018).

However, the complete elimination of the internet is not a long-term solution. Eliminating it entirely precludes the possibility of a successful professional and social life. In this way, we endorse a model for defining abuse or addiction to be more similar to an eating addiction rather than an alcohol addiction. In the former, one cannot live without consuming it, but in the latter one could forego the activity entirely and still function adaptively.

Clinical vignette 2

A patient complains during a psychotherapy session that her husband and daughter are spending hours each evening watching videos of someone opening "surprise eggs" – various shaped eggs (some in a traditional egg shape, others in the shape of a popular cultural icon such as a superhero) that have "surprises" inside – candy, small toys, stickers. Their daughter is eight years old, it was 10:30 p.m., two and a half hours past her agreed-upon bedtime, and unless something was said, the wife feels that the two surprise egg watchers would have continued for hours more. After the child is finally put in bed (she was unable to fall asleep easily due to the stimulation) the parents fight, as the father defended the choice to watch the videos as spending quality time with his daughter, even though she had school early the next morning. Seemingly both father and daughter were able to connect with the colorful, musical video that has no speaking, only human hands are seen opening the eggs, and there is nothing done with the surprises except to have them put to the side out of view. The lack of effort in interacting with their daughter has triggered the mother into feeling insecure about her husband's ability to parent and his discernment regarding obsessive behaviors. One of the videos in question was posted four years ago and as of August 2018 had received over 447 million views.

(Baby Big Mouth, 2014)

Treatment for the family beset by egg watching begins with understanding the father's psychology and seeming desire to be a good parent to his daughter, "wanting to spend quality time with her at bedtime." Yet there appears to be little social exchange as the two focus on watching the same video. While it may have initially begun with this desire, the father's own emptiness and inability to emotionally connect with his daughter have led to the use of the egg watching as a substitute for connection and a gratification of his own needs through this empty and mindless reward process. Although he may feel as though a relationship is being developed, his inner emptiness and insecure-avoidant style allows, at best, a physical proximity, not an emotional proximity. His relationship with his daughter mirrors that which he has with his wife and for which his wife is angry, but unable to verbally articulate to him.

The husband would benefit from individual psychotherapy focused on identification of his inability to engage emotionally with both his wife and daughter. This step necessitates understanding of probabilistic narcissistic wounding on behalf of the husband – a wound that taught him not to be vulnerable, otherwise those close to him can cause him intense emotional pain. His "vegging-out" watching a mindless video while seated next to his daughter is probably "just good enough" relating to another object, viewed as a bonded relationship by the husband, and potentially a distant relationship by his wife and daughter. Healing of his wounds would help him to develop a strong self-object enabling him to become more secure in his attachment, vulnerable in his interaction, and emotionally intimate with his wife.

The husband and wife could benefit from an object relations couple therapy (Scharff and Scharff, 1997). In this model, couples explore how they bonded on an unconscious level – what one spouse unconsciously views as a deficit in self is ameliorated by the corresponding asset in the other spouse. The disconnect between the couple is evident in the husband's focus on a mindless video, where he oddly finds a self-object, an object that he can control, an object that requires nothing from him, an object that somehow gives him a false sense of self. Object relations couple therapy looks to help the couple understand their unconscious projective and introjective identification in order to allow for each to be a functional form of an accurate self to the other. By allowing for identification of defenses and the associated anxieties creating the opportunity to work on their anxieties together. This process frees the couple to limit their projections of each other, engendering a love relationship based on an accurate understanding and appreciation for the true other, rather than a self-object that calmed those defended/anxious parts.

While this problem as presented is primarily to be resolved by individual, parenting, and couples work, this early intense exposure to the internet may create difficulties for the child. At a neurobiological level there may be a vulnerability in the dopamine reward system that may manifest in impaired development of adequate satisfaction and gratification in relationships. While the initial desire would be attachment and connection with her father, the introduction of the egg internet activity may have become paired with the desire for connection with her father. For the child, there is a need to replace the rewarding egg experience with rewarding and appropriate play and activities with her father, mother, and the three together. From an attachment point of view, a more genuine and deeper emotional interaction between the two will potentially help her development of a more secure base in the present and autonomy in the future.

Future internet use and abuse

Tristan Harris, a former Google design ethicist and co-founder of the organization Time Well Spent, gives a bleak view of what the internet may evolve to be if we are not consciously working to regulate our use. Harris states that businesses are "racing for our attention" and sometimes actually "hijacking" our attention. For example, on Snapchat there is a feature called "the streak," where Snapchat tallies the amount of consecutive days that you communicate with one person. This gives teens "something they don't want to lose" (Harris, 2017). In reality, nothing is actually lost (a friend will most likely still remain a friend after a streak has ended). However, adolescents and adults will avoid activities in order to keep streaks going or give someone else their phone so they can continue it. One may speculate whether the actual messages sent are even "meaningful" in the way we once thought when we communicated offline.

The virtual interaction has grown in complexity from the days of two people on separate ends of a telephone (or tin cans depending on when you were born). This interaction is now adulterated by numerous engineers monitoring your behaviors and decisions who are well versed in you psychologically and are strategically manipulating data and algorithms to ensure that you continue to use their platform (Harris, 2017). Harris lists three elements that make the internet a unique medium that may invite pathological behaviors. It is "totalizing," meaning that almost everyone is connected, it is "social," and it is "intelligent and personalized," giving you the ability to teach the technology all about your life and your inner desires with every click (Harris, 2017).

The more recent pursuits of diagnostic criteria and theories to understand internet addiction have yet to define a very heterogeneous population. Discrepancies arise in the conceptualizations of internet addiction when there are attempts to concretize the definition. It is unclear whether "internet addiction" is simply another mask of developmental and personality dysfunction or a new phenomenon an amalgamation of a social and technological reality. Regardless, the one aspect that all commonly share is that it causes substantial distress or impairment in important areas of functioning such as social or occupational roles.

The internet is a complex, decentralized, elusive network of users and is undoubtedly difficult to categorize. It is utilized in almost infinite different ways – depending on age, time of day, entertainment, geographical location, cultural values, personality, comorbid diagnoses, social conditioning, educational pursuits, financial gain, and communication for example. That being said, with the advent of big data[6] and the digitalization of almost every person's behavior and day to day decisions, the process of understanding its psychological effects on humans may soon become more readily accessible. We know now that as more users join the network and a new generation integrates this technology into their life, there may be an evolution of communication and interpersonal values. We are beginning to see that to take the internet away would be to take away one's voice. The scenario that commonly occurs is one where a group of teens log into their Xbox and turn on the game "Fortnite" where they are joined by friends all over the country. They talk about their lives over the platform during the game. They cheer each other on and they shame the loser as they revel in their defeat. We can all remember similar interactions that took place in our own lives, which, contrastingly, occurred in a physical environment such as a coffee shop, local billiards hall, community recreation center, a sports field, or a bar. We can now connect, both internally and externally, to a world where any desire or fantasy can be fulfilled in a "cyber" manner. It is a world where the anxieties, wounds, emptiness, and psychological distress from a perceived lack of attachment are "healed." However, it is also a world where those craving connection can become addicted to that perceived connection.

It is not surprising that critics have voiced concern that new virtual interaction lacks depth and meaning when one desires a connection of the person on the other end. Can one obtain the same social nourishment that is given in a face-to-face contact over the internet? Does it lack the indescribable essence that our body physically senses and seeks out in our day-to-day social interactions? If so, will social media, internet blogs, email, and forthcoming virtual reality platforms be able to supplement these subtle "human" qualities that we all feel in another's presence? In past generations, the experienced elders scoffed at revolutionary changes in technology. In 1899, when motor automobiles first came on the market, there was apprehension that prevented many consumers from adapting this new technology. Uriah Smith became very successful when he constructed a fake horse head to affix onto the front of a car to make it more acceptable to other horses (Hartzman, 2011). In the same vein, it is possible that the conventional human interactions and device-free behaviors we feel are threatened by increased internet use will result in new avenues to relate to one another. Perhaps we just need a horse head. As a result of these queries the boundaries between addiction, problematic use, and "normal" use at this current time may continue to appear pixelated. Nonetheless, it may be a call for mental health professionals everywhere to become more familiar with this modern vehicle of expression so we can help those suffering to live the life they want for themselves.

Notes

1 Eighty-nine percent of all men and 88% of all women, 89% of white, 87% of black, and 88% of Hispanic Americans actively use the internet (Pew Research Center, 2018).
2 The American Academy of Pediatrics released a report in October 2016 outlining recommendations for media use in children. Among some of the recommendations, AAP notes that screen use should be avoided in children 18 months or less, ages two to five years should limit use to one hour per day of high-quality content, for children ages six and older it suggests parents choose a "limit" on time spent on media with a max of two hours for ages 2 to 18. AAP also created a website at healthychildren.org website where families can access a Family Media Use Plan tool (Reid et al., 2016).
3 Kuss's systematic review of internet addiction highlights the more established rating scales in the literature such as Young's Internet Addiction Test, Internet Addiction Diagnostic Questionnaire, and Chen et al.'s Chinese Internet Addiction Scale (Kuss et al., 2014). Laconi's (2014) critical review of existing scales suggests that the Generalized Problematic Internet Use Scale-2 (Caplan, 2010) may be useful and reported the Compulsive Internet Use Scale (CIUS) from Meerkerk et al. (2009) scored well in reliability and validity.
4 Variable ratio reinforcement is a concept from instrumental learning theory (Skinnerian). Rewards emitted at a variable rate makes the extinction of behavior extremely difficult. This is a well-established empirical relationship.
5 Part of the basal ganglia – a region also responsible for motor and action planning, decision making, reinforcement, and motivation.
6 Big data in this context is the raw, unstructured data from an internet database that can be extracted in order to analyze human behaviors and help shape predictive models from a vast sample of people (Kim et al., 2017).

Chapter 7

Work addiction

Salman Akhtar

Effective March 30, 2018, the government of South Korea rolled out a new initiative that forced federal employees to shut down their computers at 8 p.m. each Friday. A month later, the second phase of this directive set in, requiring the office computers to shut down at 7:30 p.m. on the second and fourth Friday of the month. And, in May 2018, the third phase enforced shutting down all computers by 7 p.m. every Friday. In a related move, the national assembly passed a law that cut down the maximum permissible work week from 68 to 52 hours. South Korea is one of the countries of the world with the most overworked employees and is desperately trying to make its citizens work less!

If this is too alien for the Puritan ears of task-driven Americans, the situation is Japan in bound to shock the bejesus out of them. That country's mortality statistics include a condition called *Karoshi*, literally translated as "overwork death." The first case of *Karoshi* was reported in 1969 but the term itself was not coined until 1978 and became well-recognized by mid-to-late 1980s. The Japanese Ministry of Labor began to publish statistics on *Karoshi* around this time. A group of physicians and lawyers established *Karoshi* hotlines across the nation (Kohi, 2014) and the International Labor Organization cited the deaths of a nurse who worked 34 hour-long shifts five times a month, a bus driver who did not take a single day off in 15 years of employment, and a snack food processor who worked 110 hours a week (not a month) and suffered a heart attack at age 34 (ILO report, April 23, 2013).

Such morbid over-involvement with work is not restricted to exotic and faraway lands. It is present in the Western nations, too, where average annual work hours range from lows of 1368, 1412, and 1482 in Germany, Denmark, and France, respectively, to highs of 1789, 2033, and 2739 in the United States, Greece, and Mexico, respectively. To wit, the number of public holidays varies greatly across the world's nations with India, Philippines, and Turkey on the luxurious end (with 21, 18, and 14 national holidays annually) and the United Kingdom, Germany, and the United States at the austere end of the spectrum (with 9, 8, and 5 days off per year). Clearly, work that is ordinarily a rewarding activity has become a malady of the soul in many societies and for many people. But why? What societal and psychological variables transform a productive and enriching pursuit into a demonic force that can injure its subject and those around him? To put it bluntly, what changes work into work addiction?

I will explore this issue in a step-by-step fashion: first, dealing with the nature of work and the human need for it; next with the psychodynamics of addictions in general; and only then with the roots, manifestations, consequences, and possible remedies of addiction to work.

Work

While declaring that men, by nature, are "lazy and unintelligent" (1927, p. 7), Freud acknowledged that work is essential for their emotional well-being. He stated:

> No other technique for the conduct of life attaches the individual so firmly to reality as laying emphasis on work; for his work at least gives him a secure place in a portion of reality, in the human community. The possibility it offers of displacing a large amount of libidinal components, whether narcissistic, aggressive or even erotic, on to professional work and on to the human relations connected with it lends it a value by no means second to what it enjoys as something indispensable to the preservation and justification of existence in society.
>
> (Freud, 1930, p. 80)

Freud's statement about the importance of work to man's daily existence became the point of departure for the subsequent psychoanalytic contributions on this topic. Menninger (1942) considered work as sublimation par excellence. Hendrick (1943) went one step further and coined the term "work principle." This referred to "the principle that primary pleasure is sought by efficient use of the central nervous system for the performance of well-integrated ego functions which enabled the individual to control or alter his environment" (p. 311). Hendrick proposed that sexualized and narcissistic pleasures derived from work are secondary; work has its own rewards in terms of ego gratification. He did, however, concede that "libidinal pleasure in work is predominant in adolescent activities, in contrast to the greater pleasure in effective performance which characterizes maturity" (p. 317).

The impact of Hendrick's ideas can be discerned in later contributions to the psychoanalytic understanding of work. Lantos (1952) emphasized that capacity to work is a "proof of good adaptation to reality" (p. 439). Jacques (1960) deconstructed the process of work and identified its six stages: (1) the achievement of a particular objective is undertaken; (2) a quantum of energy is allocated to the task; (3) an integrative reticulum is elaborated within which the work is organized; (4) concentrated attention is paid; (5) elements that are fit for the purpose are gathered and linked; and (6) decisions are made at every step in the sequence in order to sustain the endeavor. Holmes (1965) noted that Freud's much cited statement on work (see preceding quote) differentiates between its two psychic functions: discharge of instinctual impulses and binding the individual more closely to reality. Holmes proposed that the former function was carried on by drive energy and the latter by neutralized energy. The two seem to be in a complementary relationship: "the greater the investment of drive energy, the less neutralized energy is available for investment in work activity" (p. 385). Furthermore, the proportion of each function is related to the individual's whole developmental history and as such remains relatively stable within a given individual.

Holmes' (1965) neutralized energy pole comes close to Hendrick's (1943) notion of "work principle." Impact of the latter is also discernable in certain ideas of Erikson (1959), White (1963), G. Klein (1976), and Wolf (1988). Erikson's (1959) placing developmental emphasis upon autonomy, initiative, and industry can be viewed as a contribution to the psychosocial underpinnings of the "work principle." He focused upon the dialectics between ego growth and social competence while minimizing the derivation of work from drive energy. White (1963) also diluted the instinctual foundations of work. He spoke of "competence" and "effectance" as forms of independent ego forces that regulated its capacity for effective action and accomplishment. G. Klein (1976) delineated many "ego pleasures" and included "pleasure in effectiveness" among them. Wolf (1988) noted that "efficacy experiences," including those related to work, strengthen the ego and provide a sense of vitality to the self.

It should, however, be acknowledged that most of these contributions did not focus directly upon work. After the few early papers just cited (Menninger, 1942; Hendrick, 1943; Lantos, 1952; Jacques, 1960; Holmes, 1965), exclusive attention to work was not given till 1997. That year saw the publication of the book, *Work and Its Inhibitions* (Socarides and Kramer, 1997). It is hardly possible here to summarize the entire content of this edited volume. I will only comment upon four outstanding essays in it.

- Blum (1997, pp. 19–34) reminded us that Anna Freud (1963) had traced a developmental line from play to work and stated that the capacity to work consolidates during latency. In Blum's opinion, however, play and work are not necessarily opposites; they may be mutually facilitating and synergetic. Moreover, there are "activities intermediate between work and play such as forms of recreational interest and hobbies which have serious intent, require considerable skill and knowledge, and involve work that is very playful" (p. 21). In general, though, work is more directly involved with reality and involves activities designed to have a desired effect.
- Meissner (1997, pp. 35–60) began by clarifying what work is not: "It is not holding down a job, having a career, or making money. Work may be involved with all of these, but it is not synonymous with any" (p. 36). He noted that work has little to do with recognition or reward; those may or may not be bestowed upon the end result of work (e.g., a painting, a scientific discovery)

but are not dynamic constituents of work itself. Work is a manifestation of the "principle of agency" (Meissner, 1997), and seeks to integrate the aims of id, ego, and superego for the purposes of accomplishing goals into external reality. At the same time, work must not be equated with producing something tangible or merely "sublimating" aggression. Work refers to a process, not to its content. Meissner put it eloquently by saying that "The work of the painter is to paint, the work of the musician to play music, the work of the intellectual to think, of the mystic to pray. The monk who spends hours quietly in prayer and meditative reflection in his cell is as much at work as when he is pouring out sweat in the field" (p. 39).

• Levine (1997, pp. 143–157) astutely noted that patients, notably adult male patients, talk a lot about their work during the early phases of analyses before the transference neurosis becomes consolidated. Work offers a repository of all sorts of externalizations. "It furnishes a never-ending supply of actors and opportunities for the actualization and enactment of the dramas of the inner world" (p. 145). Levine added that the internal conditions for successful work are based upon the capacity to relate to one's work in the context of a significant object relationship or to relate to it as an object itself. "In either case, a positive relationship to one's work task mitigates the loneliness of creation through the unconscious source of contact and well-being with one's internal objects" (p. 153).

• Bergman (1997, pp. 191–207) proposed that disavowed hostile aspects of internal relationships with parents contribute greatly to the inhibitions of creative work. Experienced as a transient block or total incapacity to work, such inhibitions emerge from the desperate hunger for a loving internal object coupled with the inability to bypass a severely critical internal presence. It is only via the modification of this love-hate economy in the favor of love (by transference interpretation and by the internalization of the analyst as a new object) can such impediments be resolved and capacity to work grow.

These essays, along with the others contained in the book, *Work and Its Inhibitions*, clarify that besides keeping instincts in abeyance (or expressing them in well-titrated and "aim-inhibited" doses), work provides a sense of esteem, coherence, identity, location in a social context, and, in Freud's words, "justification for existence in society" (1930, p. 80). A telling illustration of this is constituted by the following story, apocryphal though it might be:

An American woman goes to Mexico. There she comes across a poor village woman who is selling little ceramic bowls; some twelve of them are neatly arranged on a sheet spread in front of her on the roadside. The American woman picks one of them up and is taken by its beauty. She asks the price and, finding it reasonable, says that she will buy all twelve of the bowls. To her surprise, however, the Mexican woman refuses to sell them all at once. "What would I do the rest of the day?" she asks in mocking exasperation.

This story highlights that monetary benefit, while playing a significant role on the conscious level, is not sufficient to explain the "need to work." More is at stake here. Work provides a sense of agency, purpose, and worth that is gratifying on deeper levels of the psyche.

Work is thus necessary for mental health.[1] The organizing power of work becomes more evident when it is specialized and professional. Both internal and external worlds then come under its sway.

> An occupation represents much more than a set of skills and functions; it means a way of life. It provides and determines much of the environment, both physical and social, in which a person lives; it selects out traits that are utilized most frequently and strengthened; and it usually carries with it a status in the community and provides social rolls and patterns for living. Through determining with what sorts of persons one spends much of one's life, a vocation markedly influences value judgments and ethical standards. Occupation and personality traits are intimately related.
>
> (Lidz, 1983, p. 392)

Lidz is correct and individuals who choose (or, are unconsciously led to) occupations that best synthesize their temperament, ego attributes, and identifications are indeed fortunate.

Addiction

In declaring masturbation to be the "primal addiction," Freud (1897b, p. 287) laid the groundwork for a deeper understanding of all addictive behaviors. Implicit in this deceptively simple statement are the various psychic ingredients of addiction, including manipulation of the body in the search for pleasure, narcissistic turning away from external object relations, and replacement of genital sexuality by autoeroticism. Freud's subsequent reflections on addiction develop this basic idea while adding other potential etiologic factors. These include constitutional predisposition (1905a), attempt at managing painful affects (1917a), and narcissistic withdrawal from the pressures of external reality (1930). Freud's early followers continued to underscore the pregenital foundation of addictions. It is in this spirit that Abraham (1908) noted the similarity between addictions and perversions. Both involve a tenacious denial of the morbidity of one's behavior and a replacement of genital sexuality by pregenital aims.

While not disregarding the addict's oral eroticism, Radó (1926, 1933) emphasized the ego defects of such an individual. He traced the origin of "pharmacothymia" to the ego's readily resorting to the pleasure principle in an inability to accept the realistic limitations of life. Addiction was basically "a narcissistic disorder" (1933, p. 84). The addict felt severe pain when facing ordinary frustrations and readily mobilized yearnings to recapture his infantile omnipotence. Moreover, he pushed aside and, at times, completely ignored, the ego's devices of reality testing. He sacrificed object relations over transient subjective relief. Narcissistic regression also affects the sexual realm. Habitual attainment of pharmacogenic pleasure initiated "an artificial sexual organization which is autoerotic and modelled on infantile masturbation" (p. 85). Heterosexuality suffered, passive aims rose to the surface, and interest in sex was lost. Rado's sophisticated contribution recognized the addict's defective ego, tenuous object relations, untamed infantile omnipotence, and fragile sexuality. It accommodated the role of both severe childhood frustration and genetically preformed pathways in the genesis of addiction.

Fenichel (1945) noted that addicts are governed by the need to get something that is not merely sexual satisfaction but also security and an assurance of self-assertion, and as such essential to the person's very existence. Addiction is characterized by the urgency of this need and the final insufficiency of all attempts to satisfy it. Individuals prone to addiction display "oral and narcissistic pre-morbid personalities" (p. 379): inconsolable, intolerant of tension, and fragile in the sexual realm.

In contrast to this emphasis on drive-based explanations, more recent psychoanalytic contributions (themselves reflective of parallel shifts in the overall psychoanalytic theory) focus on structural factors, ego functions, self-states, and object relations in understanding the psychic suffering of addicts. Chein and colleagues (Chein et al., 1964), for instance, note that in addictions, the chemical gets incorporated as a diffuse pharmacological defense of the ego. The drug becomes an auxiliary ego that facilitates speaking of the unspeakable and doing of the prohibitively difficult. The subject can displace the responsibility of his utterances and deeds upon the chemical in a characteristic "evocation of a proxy" (Wangh, 1962).

Emphasizing a different aspect of ego functioning, Krystal and Raskin (1970) noted that the stimulus barrier preventing psychic helplessness and traumatization is defective in addiction-prone individuals. In addiction there is a characteristic primitivization of affects. The ideational component of affect becomes separated from its experiential and expressive components. Verbal markers of emotions recede and somatic manifestations predominate. Such regression in affects impairs their use as signals. Instead, affects are experienced as traumatic, powerful all or none phenomena, something to be quickly dissipated. When the stimulus barrier is weak, affects are powerful, and self-soothing abilities are deficient, the situation is ripe for substance abuse. Wurmser (1984b) later echoed this view by calling addiction a "pharmacologically induced denial of affect" (p. 44).

Khantzian, a major contemporary contributor to the psychoanalytic understanding of substance abuse, furthered this affect-based explanation of the development of addiction. He (1975) classified the drugs of abuse into three types: energizing, releasing, and stabilizing. Individuals with depressive proclivities, inner emptiness, boredom, and passivity, are drawn toward "energizing" substances such as amphetamines. Individuals who are constantly warding off their aggression, their need for love and forgiveness, as well as their narcissistic longings, seek the "releasing" pleasure of alcohol and barbiturates to relieve the pain related to rigid defenses. Individuals who are frequently taken over by restlessness, anger, and violent feelings, prefer the "stabilizing" effect of opiates. Viewed in this way, the use of drugs starts as an "adaptive" measure and only later comes to preclude reliance on true intrapsychic and interpersonal conflict resolutions. Addiction then begins and takes on a life of its own with an ever-increasing tendency for psychic regression and social withdrawal.

Khantzian (Khantzian, 1982, 1985; Treece and Khantzian, 1986; Bell and Khantzian, 1991) further refined this self-attempted affect-regulation hypothesis of addiction. He emphasized that addicts neither simply seek euphoria nor self-destruction. To the contrary, they attempt to regulate unmanageably distressing emotions, only to succumb to the psychostructurally deleterious impact of the substance abuse. Khantzian traced their difficulty with emotions to pronounced ego defects that "take such forms as an inability to identify and verbalize feelings, an incapacity to tolerate painful feelings such as anxiety and depression, an inability to moderate feelings, problems in activation and initiative, and a tendency to exhibit extreme manifestations of feelings" (1974, p. 166).

In a related vein, Mack (1981) portrayed alcoholism as a defect in the ego's function of "self-governance," which he saw as being concerned with "choosing or deciding, with directing and controlling" (p. 132) important matters affecting one's life. He emphasized the role of object losses and shifts in essential social supports as precipitating a dysfunction of self-governance. Such susceptibility to regression is both constitutionally and psychically based. At the same time, it remains unclear whether the self-care functions have failed to develop adequately in childhood or have been retrospectively obliterated by the substance abuse itself.

Finally, Keller (1992) pointed out the psychostructural similarities between addiction and perversion. Both conditions are characterized by the use of an external object to bring an internal, anxiety-provoking situation under illusory control. Both conditions are characterized by a collapse of the ability to symbolize, loss of transitional space, impaired genitality, and weak ties to the object world. Individuals with both conditions display a dread of intimacy, reliance on fetishlike objects, the intrapsychic mechanism of denial, and the interpersonal maneuver of secrecy. The ego's desperate failure in truly mastering inner anxieties is also evident in both disorders.

While not ignoring the role of oedipal factors, almost all the psychoanalytic investigators just cited conclude that the "fundamental wound of the addict's ego" (Simmel, 1948, p. 27) is caused by early, preoedipal damage to the personality. At the same time, they acknowledge the role of social variables and constitutional vulnerabilities, which perhaps explains the fact that not all individuals with pre-oedipal ego damage develop addiction.

Putting two plus two together

Having laid bare the essential psychological processes involved in work and in addiction, now the task at hand is to discern how and in what ways these two trajectories converge. In other words, how does "work addiction" arise? Faced with this inquiry, we find ourselves needing to tackle two basic questions. One, how can an instinct-sublimating, ego-replenishing, efficacy-rendering, superego-pacifying, and ego-ideal pleasing activity turn into an imperious and tyrannical psychic mandate? Two, how can the malady of addiction that is exemplified by the bondage to psychotoxic substances like drugs and alcohol enlist ordinary behaviors for its nefarious goals?

Work gone awry

To answer the first question, let us retrace our steps back to the psychoanalytic literature on work. There we find three or four instances that make us think that work can indeed go mad, become a merciless inner force. Freud (1895b) himself gave us a hint to this effect. He said:

> A man like me can not live without a hobby-horse, a consuming passion – in Schiller's words, a tyrant. I have found my tyrant, and in his service I know no limit. My tyrant is psychology.
>
> (p. 112)

The key words here are "consuming," "tyrant," and "no limits." And, consumed he certainly was, working long hours and often unable (unwilling?) to participate in family activities. That this industriousness and single-minded devotion to work gave the great gift of psychoanalysis to the world raises the issue of where should one draw a line between "work devotion" and "work addiction," a thorny matter to which I shall return later in this discourse.

Following Freud, Hendrick (1943), whose work has been cited previously, acknowledged that all work was not the result of sublimation and sometimes work reflected reaction formation (which by its countercathectic rigidity betrays continued instinctualization). Fenichel (1945) also spoke of the "reactive type of work" (p. 183), which is relentless, devoid of pleasure, and undertaken to keep instinctual demands in abeyance. More recently, Kernberg (1975) has talked about professional pursuits that are "pseudo-sublimatory" (p. 230) in nature and largely executed in the service of narcissism. Wolf (1997) has mentioned "work obsessions" (p. 110) whereby work becomes something more than a method to make a living or even an avenue for joyful self-fulfillment. Both Kernberg and Wolf speak of the narcissistic individuals' compulsion to work excessively since work, for them, has become the sole source of self-esteem.

Behavioral addictions

Now that we have established that work can go awry, we can move on to the second question raised at the beginning of this section. This pertained to how addictions can develop without psychotropic substances. Here too we need to take a few steps back and remind ourselves that as early as 1897, Freud declared an activity (namely masturbation) and not the overuse of a substance to be the prototypical addiction. He also referred to "addiction to bed-wetting" (1905b, p. 78) in the case of Dora and "addiction to gambling" (1928, p. 194) in his brief biographical paper on Dostoyevsky. And in his encyclopedic text on (early) psychoanalytic theory, Fenichel (1945) stated that: "the mechanisms and symptoms of addictions may also occur without the employment of any drugs, and thus without the complications brought about by the chemical effects of drugs" (p. 381). Fenichel included food, reading, and even love as the objects of such addictions. Regarding the last-mentioned, he said that "love addicts" are:

> Persons in whom the affection or the confirmation they receive from external objects plays the same role as food in the case of food addicts. Although they are unable to return love, they absolutely need an object by whom they feel loved, but only as an instrument to procure the condensed and gratification. The "love addicts" constitute a high percentage of "hypersexual persons".
>
> (p. 382)

Fascinatingly, almost 60 years passed before psychoanalytic attention returned to addictions without drugs when Khantzian and Albanese (2008) referred to pathological gambling and hypersexuality as "behavioral addictions." They declared that:

> Such behavioral addictions have much in common with chemical addictions. In our opinion, the evidence provides a basis to conclude that these addictive behaviors, much like substances of addiction, serve the need to relieve or change the stress associated with enduring painful feelings and problems with self-esteem and interpersonal relationships.
>
> (pp. 87–88)

Contemporary descriptive psychiatry also began to recognize behavioral addictions as valid nosological entities. The haloed DSM-V recognized pathological gambling as an addiction. And, three psychiatric books (Rosenberg and Feder, 2014; Ascher and Levounis, 2014; Petry, 2005) extended "behavioral addictions" to activities as wide-ranging as eating, gambling, internet surfing, exercise, tanning, kleptomania, and social networking. Only one of these books (Ascher and Levounis, 2014) includes a chapter on work addiction. In this chapter, Ascher et al. (2014) delineate two elements of work addiction: "a strong inner drive to work and working excessively hard" (p. 241). In addition to these cognitive and behavioral criteria, they propose that pleasure in work evaporates almost totally for most work-addicts except for a small proportion of "enthusiastic workaholics" (p. 241) who continue to have high work enjoyment.

This descriptive tip of the hat to the syndrome of work addiction notwithstanding, the paucity of psychoanalytic writings on "work addiction" remains striking; the PEP Web (the electronic compendium of psychoanalytic literature extending over more than a century) does not have a single paper with these words in the title. This is in contrast to the glut of books in the genres of "lay" and "pop" psychology and self-help traditions. A possible explanation for this discrepancy is the "work-addicts," glued as they are to their ego-syntonic salve against deeper wounds, do not seek psychotherapeutic help. Their spouses and children do. Thus, the lay books on strategies to "cure" work addiction are most likely devoured by those affected and not by those afflicted by this malady.[2]

Symptoms of work addiction

The manifest picture of work addiction bears many similarities to those of substance abuse and alcoholism. The term "workaholism," coined by Wayne Oates (1971), an American minister and professor of psychology of religion, captures this very point. Although the designation has remained in the colloquial realm, the entity is beginning to be recognized by professionals in the fields of clinical psychology (Robinson, 1989, 2014; Killinger, 1991), occupational therapy (Rasmussen, 2008), and psychiatry (Ascher and Levounis, 2014). The following seven features constitute its symptomatology:

- Devoting an excessive amount of time to work that somehow does not seem enough; this can be called "work hunger."
- Feeling bored when not working and, as a result, being unable to take or enjoy vacations; the phenomenon of becoming dysphoric on holidays has received many labels including "Sunday neurosis" (Ferenczi, 1919) and "leisure sickness" (Robinson, 2014).
- Working on a secret basis during family get-togethers, romantic intimacy, and even while making love; this includes "work trances," (Robinson, 2014) i.e., lapses of attention during conversations owing to inner preoccupation with work.
- Neglecting the emotional and physical needs of persons close to oneself (e.g., spouse, children, elderly parents); the colloquial phrase, "wedded to his work," refers to the deleterious effects of work addiction upon marriages.
- Attending sub-optimally to non-work-related, important aspects of one's own self (e.g., health, attire, monetary affairs).
- Striving for unrealistically high goals on either a quantitative or qualitative basis or both; in the latter case, much tension ensues between the need to be excessively productive and be excellent.
- Denying that work has become an affliction or acknowledging it only in a farcical way underneath which lurks a sadomasochistic image of moral superiority (Killinger, 1991).

Needless to add that one or the other clinical feature may be more marked in a given case of work addiction. Such subtle symptomatic variations have led some investigators to distinguish different types of work addiction. Rasmussen (2008), for instance, suggests that there are three types of "workaholics": the *compulsive type* (who cannot put off work even though feeling stressed by it), the *perfectionistic type* (who is focused on details and given to revising his work over and over), and the *ambitious type* (who strives mainly to ascend the career ladder and seems to be defending against the fear of being worthless). Robinson (2014) classified work-addicts into the *relentless type* (who work excessively and constantly), the *bulimic type* (who fluctuate between overwork and underwork), the *attention-deficit type* (who jump from task to task), and the *savouring type* (who endlessly revisit and revise their work). Rasmussen and Robinson do provide some interesting designations, but my socio-clinical experience does not confirm the existence of such pure categories. More often than not, the symptomatic picture is mixed and represents a composite portrait (see preceding) drawn from the writings of all the investigators cited previously. And even that portrayal needs to be tempered by adding two caveats: (1) this type of excessive work is not due to economic necessity; someone who has to take on additional work after one's regular job in order to feed and clothe his or her family is not suffering from "work addiction," and (2) sporadic periods of passionate devotion to work (e.g., those dictated by professional timetables or undertaken to divert attention from personal crises) also do not constitute "work addiction" which is a chronic, ego-depleting, and interpersonally disturbing condition.

Psychodynamics

In considering the psychodynamics of work addiction, we must keep in mind the "principle of multiple function" (Waelder, 1936) and the early psychoanalytic reminder (Fenichel, 1945) that all conflicts of dependence-independence, submission-defiance, and sensuality-logic can affect one's work life. "Work addiction" thus has many causes though one or the other may predominate in a given case. Four configurations especially stand out. As will be readily evident, these are arranged in order of increasing depth of the developmental level responsible for work addiction.

Proving one's goodness and avoiding unruly impulses

This is generally an oedipal level problem or, to put it more correctly, a problem of anal regression from oedipal level conflicts. Translated into daily language, this means that the individual harbors impulses of defying generational boundaries, mocking authority figures, and having sex with prohibited objects (e.g., one's parents or children) and has escaped from the moral anxiety consequent upon such impulses by replacing them with conflicts around orderliness, productivity, and compliance with societal expectations. Regression from oedipal conflicts to anal sadism and a subsequent reaction formation against the latter constitutes the central dynamic here (Fenichel, 1945). It is as if by the rapt absorption in work and by striving to be an exemplary member of society, one is running away from one's covert preserve sexuality and seeking absolution of guilt over it. Obsessional perfectionism is then deployed to allay self-doubt and external acclaim is sought to prove, over and over again, that one is "good," not "bad." Devotion to work becomes rigid, leaving little space for instinctual pleasures, especially of adult sexuality. The disregard for attire, nutrition, and even the messiness of one's workplace unconsciously gratifies regressive anal aims, however. Guilt over remnant oedipal impulses contributes to harshness of conscience and underestimation of one's task-related prowess.

Turning an ego need into a narcissistic virtue

This configuration is likely to be found in schizoid individuals. Pertinent in this context are Fairbairn's (1940) observation that schizoid individuals feel exhausted after social contacts and defend against their difficulty in emotional giving by playing roles that replace giving by showing. They are attracted to "literary and artistic activities partly due to the fact that these activities provide an exhibitionistic means of expression without involving direct contact" (p. 16). Thus the felt need to avoid emotional involvement can be replaced by exhibitionistic activities including work; a necessity is transformed into a virtue. Guntrip (1969) added further descriptive nuance to this outcome.

> The fundamental detachment [of the schizoid personality] is often masked and hidden under a façade of compulsive sociability, incessant talking, and hectic activity. . . . The emotional core of the personality is withdrawn from the self that lives in the external world. The outer self, like a skilled actor, can act even an emotional part mechanically while thinking of other things. . . . [This is] a human being who functions as an efficient robot within a restricted and safe conception of how life is to be lived. Life is the pursuit of truth, not love, the art of an ideology, and ideas become more important than people.
>
> (pp. 63, 64)

Unlike the obsessional scenario where work is a means to avoid the "naughtiness" of instincts, the schizoid scenario renders work itself into an object to whom one can relate more safely than to actual human beings who never live up to the desperate (though repudiated) expectation of utter reliability and exquisite attunement. The ego defect of mistrusting others and fearing betrayal is covered up by the "reliability" of work always being there. One becomes infatuated with work, ignoring the human lover that awaits in the wings.

Defending against the dread of indolence

Lying deeper than schizoid fears of attachment are powerful wishes to regress, become an infant, and do nothing for oneself. Once again, Guntrip (1969) provides us the understanding of such "regressive impulse to return to the safety of the womb" (p. 50) by stating that this wish is intensified in individuals who have not had a satisfactory infancy. They felt unloved by their mothers and also felt that their mothers rejected (or misunderstood) their loving gestures toward her. As a result, they now seek physical and motoric inactivity, total care by others, and provisions of simple and predictable nourishment. Their desire is to retire, do nothing, and be fed by a kind person who makes no demands upon them. However, the rational and morally driven sector of their personality is horrified by such fundamental laziness. A tinge of remorse also trickles "downwards" from this "grown up" part since this part realizes that such hunger is inconsolable and will sooner or later empty-out those who attempt to "feed" them. Reacting to exhortations and admonitions of their "mature" selves, such individuals bury their elementary indolence deep in their souls and pull themselves up by their bootstraps. They turn energetically to work.

Searching for immortality

This dynamic refers to the fact that some people undergo a "psychic death" during infancy and childhood. This death might be due to their (1) compliance with early parental wishes for them to vanish (Ferenczi, 1929), (2) profound "survivor guilt" (Niederland, 1968) over having escaped the misfortune that befell a sick or congenitally deformed sibling, and (3) identification with a loved parent who died during their childhood (Akhtar, 2011). Regardless of its etiology, people who have died first and live later often develop stoicism, pessimism, half-heartedness about life, and a sense of psychic weakness. However, given extraordinary talent, good extra-familial role models (e.g., a benevolent neighbor, an encouraging school teacher), and a serendipitous "break" or two, such "half-dead" individuals turn ferociously against mortality, as it were, and strive for achievements that will make them "immortal." Thus individuals who have lost their parents during early childhood can turn schizoid, guilty, masochistic, and even die (actually) earlier than expected (Li et al., 2014). Or, they can work tenaciously, become renowned, and achieve "immortality." The list of world-renowned people who suffered childhood parental loss includes religious figures like the Prophet Mohammad, literary giants like Leo Tolstoy, political geniuses like Thomas Jefferson,[3] civic activists like Malcolm X, and pop celebrities like Paul McCartney. A death-defying energy characterizes the work life of all of them. Far less known but still outstanding among such individuals is Korczak Ziolkowski (1908–1982), the Polish-American orphan from Boston who grew up to undertake the carving of the world's largest statue (in honor of the Indian chief, Crazy Horse); Ziolkowski has passed away but the work on that statue, taller than the famed Empire State Building, is still going on and is bound to ensure immortality to the sculptor.

In essence, work addiction can be derived from (1) reaction formation against unruly instincts, (2) substitution of relationships by work, (3) defense against indolence, and (4) search for immortality. Theses motives often coexist and reinforce each other. Moreover, their existence does not rule out the role of societal reinforcement of industriousness and productivity in the genesis of work addiction. Constitutional factors (e.g., outstanding talent, greater tolerance for hunger, lesser need for sleep) also contribute to the etiology of the malady. Not surprisingly, then, work addiction is often accompanied by vulnerability to other addictions (e.g., alcohol, drugs) as well.

Treatment possibilities

Treating work addiction may be a moot point since most individuals afflicted with it do not seek help. Their condition is largely ego-syntonic and even pleasurable. Their consumption with work provides them with social approval and monetary rewards. They are "respectable addicts" (Killinger, 1991). Further resistance is added by work being closely tied to identity, especially in the case of men. Questioning it can be experienced as an assault upon the self. And, unlike other addictions where going "cold turkey" is a potential avenue to recovery, "workaholism" is hardly suited for such a drastic measure.

Given these formidable resistances, it is not surprising that few work-addicts appear on their own at the psychoanalyst's door. The break-up of a relationship, threat of divorce by the spouse, or impending retirement may, at times, succeed in pushing them to seek help. More often, the clinician is left to deal with the "collateral damage" in the treatment of the work-addict's spouse or grown children who bitterly recount feeling marginalized and ignored. Once in a while, the ravaged spouse drags the work-addict into couples' therapy.[4] This, in turn, can become a first step toward the latter's looking into the narcissistic-masochistic traits contributing to his addiction. One other way such problems enter the analytic dialogue is via a patient's repeated cancellations of sessions and his staying stuck with work-related themes instead of settling into deeper transferences. Complaints of being too busy, rushed, and overwhelmed with work are also indications that work is being defensively used to ward off anxieties over interpersonal intimacy.

Having "diagnosed" work addiction, even if of subclinical proportions, the psychoanalyst is faced with a dilemma. On the one hand, his technique propels him toward "not directing one's notice to anything in particular and in maintaining the same "evenly suspended attention" in the face of all that one hears" (Freud, 1912, p. 111). On the other hand, psychoanalysis accommodates a step-by-step, logical, and theoretically informed process of conjecture formation (Brenner, 1976). Both methods might come in handy in discerning and understanding the patient's work addiction. The analyst might then explore and pursue the themes of childhood deprivation, lonely self-sufficiency, and desire to attract attention that underlies work addiction. In doing so, the analyst would be paying homage to the legacy of "strategy" (Levy, 1987) in psychoanalysis that dictates measured and deliberate tracks of interventions in certain circumstances. The shift that occurs from psychoanalytic to psychotherapeutic methodology during such moments might seem undesirable to tight-laced conservatives but is inevitable given the clinical task at hand. Pertinent here is Pine's (1997) declaration that he does "as much psychoanalysis as possible in context where [he does] as much psychotherapy as necessary – the latter being precisely what makes it possible to pursue the former" (p. 3).

Concluding remarks

In this contribution, I have elucidated the syndrome of work addiction. After discussing the place of work in human life and the psychodynamics of addictions in general, I have attempted to delineate seven features of addiction to work: (1) excessive work; (2) discomfort upon not working; (3) neglect of self; (4) neglect of others; (5) perfectionism; (6) covert forays into work; and (7) denial of one's affliction. Following this, I have deciphered four dynamic configurations that frequently underlie work addiction: (1) reaction formation against anal drives activated by regression from oedipal level conflict; (2) schizoid replacement of object relations with the solitary pleasure of work; (3) vehement repudiation of longings for rest, passivity, and maternal indulgence; and (4) defiant transformation of a "dead" part of the self into one that would become immortal, so to speak. I have also included constitutional and sociocultural factors as contributing to the origin and sustenance of work addiction.

Now, I wish to touch upon two other matters. The first pertains to gender. Though little literature is available on this topic, whatever does exist tends to suggest that men are more prone to work addiction than women. This may in part be due to the greater activity-proneness of the male species at large. Additionally, it may be due to the imperatives of patriarchy, which not only encourage men to work more and more but also provide them greater access to opportunities for passion-arousing lines of work. Women's propensity – co-created by evolutionary and cultural forces – to be embedded in the relational matrix of family and groups, in contrast, might serve as a prophylaxis against their being consumed by work and regarding it as the sole source of their self-esteem. To be sure, with sweeping cultural changes in offing the stability of the male-female ratio of work addiction prevalence remains to be seen.

The second and last matter involves a philosophical question. Should "work addiction" be treated at all? Imagine what our world would be like if mental health specialists had helped all its work-addicts overcome their affliction. How many scientific inventions, political uprisings, great pieces of literature, and stunning works of art would we have been deprived of if people like Tolstoy, Churchill, Edison, and Einstein had been "cured"? Let us admit it. We are vultures of epistemology. Our hunger for science and culture thrives by preying on the flesh of the work-addict's miserable devotion. However, it is also true that the work-addict causes much suffering to those around him. No one has captured this observation better than the philosopher-psychoanalyst, Allan Wheelis.

> I do not use myself up in living. A part of myself I save, like a miser, hoping to transmute it into something that will go on living for me in the future. With the quick I have little to do; the eminent dead are my models, the yet unborn my legatees. I am a time-binder, obsessed with mortality, spend my life creating an effigy to outlast me. In the graveyard, ceaselessly I carve at

my epitaph, trying to make of it something so beautiful, so compact of meaning, that people will come from afar to read.

It need not be in vain, this elaboration of self – great treasures have been so fashioned. What gets served up to the future may be a tasty dish indeed, but what shall we say of the chef, oblivious of the hungry ones around him, garnishing himself for the gourmets of the future? Rather than miss a day of painting, Cézanne did not attend his mother's funeral. Rilke could not spare time from his poetry for his daughter's wedding. The world cannot do without such people, but pity those whose lot it is to live with them.

(1975, p. 53)

What Wheelis says is true. But look carefully. Is the work-addict self-indulgent or self-depriving? And, are those around the work-addict merely suffering? Do they not bask in the narcissistic glory generated by his manic pursuit? Are the material benefits that often accompany excessive work truly irrelevant to them? Seen this way, work addiction appears more of a self-sacrificing virtue than a sadistic ailment. Think about it and tell me. Which is it? A virtue or an illness? If it is a virtue, we must leave it alone or celebrate it. If it is an illness, we must rush in and attempt to treat it.

I, for one, am reluctant to consider work addiction as a virtue *only* because it involves a socially applauded activity; in any case, not all work-addicts produce things of lasting value. I am also averse to viewing it as an illness *only* because it results in the suffering of family members. This would be dealing with the matter on a purely behavioral basis. We need to look at the phenomena from a deeper perspective. For doing so, the concept of "projective identification" (Klein, 1946) turns out to be quite useful. Seen through its lens, the neglect felt by the work addict's spouse and children represents the neglect experienced by him in his past. As a child when he desperately sought his parents' love, he was ignored and left to his own resources. It is this painful experience that is now projectively deposited in the loved ones around him. And, the narcissistic and material benefits his work confers upon others reflects his unconscious reparation for the guilt at causing distress to them. All that seems interpersonal here actually turns out to be intrapsychic. And, being suffused with pain, this intrapsychic substrate does need attention. This much seems clear. But whether the attention that the work-addict's wound needs is simply patience and forgiveness from those who love him or a professional intervention by a clinician remains unclear to me. Perhaps I need to do some more work to sort this out!

Notes

1 An exception to this perspective is to be found in Gedo's (1997a) impish essay "In Praise of Leisure." Denouncing Freud's celebration of work, Gedo says that for many people living up to one's ideal means "engaging in productive work. For others, however, it involves not productivity, but doing one's best, if only in private endeavors like raising children, reaching out for the deity, playing golf or reading Tolstoy" (p. 141).

2 A tongue-in-cheek parallel is my quip that "Victoria Secret, while offering women rightful pride and pleasure in their bodies, is actually a man's store par excellence" (Akhtar, 2005, p. 100) since it gratifies their vision-dependent eroticism!

3 Indeed 12 U.S. presidents lost a parent during childhood and the same is true of 67% of British Prime Ministers between 1799 and the beginning of World War II.

4 Clinical interventions with couples or families of work-addicts may be useful in destabilizing the erstwhile fixed, but pain equilibrium. This might lead to enhanced empathy and re-negotiation of roles and responsibilities within the interpersonal matrix (Robinson, 2014; Killinger, 1991). I am personally not experienced in such work and therefore restrict my comments to the treatment of the work-addict on a one-to-one basis.

Epilogue

Chapter 8

Addictions without drugs

Salman Akhtar and Nina Savelle-Rocklin

We begin this concluding commentary on our book with the following statements:

- Addiction is defined as a mandatory reliance upon the use of a substance or an activity that is associated with psychosocial distress, inability to free one-self of the habit, craving, risk-taking behaviors, and continuing to resort to the substance or activity despite interpersonal problems and physical harm.
- While psychodynamically akin, the broad group of addictions can be divided into two categories: (1) addiction to substances (e.g., alcohol, cocaine), and (2) addiction to activities (e.g., gambling, working).
- Psychiatric, psychoanalytic, and medical literature as well as epidemiological research and sociopolitical discourse have largely focused upon addiction to substances. This is understandable because such maladies lead to serious problems.
- In this zeal, "addictions without drugs" (Fenichel, 1945, p. 381) have become marginalized.
- Our book is aimed to fill this gap in the psychiatric and psychoanalytic literature.

The opening essay of the book is written by the eminent psychoanalyst and addiction scholar, Lance Dodes. The thrust of his contribution is threefold: (1) all addictions emanate from the ontogenetic triad of early narcissistic injury and rage, displacement of the resulting aims and objects, and attempted reversal of helpless-ness; (2) it is erroneous to regard addictions as ego-syntonic pleasure-seeking actions; many addictions become ego-dystonic over time and the euphoric accom-paniments of addictions are secondary to the inhibited/or and displaced aggres-sive drive discharge in them; and (3) treatment of addiction is best viewed as any other psychoanalytic treatment; relegating individuals suffering from addic-tions to behavioral counseling betrays a combination of analysts' underestima-tion of their therapeutic abilities and the profession's negative countertransference toward "addicts."

This challenging and powerful opening of the book leads to six thoughtful chapters that deal specifically with addictions to food, sex, gambling, shopping, internet, and work. To be sure, this list could have been enlarged to include addictions to reading, hoarding objects and animals, and so on. But we felt content with our selection of the six maladies just mentioned since these cover most, if not all, of the terrain encountered in clinical practice. The authors of these essays represent the fields of psychology, psychiatry, and psychoanalysis. Each contributor deals with the etiology, pathology, symptomology, and treatment of the particular malady under his or her purview. Without explicit reference to the opening chapter by Lance Dodes (since this was not made available to them), each contributor stays close to his proposals while also departing from them in subtle and nuanced ways. We shall explicate such concordances and discordances later in this commentary. First, we offer brief commentaries on the six main essays contained in our book. Four commentaries are co-authored by us. The commentary on a chapter by one of us is written by the other co-editor and vice versa.

The six maladies

Food addiction

Nina Savelle-Rocklin's chapter on food addiction is lucid, comprehensive, and clinically generous. Firmly grounded in psychoanalytic vision, it does not shirk the clinician's (and the theoretician's) responsibility to deal with the plebian, popular, and proselytized surface of addiction to food and eating. As a result, Savelle-Rocklin starts her discourse with the widespread notion that sugar is the main culprit in such a situation. By critically reviewing the scientific research that supports and the scientific research that opposes such reductionism, she demonstrates the superiority of the latter perspective. In doing this, she also lays the groundwork for dealing with the true issues at hand here, which are emotional, imaginary, and intrapsychic.

This leads her to survey the psychoanalytic literature pertaining to addiction. Her oeuvre is vast and impressive. She includes all the viewpoints that Pine (1988) has subsumed under his "four psychologies of psychoanalysis": drive, ego, object-relations, and the self. Savelle-Rocklin familiarizes the reader with Glover's (1932) and Radó's (1933) orality-based perspectives while also elucidating Khantzian's (1974), Wurmser's (1974) and most importantly, Dodes' (1990, 1995, 2002, 2003; see also Chapter 1 of this book) self-regulation hypotheses. From this point onwards, her review of literature becomes more specific and directed to the issue of food addiction in particular.

Six different (but surely overlapping?) pathways to food addiction are now delineated. These include: (1) self-soothing; (2) expressing unmentalized states; (3) defending against object hunger; (4) avoiding the fear of objectification; (5) filling an inner void; and (6) establishing a rhythmic predictability to existence; the fact that this last dynamic ends up backfiring (e.g., via vomiting, weight fluctuations, secondary anxieties) reminds one of Blum's (1981) concept of the "inconstant object," which by its rigidly expected unreliability paradoxically imparts a modicum of stability to a shaky psychic structure. Impressive about this section of Savelle-Rocklin's chapter are the following three features. First, each of the etiological dynamics is supported by fresh additions of pertinent psychoanalytic literature. Second, each dynamic configuration is illustrated by a clinical vignette or two. And finally, just when the reader is about to raise objection against the exclusivity of females in the clinical material presented, Savelle-Rocklin surprises and delights us by offering a vignette of her work with a male patient.

Her chapter on food addiction does not refer to Zerbe's (1993) work on eating disorders in women and Balsam's (2012) views on the erotic mysteries of the female body. However, the impact of these omissions pales in comparison to the weight that Savelle-Rocklin's textured perspective carries. Such "weight" is evident in her nuanced etiological formulations, which meaningfully integrate the social and psychological vectors of causation and assiduously side-step the oedipal-preoedipal polemic. This reflects true psychoanalytic sophistication since:

> [I]n the flow and flux of analytic clinical material, we are always in the world of "both/and." We deal constantly, and in turn, both with the oedipal where there is a coherent self, and the preoedipal, where there may not yet be; with defensive regressions and with developmental arrests; with defensive transferences and defensive resistances and with recreations of earlier traumatic and traumatized states.
>
> (Wallerstein, 1983, p. 31)

Savelle-Rocklin's therapeutic approach to food addiction also avoids formulaic interpretations. Instead, she focuses upon each individual patient's traumatic history, unconscious fantasies, and adaptive strategies. As a result, her manner of working skillfully combines patience and curiosity, empathy and insight, and reconstruction and interpretation.

Sex addiction

Lawrence Jacobson's nuanced discourse on sex addiction interweaves strands that are social and clinical, historical and contemporary, and theoretical and technical. Jacobson opens his essay with the problems of definition and terminology in this realm. He notes that nosological labels ranging from the ancient Greek "nymphomania" and "satyriasis" through Krafft-Ebings' (1886) "hypersexuality" to the current DSM-V's (2017) "paraphilic disorders" invariably reflect moral undertones, an admixture of titillation and condemnation, and a preconscious message that what is being called an "addiction" might actually be a "perversion."

This opening gambit sets up a theater of novelty. Jacobson's differentiation and linkage between "addiction" and "pervasion" is fresh, thought-provoking, and clinically astute. Addiction, for Jacobson, is always passive: the subject is an obedient servant to a power that seems to lie outside his omnipotence. Perversion, in contrast, is more active and the driving ominous force seems to reside within the individual. While thus distinguishing addiction and perversion, Jacobson puts the so-called sex addiction upside down on its theoretical head. He declares it is a perversion by stating that "sex addiction is an *addiction* to an activity that is basically perverse" (italics added). This is heady stuff and reminiscent of a colleague's response upon being asked whether he believes in God: "thank God, I'm an atheist." Despite the inherent paradox in Jacobson's proposal, the idea that sex addiction could be viewed as a perversion remains conceptually alluring.

This novel foundational step leads Jacobson to search for the essential meaning of sex addiction not in the addiction literature (including that from psychoanalytic perspective) but in the heuristic models of sexual perversion. Jacobson's search leads him to three such paradigms: (1) Freud's (1905a), which found any activity that was "pregenital" (not heterosexual and not reproductive) or sought to deny genital differences (e.g., fetishism that attributed a penis to women) as perverse; (2) Khan's (1979), which viewed the failure to rework childhood traumatic experiences of humiliation and inadequacy into viable fantasy scenarios of self-object relating (via the transitional realm of experience) as underlying sexual perversion; perverse acts were libidinized enactments of damage and revenge; and (3) Lacan's (1998), which viewed perversion as a denial of the fact that the infant-mother dyad is far from perfect and that the mother lacks and desires something beyond what the infant can provide; perverse acts, in this viewpoint, displayed a regressive repudiation of the need to tolerate separateness and psychically elaborate symbolic satisfaction instead.

Deftly, Jacobson notes that in all three models, something "good" but limit-setting is being repudiated: realty testing (acceptance of sexual and genital difference in Freud's model), bearing sadness (elaborating trauma via transitional realm in Khan's model), and accepting a lack in the self (Lacan's proposal that the mother needs the "phallus" for her complete jouissance and the infant can't provide it). It is this turning away from something good but painful that underlies the origin of perversion.

Jacobson goes on to illustrate these theoretical ideas by a brief clinical vignette. This involves a professionally successful married man (and a father of many children) who had arranged his life to be prototypically idyllic while carrying on sexual affairs on the side. A quality typical of these affairs was that no meaningful attachment was allowed to develop and psychic intimacy was kept to a minimum. In fact, it was the failure to keep feelings restricted in this manner with one particular paramour that led the patient to seek help. This man's background history revealed that his father had died when he was very young and, as an only child, he had become the sole agent of comfort for his mother. A great amount of mutual dependency and excitement developed between the two (note in this connection Khan's 1969 paper on "symbolic omnipotence"). The reactivation of this dynamic in adulthood became a source of anxiety and had to be strenuously avoided. Shallow, even though highly charged, encounters were thus preferred over deep and sustained emotional reliance upon another person.

Jacobson details the challenges of clinical work with such patients. First, one must distinguish sexual addicts from obsessively preoccupied sexual neurotics; the former lack empathy with their partners while the latter retain. Second, one must not confuse sexual promiscuity prevalent in the gay subculture with "sex addiction" (or perversion, as Jacobson has now come to call it), since men in general de-link sex and love (Kernberg, 1995); the promiscuity involving two men is not subject to the same nosological logic as that involving men and women. Here, Jacobson makes the pithy observation that "If straight women were generally as open to anonymous non-intimate sex as straight men then perhaps straight men would be having as many anonymous sexual encounters as gay men." In essence, gay promiscuity is a matter of willing partners and an enabling subculture, not psychopathology.

Jacobson proposes that the treatment of "sex addicts" has to take place at two levels: at the "secondary level" of the presenting problem (e.g., marital strife, shame at being found out, social and legal concerns) and at the level of "underlying problems" (e.g., dread of actual intimacy and the complicated affects it mobilizes), Jacobson is not averse to the idea that some patients might only be able to tolerate work on "secondary problems" and he is willing to acknowledge the potential relevance of behavioral approaches, pastoral counseling, and 12-step programs. He acknowledges that an occasional departure from neutrality and confrontative questioning of the pleasure in the patient's activities might be necessary during the course of such work. Here his ideas contain the echo of Ferenczi's (1921) "active technique" as well as those of others who have suggested that "spoiling" of ego-syntonic but destructive activities (often of preoedipal origin) is often necessary in the course of psychoanalysis (Kolansky and Eisner, 1974; Akhtar, 1996). This applies to his views about dealing with the "secondary level" issues. His greater emphasis, however, is upon working with the patient's "underlying problem," i.e., dread of genuine and sustained attachment and of the complicated emotions this invariably mobilizes. An important constituent of this work is to help the patient become curious not about what internal states and sensations he is seeking by having sex but about what internal states and sensations he is avoiding by having sex. This brings Jacobson full-circle back to reassert his proposal that the designation "addiction" lacks heuristic anchor, personal responsibility, and therapeutic traction offered by the label "perversion." It is best then to end this commentary on Jacobson's chapter by citing his own concluding words:

> To understand perversion as a creativity that has gone seriously awry provides, I think, a further reason to prefer the rubric of perversion to addiction, granting to "perversion" a therapeutic traction that I find "addiction" lacks. Leave aside the question of which word to use with patients, who generally provide the word themselves (some find the notion of "perversion" intriguing, while others would be horrified at its being applied to them). At the secondary level of inducing the patient to tolerate sensations that he or she is short-circuiting through sexual activity, and of arousing curiosity about what

may emerge in those sensations, I find that bearing in mind the normality of "perversion," its status as structure of desire, and its relation to creativity, it is more helpful than the externalization and passivity implicit in "addiction."

Gambling addiction

In his fascinating and detailed chapter on gambling, Rosenthal delves into its historical and religious underpinnings, skillfully relating them to psychoanalytic principles. In a brief historical overview, he notes that gambling signifies belief in an ambient underlying system of divine justice. If people live by a moral code, surely the heavens will reward them in some manner. He points out numerous examples in the Old Testament in which lots are cast as a means of making decisions. In ancient times, lots were drawn to "choose leaders, settle major disputes, determine guilt or innocence. The winning throw was thought to represent the will of God." This reference to drawing lots brings to mind the chilling scene in Shirley Jackson's (1948) novella, *The Lottery*, in which a game of chance, tradition, and blind faith culminate in human sacrifice.

The prevailing belief in early psychoanalytic literature was that gambling is invariably related to masochism. Freud (1928) proposes that the gambler wants to lose as a way to punish himself for conflicted feelings toward his father, and thus assuage his guilt. Subsequent theorists suggest that pathological gambling represents a wish to rebel against parental authority (Bergler, 1936, 1943, 1958), a means of expressing hidden hostility toward parents (Lindner, 1950) or as a way of creating self-punishment for unconscious guilt.

Rosenthal challenges the idea that gambling is always rooted in masochism. He acknowledges that "all neurotic and mentally disordered behavior is self-defeating," but goes on to state that "are we to therefore infer that all our patients are masochists?" He reminds us that masochism was originally conceived as a specific sexual perversion. Freud wrote a series of papers in which he used the term "masochism" in increasingly different ways, originally regarding the coexistence of sadism and masochism as necessary elements of sexuality, and later proposing that masochism was a manifestation of the death instinct, and still later, introducing the idea it was related to unconscious guilt. Various psychoanalytic writers used the term in different ways, creating some confusion as to whether masochism referred to perversion, sexuality, or oedipal guilt.

Rosenthal does a masterful job in clarifying the various types of masochistic behavior, elucidating the differences between sexual masochism, which is specific to achieving sexual excitement and orgasm, and typically involves some kind of pain, humiliation and abdication of control, and nonsexual masochism. This latter definition refers to a personality organization in which people have a life-long pattern of unconsciously creating failures and problems in multiple areas of functioning. He explains the problem of relational masochism, in which suffering is seen as a necessary ingredient for being in relationship. He further elucidates seven reasons why people seek out pain, including: (1) to atone for guilt; (2) to avoid some greater pain; (3) to manipulate and control a powerful person; (4) to please a parent; (5) to reenact a traumatic situation, turning passive to active; (6) to protect love objects from destruction; and (7) to inflict suffering on others. He proposes the term "self-defeating behavior disorder" as a more appropriate way of describing those who show masochistic traits and presents several brief clinical vignettes to illustrate these ideas.

He then delves into the treatment of Ms. K, a recovering alcoholic whose gambling addiction began soon after winning a scratch-off lottery ticket. Ms. K's recollections of feeling loved all followed incidents of sexual abuse by her father. She experienced oral copulation and partial penetration by this father, followed by his declarations of love. Her father called her his "princess" and told her that he loved her. Her mother's general reaction to any of Ms. K's requests was to object, "Why should you have that? I never did."

Ms. K's description of gambling as "exciting in a negative way" and her sexual arousal at the notion of sitting at a winning slot machines confirms the connection between gambling and masochism. Notably, gambling is similar to masturbation in that, "Both involve arousal, excitement and climax. Both deploy punishment for the activity per se as a plea bargain for keeping the fantasies involved in them unconscious" (Akhtar, 2009, p. 75). At the time of Ms. K's hospitalization and therapy with Rosenthal, she was engaged to a loving man, yet she found the prospect of being in a caring relationship to be terrifying. Although she was sober and believed she was "working a good program," she had, unbeknownst to her, exchanged one form of addictive behavior for another, shifting from drinking to gambling. In treatment, she came to recognize that she was unconsciously recapitulating the abuse and neglect of childhood through these addictions. Gambling allowed her to repeat the "chaos, terror, panic, reward and punishment" of childhood. She also converted emotional pain to physical, suffering a variety of physical aches as a way of expressing underlying pain. The simultaneous experience of excitement and pain provided a sense of aliveness that otherwise eluded her. Pain was a confirmation that she was alive, and pain was preferable to the sense of "floating in space" and dissociation that she correlated to her rejecting mother.

Through the presentation of this moving and interesting clinical material, Rosenthal makes the point that compulsive gambling represents a plethora of unconscious conflicts, reenactments, and meanings. Treatment modalities such as 12-step programs address the symptoms but not the cause of deleterious behaviors such as compulsive gambling. Only by recognizing the underlying masochistic agenda, whether it be suffering as a means of relieving guilt, turning passive to active, or obtaining love, power or validation, can gamblers find relief. Rosenthal warns against the complacency of most treatment programs, noting that only through psychoanalysis or psychodynamic therapy can masochistic gamblers "understand the meaning and purpose of their behavior."

Ms. K is currently happily married, free of addiction to both gambling and alcohol, and employed in the field of chemical dependency. Although the specifics of working through the dread and hope of detaching from pain were not detailed, the outcome suggests that her relinquishment of addictive behavior is a testament to the healing and transformational experience of psychoanalytic treatment. It seems fitting for us to end this commentary by sharing Freud's (1928) thoughts on Dostoyevsky's mania for gambling:

> He never rested until he had lost everything. For him gambling was another method of self-punishment. . . . When his sense of guilt was satisfied by the punishments he had inflicted on himself, the inhibitions on his work became less severe and he allowed himself to take a few steps along the way to success.
>
> (pp. 190–191)

Shopping addiction

We live in a world in which jokes about "retail therapy" abound, both in our culture and in the consulting room. Shopping is often viewed as a relatively innocuous way to resolve anxiety, but compulsive shopping is a disorder that simultaneously hides and expresses a plethora of intrapsychic and interpersonal conflicts and deficits. In this chapter, Ricardo Rieppi and Jean Petrucelli explore the multi-determined etiology of compulsive shopping, which they define as, "a maladaptive preoccupation with shopping or buying that either (1) is experienced as overpowering, intrusive, with irresistible urges or (2) frequently leads to spending more money or buying more items than intended, buying unnecessary items, and/or spending more time shopping than intended." They note that compulsive shoppers suffer significant emotional, social, occupational, and financial distress as a result of their compulsive behavior, yet there is a dearth of psychoanalytic inquiry into this subject. The chapter is organized into four sections: (1) psychoanalytic perspectives on money; (2) contemporary psychoanalytic perspectives on compulsive shopping and buying; (3) treatment of compulsive shopping; and (4) clinical material that illustrates the issues pertinent to the treatment of compulsive shopping.

Rieppi and Petrucelli delve into the historical and psychoanalytic perspectives on money, examining how these attitudes toward money impact the understanding and treatment of compulsive shopping. They state that money is "located on the boundary between the concrete and the symbolic" and thus may serve to alleviate unconscious anxieties. Beginning with Freud's (REF) conceptualization of the unconscious relationship between money and defecation, they describe the early psychoanalytic thinking along the lines of a money = feces equation, including the developmental perspective of Sandor Ferenczi (1916), and the notion proposed by Karl Abraham (1908) that stinginess is not due to anal fixation per se, but instead actually results from regression to the anal level due to genital conflicts. Later theorists such as Otto Fenichel (1938) view money as a primary source of narcissistic supplies and understand the wish to acquire more money and possessions as a means of protecting against a diminution of the ego.

After an overview of classical psychoanalytic thought with respect to money, the authors bring in viewpoints outside of the Freudian tradition, including that of Erich Fromm, who posits that socialization is a factor in the development of character orientations relating to the various usages of money. They include the contemporary analytic perspective that an individual's unique developmental experiences, as well as identifications both personally and societally, informs conflicts about money.

At this point, Rieppi and Petrucelli turn their attention to compulsive shopping. Interestingly, the first formal reference to this disorder was over a century ago when Emil Kraepelin (1915) first wrote of "buying maniacs" and conceptualizes the behavior as a type of impulsivity along the lines of kleptomania. Many decades later, Lance Dodes (1996) proposed that, "addictions are always compulsions, while compulsions frequently take on the characteristics of addictions and in these cases may be more usefully thought of as addictions" (p. 815). Although Dodes did not make specific reference to shopping, this conceptualization of addiction and compulsion is helpful in understanding compulsive shoppers.

In terms of the treatment of compulsive shopping, the authors elucidate four relevant analytic perspectives on addiction. These viewpoints encompass the following: (1) affect regulation and management; (2) the somatization of affect and psychosomatic illness; (3) limited access to fantasy, play, and symbolization; and (4) unique characteristics of the transference-countertransference. Compulsive shoppers often have difficulty identifying and differentiating between affective states, a problem compounded by their inability to respond to painful or upsetting states in a reassuring and calming manner. They distract themselves from distress by shopping and remain unaware of the internal conflicts and emotions that may be facilitating the behavior. These features have much in common with eating disorder patients, who often use food as a means of managing emotions and symbolically expressing conflict. This is consistent with our experience of such patients, who may alternate between eating binges and shopping binges, or restrict food yet express all their emotional hunger through shopping sprees. It is not unusual to find that a bulimic patient also displays financial bulimia, going on a buying spree and later returning all the items.

A second outlook is that addiction represents a somatization of affect and psychosomatic illness. The authors cite the work of several authors, including Krueger (1989, 2000) who describes the difficulty that many patients have in achieving a sense of self-representation due to arrested development of the body self, along with an overvaluation of the perceptions of others in terms of identity. Compulsive shopping is a means of finding a relational experience that was either lost or never experienced. Since the addict is "functioning at a concrete, non-symbolic level of operation," purchased items are "seen as original objects rather than substitutes" and the shopper must continue to spend as a means of soothing, calming, or restoring some internal equilibrium. This lack of ability to symbolize also extends to the arena of fantasy, the third area of inquiry. Many addicts have difficulty self-soothing, because they cannot access internal good objects. These patients struggle to conceptualize what the authors term "emotional cause and effect" and their specific actions around shopping must be closely understood as a means of helping them understand the relationship between internal experience and shopping behavior. Psychoanalysts must "provide a bridge between action and meaning, purchased items and object, act of shopping and underlying relational needs."

Last, the authors describe the transference and countertransference issues in the treatment of compulsive shopping. The importance of working through enactments is stressed, as is the difficulty working with patients who may be alexithymic and dissociative, and distrustful of the analytic relationship.

Petrucelli then provides the clinical example of her work with Tina, a charismatic young woman married to an older, wealthy man. Tina's symptoms initially include compulsivity in a number of areas, including shopping. She is also bright, engaging, and hypervigilant – for good reason, as she was abandoned both physically and emotionally by both parents. Her father left her when she was six years old, leaving her in the care of an alcoholic, hoarder, promiscuous mother who was incapable of caring for a child. Tina's early life was one of chaos and poverty both monetary and emotional. She later became a model, and through her work, she met a wealthy older man, got pregnant and quickly married at the age of 19.

In treatment, Tina initially wears different outfits to depict different parts of herself, expressing her internal world through her external appearance. She dresses Goth one day, designer suits another, floral dresses, or grunge, depending on her internal state. Dr. Petrucelli does a masterful job of helping Tina become attuned to the range of longings, pain, disappointment, and anger that lay within, and to understand herself in a new way. Tina slowly learns to use words instead of action, and to trust the bond between herself and her analyst, and she slowly relinquishes the sartorial armor in favor of actual human relatedness.

Tina initially had entered psychotherapy at the husband's request, but it is unclear what motivated him to suggest or "demand" treatment. He is described as a wealthy, older man whose response to Tina's spending is to "quickly tell the accountant to replenish her account – never getting angry at her about it." Petrucelli interprets that "her husband treats her more like a mistress than a wife, never asking where her new things come from and often not noticing." As we considered this, a scene from the movie *Annie* came to mind about the relationship between Daddy Warbucks and Annie: after rescuing her from the street, he eventually comes to love her and adopt her as his own. Did Tina's husband treated her more like a daughter than a mistress, as he has the feel of an indulgent father along the lines of Daddy Warbucks?

The sense of Tina's father hunger is palpable in this treatment. When Tina dreams that Barneys is closed, she thinks in the dream, "Where am I going to get my grilled cheese?" Grilled cheese is the one food that she recalls her father preparing for her, before he abandoned her. Was it possible that her husband represented a paternal figure to her, and that by draining his bank accounts she was taking symbolic action against her abandoning parent? Would she continue to drain his resources and leave him the empty one, instead of her?

Finally, we had one additional thought for consideration: What about Tina's child or children? Reference is made to two nannies, and we would have liked to know more about her experience as a mother and how her own maternal experience impacted her relationship to herself and to Petrucelli. Did she show maternal aptitude toward her child or children? Did she buy things only for herself or did she give things to her children?

These questions remain unanswered, but the fact that Tina lingers in our minds is evidence of the impressive analytic work by Petrucelli. In this broad-reaching and ambitious chapter, detailing the historical and contemporary psychoanalytic conceptualization of money and its uses, with emphasis on the relationship to shopping, Rieppi and Petrucelli contribute a great deal to our understanding of the understanding and treatment of compulsive shopping.

Internet addiction

In their comprehensive chapter on internet addiction, Charles Wisniewski, Stanley Kletkewicz, and April Fallon delve into the etiology of this relatively new form of addictive behavior, identifying its origins, examining the theories on neurobiology and attachment that contribute to our understanding of the disorder, and providing treatment recommendations. This ambitious chapter opens with a report of a South Korean couple who are so taken by an online "virtual" child that they ignore their own three-month-old baby, who starves to death. This shocking account highlights the severity of the problem of internet addiction, which can lead to devastating consequences. Having grabbed our attention, the authors then present an overview of the origins of cyber communication and the evolution of today's internet, noting the prevalence of internet communication via mobile devices in third world countries.

Wisniewski et al. distinguish between use and abuse of the internet, presenting the case of two brothers in New Delhi who played multiplayer games online to the point where they devoted almost every waking hour to the activity, eschewing family, work, and social relationships to the point where they urinated and defecated in their clothes rather than miss a moment of gaming. This is clearly an example of egregious abuse, but absent such extreme behavior, it may be difficult to differentiate between normal and pathological use of the internet. As the authors put it, "Is checking your email 15 times per day a necessity for work, an uncontrolled desire for connectivity or a fear of missing or being left out?" In an attempt to define what constitutes abuse, the World Health Organization recently (2018) defined gaming addiction abuse as that which has a duration of at least 12 months of "impaired control over gaming, increasing priority given to gaming to the extent that gaming takes precedence over other life interests and daily activities and continuation or escalation of gaming despite the occurrence of negative consequences as well as significant impairment in functioning."

Other theorists on the subject (Andreassen and Pallesen, 2014, p. 4057) define social networking addiction as behavior where individuals spend so much time on social networking sites that, "it impairs other social activities, education/job, personal relationships and/or psychological health and well-being." A plethora of variables influence the demarcation point between use and abuse, including age, sociodemographic variables, psychosocial factors, and gender, rendering it difficult to diagnose. Additionally, excessive online use may represent a solution to underlying psychological conflicts or issues. Internet use may serve as a means of coping with painful or difficult life events or conflicts and must be understood as a deleterious coping mechanism.

At this point, Wisniewski et al. turn their attention to the neurobiology of internet addiction, pointing out that the brain physiology in internet addicts is similar to that addicts who abuse substances. They explicate the role of the neurotransmitter dopamine in the phenomenon of both addictions and highlight how the reward system of the brain makes certain individuals more susceptible to deleterious patterns of behavior such as internet addiction.

After a brief overview of the psychological motivations for internet addiction, such as fear of missing out or concerns about social connections, the authors explore the role of attachment and object-relatedness in internet addiction. Noting that insecure attachment is one of the strongest predictors of internet addiction (Cerniglia et al., 2017), they examine how various cyber interactions keep attachment anxieties at bay. They report that, "Email, snapchat, instagram and texting offer stellar platforms to quell anxieties concerning connectedness." From a self-psychological perspective, this urge to connect online may serve the purpose of helping individuals hold onto a sense of themselves. Internet addicts connect with other people online, and these others are unconsciously experienced as an extension of the self, which in turn, "serves as a support for the delicate sense of self."

The internet can provide an opportunity to connect with real objects. The internet may also be utilized as a means of replacing reality with fantasy. An example is given of a male graduate student who created a plethora of identities, ranging from a young boy, rock star, gay male, and gay female, none of which he identified with in his actual life. He created these online personas and established connections with others online as a means of avoiding the disappointment and potential pain of actual relationships in the real world. This escape into fantasy represents an extreme of a continuum ranging from those who seek safe connections online to those who use online applications as a replacement for the real world.

In terms of treatment, the authors point out that the varied degrees of internet addiction suggest the need for markedly different clinical responses. They summarize a case of a 14-year-old boy who was unable to stop gaming and became physically aggressive at the prospect of his gaming system being taken away. He eventually stopped going to school. This boy needed residential treatment to "help break neural pathways associated with their maladaptive use pattern." Another example involves a family in which a father and eight-year-old daughter are consumed with watching videos of people opening surprise eggs – plastic eggs – that have candy, small toys, or stickers inside. The father's inability to meaningfully connect with his young daughter is one factor that led to using the surprise egg videos as a substitute for parenting. Notably, the father also had a similar difficulty in relating to his wife. The therapeutic recommendation was for this patient to explore this inability to meaningfully connect with his daughter and wife on an emotional level. Object relations couples therapy was suggested as beneficial, so that both husband and wife could come to recognize the unconscious repetitions that brought them together and now keep them stuck in a painful and distant relatedness. By resolving the past and creating new patterns of relating, reliance of the internet as a substitute for attachment will diminish.

There is no doubt that internet abuse is deleterious to individual functioning. Yet in certain circumstances such use may facilitate positive change. We recall a patient who joined an online "wolf pack" as a teenager. She experienced little meaningful connection with her workaholic father and an alcoholic mother, and was often left to her own devices. Desperate for a sense of connection, she joined the wolf pack. Participants in this online community took on the personas of wolves and related to each other as a pack. This patient spent hours each day with her "wolf family," which helped fill the void she felt with her actual family. This experience gave her a sense of what familial connection can feel like, sparking hope that she might one day find that sense of connection and community in the real world. Internet use, though excessive, served here as a bridge between personal isolation and hope for actual relationships in real life.

At the close of their comprehensive paper, Wisniewski et al. caution us that the internet is, "a world where the anxieties, wounds, emptiness and psychological distress from a perceived lack of attachment are "healed." However, it is also a world where those craving connection can become addicted to that perceived connection." They ask us to ponder whether virtual interaction can ever hold the resonance of actual physical interaction. Upon first contemplation, it may seem not. Yet, perhaps we are in a new zeitgeist, a period in which cyber connection is evolving as a new alternative to face-to-face connection. As John F. Kennedy stated in his 1960 speech upon accepting the nomination of president, "We stand today on the edge of a new frontier, a frontier of unknown opportunities and perils . . . of unfilled hopes and unfilled threats." What is evident is that the new frontier of internet technology and its implication in human relatedness leaves us with more questions than answers.

Work addiction

Salman Akhtar's expansive and thought-provoking chapter seeks to answer the question: what turns work into work addiction? He begins by conveying the scope of our cultural addiction to work, taking particular note of the Japanese condition of *Karoshi*, which literally translated means "overwork death." This focus on working at the expense of enjoying life is an attitude not limited to Asian cultures, but is also well entrenched in Western society.

After reviewing the historical perspective on what makes work a crucial part of our lives, Akhtar explores its place in our self-esteem and emotional well-being. Beginning with Freud's (1930) assertion that, "No other technique for the conduct of life attaches the individual so firmly to reality as laying emphasis on work; for his work at least gives him a secure place in a portion of reality, in the human community" (p. 80), he deftly distinguishes between the psychosocial underpinnings of work and the intrapsychic forces that facilitate our ability to work and sometimes overwork. Akhtar cautions that work is not to be equated with the production of something tangible, reminding us that work refers to a process, not to its content. He notes that work provides a sense of self-worth that is profound and resonates with many levels of our psyche, both conscious and unconscious.

We then get to the heart of the matter, the mechanism that turns work into a work addiction. Akhtar first delves into the historical perspective on addiction, ranging from the drive theory perspective of early analytic thinkers to contemporary views which posit a range of different reasons for addiction. Most of these authors refer to substance addiction rather than behavioral addiction. Some (Chein et al., 1964) take the view that substances serve as an auxiliary ego allowing addicts to speak and act in ways they cannot do while sober. Others (Krystal and Raskin, 1970) emphasize the relationship between helplessness and addiction. Khantzian (1982, 1985) expands on the notion that addiction represents an attempt at affect regulation that has gone awry.

In attempting to elucidate the relationship between addiction to psychotropic substances and behavioral addictions, Akhtar considers how and why individuals become addicted to work. He reminds us that Fenichel (1945) warned specifically of behavioral addictions when he stated, "the mechanisms and symptoms of addictions may also occur without the employment of any drugs" (p. 381). Fenichel included food, reading, and love as examples of such behavioral addictions. Fascinatingly, behavioral addictions did not become a focus of psychoanalytic thought for nearly six decades following Fenichel's observations, and even then there remained a dearth of psychoanalytic literature on work addiction. From whatever little did exist and from "lay" writings, Akhtar culls seven basic features of such addiction: (1) devoting an excessive amount of time to work, yet it does not seem like enough; (2) feeling bored when not working and thus being unable to enjoy time off or vacations; (3) secretly working while occupied with other activities such as family time and intimacy; (4) neglecting the emotional and physical needs of others; (5) neglecting the basic needs of self; (6) striving for unrealistically high goals; and (7) denying that work has become an obsession or affliction, or admitting it only in a joking manner.

At this point the chapter deepens into a thoughtful exploration of the multiple psychodynamics of work addiction. One such reason is a wish to prove one's goodness and avoid unruly impulses. Akhtar explains that this represents anal sadism as a regression from oedipal level conflicts. Workaholics suffer unconscious guilt about defying authority and turn conflicts against aggressive or inappropriate impulses into conflicts about productivity. Oedipal level conflicts are thus left behind in a regression to anal sadism. Addicts essentially use their addiction to working to prove over and over again that they are good and not bad.

Another dynamic that undergirds work addiction is turning an ego need into a narcissistic virtue. This psychodynamic solution is found most often in schizoid individuals, who defend against their difficulty in giving emotionally by replacing giving with showing. Guntrip (1969) observes that the fundamental detachment of the schizoid personality is often masked and hidden; however, the emotional core of the personality is withdrawn from the self that lives in the external world. Schizoid individuals relate more easily to work than to people. Work can be counted on to be reliable, whereas people felt to be unpredictable or unavailable. As Akhtar poignantly puts it, "One becomes infatuated with work, ignoring the lover that awaits in the wings."

Akhtar also delineates other etiologies that contribute to the development of work addiction. These include a defense against the dread of indolence, in which a wish to regress into infancy or the safety of the womb is turned into its opposite. Work addiction as a means of searching for immortality is yet another reason. Those who experienced a psychic death during childhood or who lost a beloved parent use work as a means of achieving a type of immortality in which their work, whether in the realm of religion, literature, civic activism or art, would live on long after they are gone.

Since most who are afflicted with work addiction view it as ego-syntonic, few enter treatment. Akhtar asks us to consider whether work addiction is a virtue or a vice. And herein lies the conundrum, which is that work addiction brings many compelling benefits (e.g., financial gains, societal adulation) and energized sense of well-being. Yet it also creates suffering and keeps those who are work addicts from living their lives more fully. One cannot truly connect with others if one is working all the time. Workaholics must come to terms with their conflicts and repressed wishes instead of acting them out. Akhtar points out that those who suffer the most are the loved ones of work addicts. The spouse and children of a work addict are left to experience the sense of being ignored or neglected that the addict originally suffered, but is now projectively deposited into loved ones around him rather than being mourned and worked through.

All in all, Akhtar's essay is a novel and significant contribution to our understanding of work addiction. However, it leaves one wanting. Many questions arise. Could the workplace become a stage for reenacting the conflicts and traumas of childhood? Could workaholism be a means of recapitulating the family of origin's situation in order to effect a different outcome? Besides these questions, one misses actual examples of patients who suffered from and, with treatment, overcame work addiction. Akhtar points out that workaholism is positively reinforced in our culture so there is little clinical material on the subject. Yet the readers long for clinical vignettes, especially if they have themselves been exposed, during childhood, to "workaholic" parents. And, it is hardly surprising that many of our readers might belong to such a group.

Concluding remarks

This summary and critique of our book's foregoing contents prepares the final ground for sorting out certain thorny phenomenological and therapeutic issues in this realm. To be sure, etiological matters also need revisiting but there seems a greater consensus about them. Almost all the contributors avoid the lure of oedipal-preoedipal ease of nosology and understand the suffering of their patients as arising from early deprivation, helplessness, displacement, and defensive search for self-repair and omnipotence. It is in the phenomenological realm that the cracks begin to show. Two features especially draw our attention. The first pertains to the use of the word "compulsion" in connection with the addictions that form the topic of this book. The second involves the similarities and distinctions between addiction and perversion. The former overlap is evident in Dodes' proposals (Chapter 1 of this book) and in Rieppi and Petrucelli's perspective (Chapter 5 of this book). The latter overlap is implicit in Jacobson's viewpoint (Chapter 3 of this book). Consequently, it becomes necessary to delineate the boundaries between addiction and compulsion on the one hand, and between addiction and perversion on the other. Let us take a closer look at these areas one by one.

The use of the word "compulsion" or its adjective form, "compulsive," in connection with addiction is questionable, in our opinion. We acknowledge that there is a certain overlap between the two conditions insofar as both the compulsive and the addict feel a pressure to perform certain actions (the former to touch a door knob, for instance, and the latter to have a drink) and both might feel a vague sense of embarrassment at their "weakness." We also recognize that it has become common practice to employ phrases like "compulsive sexuality," "compulsive gambling," "compulsive eating," "compulsive shopping," and so on. We question this practice, however. To the best of our reading of classical descriptive psychiatry (Jaspers, 1949; Fish, 1958; Slater and Roth, 1969), a compulsion is a psychic or motor act (e.g., quietly saying "one-two-three" in one's mind, or washing one's hands repeatedly) that is reluctantly performed in order to relieve the anxiety building from the obsession that precedes it (Akhtar et al., 1975); both obsession and compulsion are, by definition, ego-dystonic. Moreover, a compulsion only provides negative relief. It does not offer instinctual pleasure or euphoria. This is underscored repeatedly in the history of psychiatry, ranging from the statement by the doyen of British descriptive psychiatry, Sir Aubrey Lewis, that "the more enjoyable an act is, the less likely it is to be compulsive in origin," (1936, p. 327) to the current DSM-V which says that a compulsion is "aimed at preventing or reducing anxiety or distress, or preventing some dreaded event or situation" (2017, p. 237) without any mention of it providing pleasure. If this is true, and believe that it is, then why such prevalence of the prefix "compulsive" with the pleasurable behaviors of promiscuous sex, gleeful shopping, and obligatory gambling? The answer regrettably resides in linguistic sloppiness which blurs the line between the descriptive and the dynamic, and worse, between the scientific and the popular. The hard fact is that these phenomena reflect what Kernberg (1975) has termed "structured impulsivity." He uses this designation for impulsive actions that are ego-syntonic, and even enjoyable, at the time of their occurrence. In his own words, under these circumstances,

> there is chronic, repetitive eruption of an impulse which gratifies instinctual needs in a way which is ego-dystonic outside of the "impulse-ridden" episodes, but which is ego-syntonic and actually highly pleasurable during the episode itself. Alcoholism, drug addictions, certain forms of psychogenic obesity, and kleptomania are all typical examples. This group actually merges with those forms of sexual deviation in which the perverse symptom appears in an eruptive, episodic way, while other than during such specific episodes the perverse impulse is ego-dystonic and even strongly rejected.
>
> (p. 12)

Kernberg's parting comment brings up the second phenomenological conundrum mentioned previously, namely, the relationship between addiction and perversion. Here we will do best by starting from Freud's (1924b) differentiation between neuroses and psychoses. According to him, the main difference between the two conditions resided in the allegiance of the ego to reality in neuroses and to instincts in psychoses. In neuroses, the narrative that is repudiated consists of instinctual clamoring for expression. In psychoses, the narrative that is repudiated consists of societal dictates for conformity. Freud then went on to create the space for a third alternative, namely perversion. He stated that at times, it is possible

> for the ego to avoid a rupture in any direction by deforming itself, by submitting to encroachments on its own unity, and even perhaps by effecting a cleavage or division of itself. In this way the inconsistencies, eccentricities and follies of men would appear in a similar light to their sexual perversions.
>
> (p. 153)

To reiterate, there are three pathways open to a conflicted ego: neurosis, psychosis, and perversion. But where does addiction fit in this scheme? It is our contention that addiction also occupies the space (along with perversion) that lies between neuroses and psychoses. Addiction and perversion are not identical, although they are dynamic and structural twins. We support this proposal by noting the following similarities and differences between the two conditions. Their *similarities* include: (1) both originate from early, severe, and sustained trauma; (2) both are aimed at warding off unbearable affects consequent upon humiliation, exclusion, and helplessness; (3) both involve the body in their symptomatic expressions; (4) both manifest through behaviors that are largely ego-syntonic; and (5) both can exist "subclinically," coming to the attention of mental health professionals only upon the urging of family members or legal agencies. Their *differences* are: (1) addictions mostly have a hereditary basis (in addition to their psychogenesis) whereas perversions may not; (2) addictions are primarily masochistic whereas perversions are primarily sadistic (though, of course, the inverse flow of aggression also occurs in each of them); (3) addictions replace sexuality by nonsexual acts whereas perversions recruit nonsexual acts into the service of sexuality; (4) addictions seek retreat from object relations whereas perversions exert narcissistic control over object relations; and (5) addictions attempt to drown the fantasy life into oblivion whereas perversions hold on to the rigid repetition of a well-tailored fantasy. Based upon these phenomenological nuances, it is our conclusion that addiction (with or without substances) are definitely not compulsions and are also considerably distinct from perversions.

This brings us to treatment issues. We strongly agree with the contributors to this volume who have, with various intensities, emphasized the following three points. *First*, addictions lie on the far end of the spectrum of treatability, or, to use an old expression, "analyzability." Given their ego-syntonic and largely pleasurable nature, the individual's motivation for seeking help is weak and, as a result, the prognosis guarded. This, however, does not mean that one should refrain from treating these conditions; in fact, the containment of some hopelessness might be a first and necessary step in the devoted work that needs to follow (Akhtar, 1996; Shah, 2015). *Second*, the treatment approach must take into account the two levels of concern in patients with addictions. One pertains to the external ramifications of risky behaviors (e.g., family strife, legal entanglements, physical ailments) and the other to the underlying anguish that drives such behaviors. Like our contributors, we advocate the need of interventions at both these levels and are not averse to behavioral control strategies, 12-step programs, and group therapy, especially when the risky behaviors are pronounced and out-of-control. Also like our contributors, we believe that addressing the underlying affective states, unmasking defensive operations, making ego-syntonic acts ego-dystonic, reconstructing the traumatic origins of anguish, and straddling between "holding" character resistances and interpreting their gradually emerging transference-based aims constitute the essential ingredients of the deeper work that such patients need. Those patients who realistically and psychostructurally can "afford" to participate in this sort of long-term self-investigation can overcome their afflictions. An addiction-free life of deeper relatedness to fellow human beings in general and to their loved ones in particular then awaits them. Their night recedes and their new day dawns. Finally.

References

Abraham, K. (1908). The psychological relation between sexuality and alcoholism. In: *Selected Papers of Karl Abraham*, pp. 80–89. London: Hogarth Press, 1954

Abraham, K. (1923). Contributions to the theory of the anal character. *International Journal of Psychoanalysis* 4: 400–418.

Ahmed, R., Hanif, M., and Meenai, Y.A. (2015). Relationship between demographic and internet usage. *Journal of Information Engineering and Applications* 5: 8–14.

Akhtar, S. (1996). "Someday . . ." and "if only . . ." fantasies: Pathological optimism and inordinate nostalgia as related forms of idealization. *Journal of American Psychoanalytic Association* 44: 723–753.

Akhtar, S. (2005). *Objects of Our Desire*. New York, NY: Harmony Press.

Akhtar, S. (2009). *Turning Points in Dynamic Psychotherapy: Initial Assessment, Boundaries, Money, Disruptions, and Suicidal Crises*. London: Karnac Books.

Akhtar, S. (2011). Orphans. In: *Matters of Life and Death: Psychoanalytic Reflections*, pp. 147–180. London, UK: Karnac Books.

Akhtar, S., Wig, N.N., Prashad, D., and Verma, S.K. (1975). A phenomenological analysis of symptoms in obsessive compulsive neurosis. *British Journal of Psychiatry* 127: 342–348.

Albayrak, O., Wölfle, S.M., and Hebebrand, J. (2012). Does food addiction exist? A phenomenological discussion based on the psychiatric classification of substance-related disorders and addiction. *Obesity Facts* 5: 165–179.

American Psychiatric Association. (2013). *Diagnostic and Statistical Manual of Mental Disorders*, 5th Edition. Arlington, VA: American Psychiatric Publishing.

Andreassen, C.S., and Pallesen, S. (2014). Social network site addiction: An overview. *Current Pharmaceutical Design* 20: 4053–4061.

Aron, L., and Hirsch, I. (1992). Money matters in psychoanalysis: A relational approach. In: *Relational Perspectives in Psychoanalysis*, eds. N. Skolnick and S. Warshaw, pp. 239–256. Hillsdale, NJ: Analytic Press.

Asch, S.S. (1988). The analytic concepts of masochism: A re-evaluation. In: *Masochism: Current Psychoanalytic Perspectives*, eds. R.A. Glick and D.I. Meyers, pp. 93–115. Hillsdale, NJ: Analytic Press.

Ascher, M., Avery, J., and Holoshitz, Y. (2014). Work-addiction. In: *The Behavioral Addictions*, eds. M. Ascher and P. Levounis, pp. 237–249. Arlington, VA: American Psychiatric Publishing.

Ascher, M., and Levounis, P., eds. (2014). *The Behavioral Addictions*. Arlington, VA: American Psychiatric Publishing.

Avena, N.M., Rada, P., and Hoebel, B.G. (2008). Evidence for sugar addiction: Behavioral and neurochemical effects of intermittent, excessive sugar intake. *Neuroscience and Biobehavioral Reviews* 32: 20–39.

AWESMR kids. (2014). 20 Surprise eggs unwrapping! Retrieved from https://www.youtube.com/watch?v=OLIIKJpqeWY.

Baby Big Mouth. (2014). NEW Huge 101 Surprise Egg Opening Kinder Surprise Elmo Disney Pixar Cars Mickey Minnie Mouse. Retrieved from https://www.youtube.com/watch?v=h6szTEZn1m4

Bach, S. (1994). *The Language of Perversion and the Language of Love*. Northvale, NJ: Jason Aronson.

Ballarotto, G., Volpi, B., Marzilli, E., and Tambelli, R. (2018). Adolescent internet abuse: A study on the role of attachment to parents and peers in a large community sample. *BioMed Research International*: 1–10.

Balsam, R. (2012). *Women's Bodies in Psychoanalysis*. London: Routledge.

Barth, D. (1998). Speaking of feelings: Affects, language and psychoanalysis. *Psychoanalytic Dialogues* 8: 685–705.

Barth, D. (2000). Eating and shopping: Companion disorders. In: *I shop, Therefore I Am: Compulsive Buying and the Search for Self*, ed. A.L. Benson, pp. 268–287. Northvale, NJ: Jason Aronson.

Baumeister, R.F. (1988). Masochism as escape from self. *Journal of Sex Research* 25: 28–59.

Bell, C.M., and Khantzian, E.J. (1991). Contemporary psychodynamic perspectives and the disease concept of addiction: Complementary or competing models? *Psychiatric Annals* 21: 273–281.

Benjamin, J. (1992). Recognition and destruction: An outline of subjectivity. In: *Relational Perspectives in Pychoanalysis*, eds. N. Skolnick and S. Warshaw, pp. 43–60. Hillsdale, NJ: Analytic Press.

Benson, A.L. (2000). *I Shop, Therefore I Am: Compulsive Buying and the Search for Self*. Northvale, NJ: Jason Aronson.

Benson, A., Dittmar, H., and Wolfsohn, R. (2010). Compulsive buying: Cultural contributors and consequences. In: *Impulse control disorders*, eds. E. Aboujaoude and L.M. Koran, pp. 23–33. New York: Cambridge University Press.

Benton, D. (2009). The plausibility of sugar addiction and its role in obesity and eating disorders. *Clinical Nutrition* 29: 288–303.

Bergler, E. (1936). On the psychology of the gambler. *Imago* 22: 409–441.

Bergler, E. (1943). The gambler: A misunderstood neurotic. *Journal of Criminal Psychopathology* 4: 379–393.

Bergler, E. (1958). *The Psychology of Gambling*. New York: International Universities Press.

Bergman, M.V. (1997). Creative work, work inhibitions, and their relation to internal objects. In: *Work and Its Inhibitions: Psychoanalytic Essays*, eds. C.W. Socarides and S. Kramer, pp. 191–207. Madison, CT: International Universities Press.

Berliner, B. (1947). On some psychodynamics of masochism. *Psychoanalytic Quarterly* 16: 459–471.

Berliner, B. (1958). The role of object relations in moral masochism. *Psychoanalytic Quarterly* 27: 38–56.

Bettelheim, B. (1987). *A Good Enough Parent: A Book on Child Rearing*. New York: Knopf.

Bion, W.R. (1970). *Attention and Interpretation*. London: Tavistock.

Blackwell, D., Leaman, C., Tramposch, R., Osborne, C., and Liss, M. (2017). Extraversion, neuroticism, attachment style and fear of missing out as predictors of social media use and addiction. *Personality and Individual Differences* 116: 69–72.

Blanton, S. (1976). The hidden faces of money. In: *The Psychoanalysis of Money*, ed. E. Borneman, pp. 253–270. New York: Urizen Books.

Bleuler, E. (1930). *Textbook of Psychiatry*. New York: Macmillan.

Blum, H.P. (1981). Object inconstancy and paranoid conspiracy. *Journal of American Psychoanalytic Association* 29: 789–813.

Blum, H.P. (1997). Psychoanalysis and playful work. In: *Work and Its Inhibitions: Psychoanalytic Essays*, eds. C.W. Socarides and S. Kramer, pp. 19–34. Madison, CT: International Universities Press.

Bollas, C. (1987). *The Shadow of the Object: Psychoanalysis of the Unthought Known*. New York: Columbia University Press.

Bower, M., Hale, R., and Wood, H., eds. (2013). *Addictive States of Mind*. London: Karnac Books.

Brand, M., Young, K.S., Laier, C., Wölfling, K., and Potenza, M.N. (2016). Integrating psychological and neurobiological considerations regarding the development and maintenance of specific internet-use disorders: An Interaction of Person-Affect-Cognition-Execution (I-PACE) model. *Neuroscience and Biobehavioral Reviews* 71: 252–266.

Brenner, C. (1976). *Psychoanalytic Technique and Psychic Conflict*. New York: International Universities Press.

Breuer, J. and Freud, S. (1895). Studies on hysteria. *Standard Edition* 2: 1–309.

Bromberg, P.M. (1993). Shadow and substance: A relational perspective on clinical process. *Psychoanalytic Psychology* 10: 147–168.

Bromberg, P. (1998). *Standing in the Spaces: Essays on Clinical Process, Trauma, and Dissociation*. Hillsdale, NJ: Analytic Press.

Bromberg, P. (2010). Minding the dissociative gap. *Contemporary Psychoanalysis* 46: 19–31.

Brown, V. (2016, June 8). China now has a boot camp for the internet-addicted. Retrieved December 1, 2018, from https://www.news.com.au/lifestyle/health/health-problems/the-digital-addiction-that-has-teens-wearing-nappies-so-they-dont-need-a-toilet-break/news-story/5e0d321846a93337dc9f0260fc0ffc23.

Bruch, H. (1969). Obesity and orality. *Contemporary Psychoanalysis* 5: 129–143.

Bychowski, G. (1950). On neurotic obesity. *Psychoanalytic Review* 37: 301–319.

Cambridge, E. (2018, June 21). Boy, 10, needs bowel surgery after his parents let him play World of Warcraft for 8 hour binges without going to toilet. *The Sun*. Retrieved from https://www.thesun.co.uk/news/6586978/boy-addicted-world-warcraft-bowel-surgery/

Campbell-Kelly, M., and Garcia-Swartz, D.D. (2013). The history of the internet: The missing narratives. *Journal of Information Technology* 28: 18–33.

Caplan, P.J. (1985). *The Myth of Women's Masochism*. New York: Dutton.

Caplan, S.E. (2010). Theory and measurement of generalized problematic internet use: A two-step approach. *Computers in Human Behavior* 26: 1089–1097.

Carrington, A. (2015). *Money as Emotional Currency*. London: Karnac Books.

Casale, S., Rugai, L., and Fioravanti, G. (2018). Exploring the role of positive metacognitions in explaining the association between the fear of missing out and social media addiction. *Addictive Behaviors* 85: 83–87.

Celenza, A. (2014). *Erotic Revelations: Clinical Applications and Perverse Scenarios*. London: Routledge.

Cerniglia, L., Zoratto, F., Cimino, S., Laviola, G., Ammaniti, M., and Adriani, W. (2017). Internet addiction in adolescence: Neurobiological, psychosocial and clinical issues. *Neuroscience and Biobehavioral Reviews* 76: 174–184.

Chasseguet-Smirgel, J. (1984). *Creativity and Perversion*. New York: W.W. Norton.

Chein, I., Gerard, D., Lee, R., and Rosenfeld, E. (1964). *The Road to H: Narcotics, Delinquency, and Social Policy*. New York: Basic Books.

Choi, J., Cho, H., Kim, J.-Y., Jung, D.J., Ahn, K.J., Kang, H.-B., and Kim, D.-J. (2017). Structural alterations in the prefrontal cortex mediate the relationship between internet gaming disorder and depressed mood. *Scientific Reports* 7: 1245.

Christenson, G.A., Faber, R.J., DeZwaan, M., Raymond, N.C., Specker, S.M., Ekern, M.D., Mackenzie, T.B., Crosby, R.D., Mussel, M.P., and Mitchell, J.E. (1994). Compulsive buying: Descriptive characteristics and psychiatric comorbidity. *Journal of Clinical Psychiatry* 55: 5–11.

Collins, J. (2018, November 6). The top 10 most popular sites of 2018. Retrieved December 1, 2018, from https://www.lifewire.com/most-popular-sites-3483140.

Comings, D.E. (1994). Role of genetic factors in human sexual behavior based on studies of Tourette syndrome and ADHD probands and their relatives. *American Journal of Medical Genetics* 54: 227–241.

Comings, D.E., Rosenthal, R.J., Lesieur, H.R., Rugle, L., Muhleman, D., Chiu, C., Dietz, G., and Gade, R. (1996). A study of the dopamine D2 receptor gene in pathological gambling. *Pharmacogenetics* 6: 223–234.

Cooper, A.M. (2009). The narcissistic-masochistic character. *Psychiatric Annals* 39: 904–912.

Corsica, J.A. and Pelchat, M.L. (2010). Food addiction: True or false? *Current Opinions in Gastroenterology* 26: 165–169.

Cruz, J., Joiner, T.E., Johnson, J.G., Heisler, L.K., Spitzer, R.L., and Pettit, J.W. (2000). Self-defeating personality disorder reconsidered. *Journal of Personality Disorders* 14: 64–71.

Davies, J.M. (1996a). Dissociation, repression, and reality testing in the countertransference: The controversy over memory and false memory in the psychoanalytic treatment of adult survivors of childhood sexual abuse. *Psychoanalytic Dialogues* 6: 189–218.

Davies, J.M. (1996b). Linking the "pre-analytic" with the postclassical: Integration, dissociation, and the multiplicity of unconscious process. *Contemporary Psychoanalysis* 32: 553–576.

Davies, J.M. and Frawley, M.G. (1994). *Treating the Adult Survivor of Childhood Sexual Abuse: A Psychoanalytic Perspective*. New York: Basic Books.

De Monchy, R. (1950). Masochism as a pathological and as a normal phenomenon in the human mind. *International Journal of Psychoanalysis* 31: 95–97.

Desarbo, W.S. and Edwards, E. A. (1996). Typologies of compulsive buying behavior: A constrained clusterwise regression approach. *Journal of Consumer Psychology* 5(3): 231–262.

Di Chiara, G. (2005). Dopamine in disturbances of food and drug motivated behavior: A case of homology? *Physiology & Behavior* 86: 9–10.

Dimen, M. (1994). Money, love, and hate: Contradiction and paradox in psychoanalysis. *Psychoanalytic Dialogues* 4(1): 69–100.

Director, L. (2002). The value of relational psychoanalysis in the treatment of chronic drug and alcohol use. *Psychoanalytic Dialogues* 12: 551–579.

Dodes, L.M. (1990). Addiction, helplessness, and narcissistic rage. *Psychoanalytic Quarterly* 59: 398–419.

Dodes, L.M. (1995). Psychic helplessness and the psychology of addiction. In: *The Psychology and Treatment of Addictive Behavior*, ed. S. Dowling, pp. 133–145. Monograph of the Workshop Series of the American Psychoanalytic Association. Madison, CT: International Universities Press.

Dodes, L.M. (1996). Compulsion and addiction. *Journal of the American Psychoanalytic Association* 44: 815–835.

Dodes, L.M. (2002). *The Heart of Addiction*. New York: HarperCollins.

Dodes, L.M. (2003). Addiction and psychoanalysis. *Canadian Journal of Psychoanalysis* 11: 123–134.

Dodes, L.M. (2009). Addiction as a psychological symptom. *Psychodynamic Practice* 15: 381–393.

Dodes, L.M. (2011). *Breaking Addiction: A 7-Step Handbook for Ending Any Addiction*. New York: HarperCollins.

Dong, G., Li, H., Wang, L., and Potenza, M.N. (2017). Cognitive control and reward/loss processing in internet gaming disorder: Results from a comparison with recreational internet game-users. *European Psychiatry* 44: 30–38.

Duggan, M. (2017, September 12). Gaming and gamers. Retrieved August 2018 from Pew Research Center Internet & Technology: http://www.pewinternet.org/2015/12/15/gaming-and-gamers/

Durkee, T., Kaess, M., Carli, V., Parzer, P., Wasserman, C., Floderus, B., and Wasserman, D. (2012). Prevalence of pathological internet use among adolescents in Europe: Demographic and social factors: Pathological internet use among adolescents. *Addiction* 107: 2210–2222.

Elliot, R. (1994). Addiction consumption: Function and fragmentation in postmodernity. *Journal of Consumer Policy* 17: 159–179.

Ellman, S. and Moskowitz, M., eds. (1998). *Enactment: Toward a New Approach to the Therapeutic Relationship*. Northvale, NJ: Aronson.

Erikson, E. (1959). *Identity and the Life Cycle: Psychological Issues Monograph: I*. New York, NY: International Universities Press.

Eshel, O. (1998). "Black holes", deadness and existing analytically. *International Journal of Psychoanalysis* 79: 1115–1130.

Essig, T. (2012). The addiction concept and technology: Diagnosis, metaphor, or something else? A psychodynamic point of view: addiction concept. *Journal of Clinical Psychology* 68: 1175–1184. https://doi.org/10.1002/jclp.21917.

Faber, R.J., and Christenson, G.A. (1996). In the mood to buy: Differences in the mood states experienced by compulsive buyers and other consumers. *Psychology and Marketing* 13: 803–819.

Faber, R.J., and O'Guinn, T.C. (1992). A clinical screener for compulsive buying. *Journal of Consumer Research* 19: 459–469.

Facebook, Inc. (2018). Facebook Reports First Quarter 2018 Results (Press Release) (p. 8). Facebook, Inc. Retrieved from https://s21.q4cdn.com/399680738/files/doc_financials/2018/Q1/Q1-2018-Press-Release.pdf

Fairbairn, W.R.D. (1940). Schizoid factors in the personality. In: *An Object Relations Theory of Personality*, pp. 3–27. New York, NY: Basic Books, 1952.

Female Perversions (1996). Directed by S. Streitfield. Produced by October Films.

Fenichel, O. (1938). The drive to amass wealth. *Psychoanalytic Quarterly* 7: 69–95.

Fenichel, O. (1942). The misapprehended oracle. *American Imago* 3: 14–21.

Fenichel, O. (1945). Nature and classification of the so-called psychosomatic phenomena. *Psychoanalytic Quarterly* 14: 287–312.

Fenichel, O. (1946). *The Psychoanalytic Theory of Neurosis*. New York: Kegan Paul.

Ferenczi, S. (1916). The ontogenesis of the interest in money. In: *Contributions to Psychoanalysis*, pp. 269–279. Toronto, CN: Richard G. Badger.

Ferenczi, S. (1919). Sunday neuroses. In: *Further Contributions to the Theory and Technique of Psychoanalysis*, pp. 174–177. New York: Boni and Liveright.

Ferenczi, S. (1921). The further development of the active therapy in psychoanalysis. In: *Further Contributions to the Theory and Technique of Psychoanalysis*, pp. 198–217. London, UK: Hogarth Press, 1955.

Ferenczi, S. (1929). The unwelcome child and his death instinct. *International Journal of Psychoanalysis* 10: 125–129.

Fiester, S.J. (1996). Self-defeating personality disorder. In: *DSM-IV Sourcebook*, Volume 2, eds. T.A. Widiger, A.J. Frances, H.A. Pincus, R. Ross, M.B. First, and W.W. Davis, pp. 833–847. Washington, DC: American Psychiatric Association.

Fink, B. (1997). *A Clinical Introduction to Lacanian Psychoanalysis: Theory and Technique*. Cambridge, MA: Harvard University Press.

Fish, F. (1958). *Clinical Psychopathology*. Bristol, UK: John Wright and Sons.

Flahive, E. (2017, December 13). 36 Mind Blowing YouTube Facts, Figures and Statistics – 2017 (re-post). Retrieved December 1, 2018, from http://videonitch.com/2017/12/13/36-mind-blowing-youtube-facts-figures-statistics-2017-re-post/

Forrest, G.G. (1984). *Intensive Psychotherapy of Alcoholism*. Northvale, NJ: Jason Aronson, 1994.

Freud, A. (1963). The concept of developmental lines. *Psychoanalytic Study of the Child* 18: 245–265.

Freud, A. (1966). Obsessional neurosis: A summary of psycho-analytic views as presented at the congress. *International Journal of Psychoanalysis* 47: 116–122.

Freud, S. (1894). The neuro-psychoses of defence. *Standard Edition* 3: 41–61.

Freud, S. (1895a). Studies on hysteria. *Standard Edition* 2: 1–323.

Freud, S. (1895b). Letter to Wilhelm Fleiss, May 25, 1895. In: *The Complete Letters of Sigmund Freud to Wilhelm Fliess, 1887–1904*, transl. and ed. J.M. Masson, p. 112. Cambridge, MA: Harvard University Press.

Freud, S. (1897a). *The Complete Letters of Sigmund Freud to Wilhelm Fliess, 1887–1904*. transl. and ed. J.M. Masson. Cambridge, MA: Harvard University Press, 1985.

Freud, S. (1897b). Letter 79: Extracts from the Fliess papers. *Standard Edition* 1: 272–273.

Freud, S. (1905a). Three essays on the theory of sexuality. *Standard Edition* 7: 135–243.

Freud, S. (1905b). Fragment of an analysis of a case of hysteria. *Standard Edition* 7: 1–122.

Freud, S. (1908). Character and anal erotism. *Standard Edition* 9: 167–176.

Freud, S. (1909). Notes upon a case of obsessional neurosis. *Standard Edition* 10: 155–318.

Freud, S. (1912). Recommendations to physicians practicing psychoanalysis. *Standard Edition* 12: 109–120.

Freud, S. (1913). On beginning the treatment: Further recommendations on the technique of psychoanalysis. *Standard Edition* 12: 121–144.

Freud, S. (1916). Some character types met with in psycho-analytic work. *Standard Edition* 16: 311–333.

Freud, S. (1917a). Mourning and melancholia. *Standard Edition* 14: 237–258.

Freud, S. (1917b). On transformations of instinct as exemplified in anal eroticism. *Standard Edition* 17: 127–133.

Freud, S. (1924a). The economic problem of masochism. *Standard Edition* 19: 157–170.

Freud, S. (1924b). Neurosis and psychosis. *Standard Edition* 19: 149–153.

Freud, S. (1926). Inhibitions, symptoms and anxiety. *Standard Edition* 20: 75–175.

Freud, S. (1927). Fetishism. *Standard Edition* 21: 152–157.

Freud, S. (1928). Dostoevsky and parricide. *Standard Edition* 21: 175–196.

Freud, S. (1930). Civilization and its discontents. *Standard Edition* 21: 64–145.

Freud, S. (1938). An outline of psychoanalysis. *Standard Edition* 23: 139–207.

Fromm, E. (1947). *Man for Himself.* New York: Rinehart and Co.

Fuqua, P.B. (1986). Classical psychoanalytic views of money. In: *The Last Taboo: Money as Symbol and Reality in Psychotherapy and Psychoanalysis*, ed. D.W. Krueger, pp. 17–23. New York: Brunner/Mazel.

Gabbard, G.O. (2000). On gratitude and gratification. *Journal of the American Psychoanalytic Association* 48: 697–716.

Gabbard, G.O. (2012). Masochism as a multiply-determined phenomenon. In: *The Clinical Problem of Masochism*, eds. D. Holtzman and N. Kulish, pp. 103–111. Lanham, MD: Jason Aronson.

Goldberg, I. (1995). Internet addictive disorder (IAD) diagnostic criteria. Retrieved from http://www.psycom.net/iadcriteria.html.

Greenfield, D. (2010). The addictive properties of Internet usage. In: *Internet Addiction: A Handbook and Guide to Evaluation and Treatment*, eds. K.S. Young and C.N. de Abreu, pp. 135–154. New York, NY: John Wiley & Sons.

Gearhardt, A.N., Corbin, W.R., and Brownell, K.D. (2009). Preliminary validation of the Yale food addiction scale. *Appetite* 52: 430–436.

Gedo, J.E. (1997a). In praise of leisure. In: *Work and Its Inhibitions: Psychoanalytic Essays*, eds. C.W. Socarides and S. Kramer, pp. 133–142. Madison, CT: International Universities Press.

Gedo, J.E. (1997b). The primitive psyche, communication, and the language of the body. *Psychoanalytic Inquiry* 17: 192–203.

Geistwhite, R. (2000). Inadequacy and indebtedness: No-Fee psychotherapy in county training programs. *The Journal of Psychotherapy Practice and Research* 9(3): 142–148.

Gentile, D. (2009). Pathological video-game use among youth ages 8 to 18: A national study. *Psychological Science* 20: 594–602.

Glatt, M.M., and Cook, C.C. (1987). Pathological spending as a form of psychological dependence. *British Journal of Addictions* 82: 1257–1258.

Glick, R.A. and Meyers, D.I. (1988). Introduction. In: *Masochism: Current Psychoanalytic Perspectives*, eds. R.A. Glick and D.I. Meyers, pp. 1–25. Hillsdale, NJ: Analytic Press.

Glickauf-Hughes, C., and Wells, M. (1991). Current conceptualizations on masochism: Genesis and object relations. *American Journal of Psychotherapy* 45: 53–68.

Glover, E. (1925). Notes on oral character formation. *International Journal of Psychoanalysis* 6: 131–154.

Glover, E. (1932). On the aetiology of drug addiction. *International Journal of Psychoanalysis* 13: 298–328.

Glover, E. (1956). *On the Early Development of Mind.* New York: International Universities Press.

Goldberg, H. (1978). *Money Madness.* New York: Signet.

Goldstein, A. (1972). Heroin addiction and the role of methadone in its treatment. *Archives of General Psychiatry* 26: 291–298.

Greenson, R. (1947). On gambling. *American Imago* 4: 61–77.

Grossman, S. (2014). Teenage British selfie addict attempts suicide over failed photos, March 24. Retrieved July 23, 2018, from time.com.

Grossman, W.I. (1986). Notes on masochism: A discussion of the history and development of a psychoanalytic concept. *Psychoanalytic Quarterly* 55: 379–413.

Grossman, W.I. (1991). Pain, aggression, fantasy, and concepts of sadomasochism. *Psychoanalytic Quarterly* 60: 22–52.

Grotstein, J. (1990). The "black hole" as the basic psychotic experience: Some newer psychoanalytic and neuroscience perspectives on psychosis. *Journal of the American Academy of Psychoanalysis* 18: 129–146.

Guntrip, H. (1969). *Schizoid Phenomena, Object Relations and the Self.* New York: International Universities Press.

Guyenet, S. (2017). *The Hungry Brain: Outsmarting the Instincts That Make Us Overeat.* New York: Flatiron Books.

Ha, J.H., Kim, S.Y., Bae, S.C., Bae, S., Kim, H., Sim, M., and Cho, S.C. (2007). Depression and internet addiction in adolescents. *Psychopathology* 40: 424–430.

Hamburger, W.W. (1951). Emotional aspects of obesity. *Medical Clinics of North America* 35: 483–499.

Harris, T. (2017, October 13). Manipulation. *NPR*. Retrieved December 1, 2018. www.npr.org/programs/ted-radio-hour/557417264/manipulation

Hartzman, M. (2011). A touch of knowledge: The horsey horseless carriage. *The Huffington Post*, September 28. Retrieved August 29, 2018, from www.huffingtonpost.com/marc-hartzman.

Hendrick, I. (1943). Work: Thoughts on the pleasure principle. *Psychoanalytic Quarterly* 12: 311–329.

Hennig, M. (1974). Family dynamics and the successful woman executive. In: *Women and Success: The Anatomy of Achievement*, eds. J. Kundsin. New York: Morrow.

Hoffer, A., and Buie, D.H. (2016). Helplessness and the analyst's war against feeling it. *American Journal of Psychoanalysis* 76: 1–17.

Holden, C. (2001). Behavioral addictions debut in proposed DSM-V. *Science* 327: 935.

Hollander, E., Kwon, J.H., Stein, D.J., Broatch, J., Rowland, C.T., and Himelein, C.A. (1996). Obsessive-compulsive and spectrum disorders: Overview and quality of life issues. *Journal of Clinical Psychiatry* 57S: 3–6.

Holmes, D. (1965). A contribution to a psychoanalytic theory of work. *Psychoanalytic Study of the Child* 20: 384–393.

Hong, S.-B., Kim, J.-W., Choi, E.-J., Kim, H.-H., Suh, J.-E., Kim, C.-D., and Yi, S.-H. (2013). Reduced orbitofrontal cortical thickness in male adolescents with internet addiction. *Behavioral and Brain Functions* 9: 11–18.

Huang, Z., Wang, M., Qian, M., Zhong, J., and Tao, R. (2007). Chinese internet addiction inventory: Developing a measure of problematic internet use for Chinese college students. *CyberPsychology and Behavior* 10: 805–812.

Huprick, S.K., Zimmerman, M.A., and Chelminski, I. (2006). Should self-defeating personality disorder be revisited in the DSM? *Journal of Personality Disorders* 20: 388–400.

Jackson, M. (1993). Manic-depressive psychosis: Psychopathology and individual psychotherapy within a psychodynamic milieu. *Psychoanalytic Psychotherapy* 7: 103–133.

Jackson, S. (1948). The lottery. *The New Yorker*, June 26.

Jacoby, R.J., and Baldelomar, R. (2016). *Sugar Crush: How to Reduce Inflammation, Reverse Nerve Damage, and Reclaim Good Health.* New York: Harper Wave.

Jaspers, K. (1949). *General Psychopathology*, transl. M.W. Hamilton. London: Manchester University Press.

Jacques, E. (1960). Disturbances in the capacity to work. *International Journal of Psychoanalysis* 41: 357–367.

Jia, R., and Jia, H.H. (2016). Maybe you should blame your parents: Parental attachment, gender, and problematic internet use. *Journal of Behavioral Addictions* 5: 524–528.

Jones, E. (1918). Anal-erotic character traits. In: *Papers on Psychoanalysis*, pp. 413–437. London: Baillierre, Tindall, and Cox, 1950.

Jorgenson, A.G., Hsiao, R.C.-J., and Yen, C.-F. (2016). Internet addiction and other behavioral addictions. *Child and Adolescent Psychiatric Clinics of North America* 25: 509–520.

June, K.J., Sohn, S.Y., So, A.Y., Yi, G.M., and Park, S.H. (2007). A study of factors that influence internet addiction, smoking, and drinking in high school students. *Journal of Korean Academy of Nursing* 37: 872–878.

Kaplan, L. (1991). *Female Perversions*. New York, NY: Anchor Books.

Kaplan, L.J. (2000). Further thoughts on female perversions. *Studies in Gender and Sexuality* 1: 349–370.

Kardefelt-Winther, D. (2014). A conceptual and methodological critique of internet addiction research: Towards a model of compensatory internet use. *Computers in Human Behavior* 31: 351–354.

Kardefelt-Winther, D. (2016). Conceptualizing internet use disorders: Addiction or coping process? *Psychiatry and Clinical Neurosciences* 71: 459–466.

Kardefelt-Winther, D. (2017). Conceptualizing Internet use disorders: Addiction or coping process? *Psychiatry and Clinical Neurosciences* 71: 459–466. https://doi.org/10.1111/pcn.12413.

Kass, F., Spitzer, R.L., Williams, J.B.W., and Widiger, T. (1989). Self-defeating personality disorder and DSM-III-R: Development of the diagnostic criteria. *American Journal of Psychiatry* 146: 1022–1026.

Kaufman, W. (1976). Some emotional uses of money. In: *The Psychoanalysis of Money*, ed. E. Borneman, pp. 227–252. New York: Urizen Books.

Keller, L.E. (1992). Addiction as a form of perversion. *Bulletin of the Menninger Clinic* 56: 221–231.

Kernberg, O.F. (1975). *Borderline Conditions and Pathological Narcissism*. New York: Jason Aronson.

Kernberg, O.F. (1988). Clinical dimensions of masochism. *Journal of the American Psychoanalytic Association* 36: 1005–1029.

Kernberg, O.F. (1992). Masochistic pathology and love relations. Presented at the Fall Meeting of the American Psychoanalytic Association, New York.

Kernberg, O.F. (1995). *Love Relations: Normality and Pathology*. New Haven, CT: Yale University Press.

Kessler, R.M., Hutson, P.H., Herman, B.K. & Potenza, M.N. (2016). The neurobiological basis of binge eating disorder. *Neuroscience & Biobehavioral Review*. April; 63; 223–238.

Khan, M.M.R. (1979). *Alienation in Perversions*. London: Hogarth Press.

Khantzian, E.J. (1974). Heroin use as an attempt to cope: Clinical observations. *American Journal of Psychiatry* 131: 160–164.

Khantzian, E.J. (1975). Self-selection and progression in drug dependence. *Psychiatry Digest* 36: 12–22.

Khantzian, E.J. (1978). The ego, the self and opiate addiction: Theoretical and treatment considerations. *International Journal of Psychoanalysis* 5: 189–198.

Khantzian, E.J. (1982). Psychological (structural) vulnerabilities and the specific appeal of narcotics. *Annals of the New York Academy of Science* 398: 24–32.

Khantzian, E.J. (1985). The self-medication hypothesis of addictive disorders: Focus on heroin and cocaine dependence. *American Journal of Psychiatry* 142: 1259–1264.

Khantzian, E.J. (1995). Self-regulation vulnerabilities in substance abusers: Treatment implications. In: *The Psychology and Treatment of Addictive Behavior*, ed. S. Dowling, pp. 17–41. Monograph of the Workshop Series of the American Psychoanalytic Association. Madison, CT: International Universities Press.

Khantzian, E.J. (1997). The self-medication hypothesis of substance use disorders: A reconsideration and recent applications. *Harvard Review of Psychiatry* 4: 231–244.

Khantzian, E.J. (2003). Understanding addictive vulnerability: An evolving psychodynamic perspective. *Neuropsychoanalysis* 5: 5–21.

Khantzian, E.J., and Albanese, M.J. (2008). *Understanding Addiction as Self-Medication.* Lanham, MD: Rowman and Littlefield.

Khantzian, E.J., and Mack, J.E. (1983). Self-preservation and the care of the self: Ego instincts reconsidered. *Psychoanalytic Study of the Child* 38: 209–232.

Killinger, B. (1991). *Workaholics: The Respectable Addicts.* Toronto, CN: Key Porter Books Ltd.

Kim, S.J., Marsch, L.A., Hancock, J.T., and Das, A.K. (2017). Scaling up research on drug abuse and addiction through social media big data. *Journal of Medical Internet Research* 19: e353.

Kinsey, A., Pomeroy, W., and Martin, C. (1948). *Sexual Behavior in the Human Male.* New York: W.B. Saunders.

Kinsey, A.C., Pomeroy, W.B., Martin, C.E., and Gebhard, P.H. (1953). *Sexual Behavior in the Human Female.* Philadelphia: W.B. Saunders.

Klein, G. (1976). *Psychoanalytic Theory.* New York, NY: International Universities Press.

Klein, M. (1935). A contribution to the psychogenesis of manic depressive states. In: *Love, Guilt and Reparation and Other Works: 1921–1945*, pp. 262–289. New York: Free Press, 1975.

Klein, M. (1937). Love, guilt, and reparation. In: *Love, Guilt and Reparation and Other Works: 1921–1945*, pp. 306–343. New York, NY: Free Press, 1975.

Klein, M. (1946). Notes on some schizoid mechanisms. *International Journal of Psychoanalysis* 27: 99–110.

Kohon, G. (1987). Fetishism revisited. *International Journal of Psychoanalysis* 68: 213–228.

Kohut, H. (1972). Thoughts on narcissism and narcissistic rage. *Psychoanalytic Study of the Child* 27: 360–400.

Kohut, H. (1977). *The Restoration of the Self.* New York, NY: International Universities Press.

Kohut, H. (1978). Preface to "Der falshe weg sum Selbst. Studien zur Drogenkarriere by Jurgen vom Scheldt". In: *The Search for the Self*, Volume 2, ed. P.H. Ornstein, pp. 845–850. New York: International Universities Press.

Kohut, H. (1984). *How Does Analysis Cure?* Chicago, IL: University of Chicago Press.

Kohut, H., and Wolf, E.S. (1978). The disorders of the self and their treatment: An outline. *International Journal of Psychoanalysis* 59: 413–425.

Kolansky, H., and Eisner, H. (1974). The psychoanalytic concept of preoedipal developmental arrest. Paper presented at the fall meetings of the American Psychoanalytic Association. Cited in: *Inner Torment: Living Between Conflict and Fragmentation*, ed. S. Akhtar, p. 231. Northvale, NJ: Jason Aronson, 1999.

Kraepelin, E. (1915). *Psychiatrie*, 8th Edition. Leipzig, Germany: Barth.

Krafft-Ebing, R.V. (1886). *Psychopathia Sexualis*, transl. F.J. Rebman. New York: Rebman Company, 1906.

Krueger, D. (1986). *The Last Taboo: Money as Symbol and Reality in Psychotherapy and Psychoanalysis*. New York: Brunner/Mazel.

Krueger, D. (1988). On compulsive shopping and spending: A psychodynamic inquiry. *American Journal of Psychotherapy* 42: 574–584.

Krueger, D. (1989). *Body Self and Psychological Self: Developmental and Clinical Integration in Disorders of the Self*. New York: Brunner/Mazel.

Krueger, D.W. (1991). Money meanings and madness: A psychoanalytic perspective. *Psychoanalytic Review* 78(2): 209–224.

Krueger, D. (2000). The use of money as an action symptom: A psychoanalytic view. In: *I Shop, Therefore I Am: Compulsive Buying and the Search for Self*, ed. A. Benson. New York: Jason Aronson.

Krueger, R.B. (2010). The DSM diagnostic criteria for sexual masochism. *Archives of Sexual Behavior* 39: 346–356.

Krystal, H. (1974). The genetic development of affects and affect regression. *The Annual of Psychoanalysis* 2: 98–126. New York: International Universities Press.

Krystal, H. (1982). Adolescence and the tendencies to develop substance dependence. *Psychoanalytic Inquiry* 2: 581–617.

Krystal, H. (1995). Disorders of emotional development in addictive behavior. In: *The Psychology and Treatment of Addictive Behavior*, ed. S. Dowling, pp. 65–100. Madison, CT: International Universities Press.

Krystal, H., and Raskin, H.A. (1970). *Drug Dependence: Aspects of Ego Function*. Detroit, MI: Wayne State University Press.

Kuss, D.J. (2013). Internet gaming addiction: Current perspectives. *Psychology Research and Behavior Management* 6: 125–137.

Kuss, D.J., Griffiths, M.D., Karila, L., and Billieux, J. (2014). Internet addiction: A systematic review of epidemiological research for the last decade. *Current Pharmaceutical Design* 20: 4026–4052.

Kuss, D.J., and Lopez-Fernandez, O. (2016). Internet addiction and problematic internet use: A systematic review of clinical research. *World Journal of Psychiatry* 6: 143–156. https://doi.org/10.5498/wjp.v6.i1.143.

Lacan, J. (1998). *The Seminar of Jacques Lacan: Book XI: The Four Fundamental Concepts of Psychoanalysis*, ed. J.-A. Miller, transl. A. Sheridan. New York: W. W. Norton.

Lacan, J. (2007). *Ecrits*, transl. B. Fink. New York: W. W. Norton.

Laconi, S., Rodgers, R.F., and Chabrol, H. (2014). The measurement of internet addiction: A critical review of existing scales and their psychometric properties. *Computers in Human Behavior* 41: 190–202.

Laforgue, R. (1930). On the eroticization of anxiety. *International Journal of Psychoanalysis* 11: 312–321.

Lantos, B. (1952). Metapsychological considerations on the concept of work. *International Journal of Psychoanalysis* 33: 439–443.

Laplanche, J., and Pontalis, J.B. (1973). *The Language of Psycho-Analysis*. New York: W.W. Norton.

Latzer, Y., and Gerzi, S. (2000). Autistic patterns: Managing the "black hole" in eating disorders. *Psychoanalytic Social Work* 7: 29–55.

Lawrence, L. (1990). The psychodynamics of the compulsive female shopper. *American Journal of Psychoanalysis* 50(1): 67–70.

Lebe, D. (1997). Masochism and the inner mother. *Psychoanalytic Review* 84: 523–540.

Lejoyeux, M., Ades, J., Tassain, V., and Solomon, J. (1996). Phenomenology and psychopathology of uncontrolled buying. *American Journal of Psychiatry* 153: 1524–1529.

Lejoyeux, M., Haberman, N., Solomon, J., and Ades, J. (1999). Comparison of buying behavior in depressed patients presenting with or without compulsive buying. *Comprehensive Psychiatry* 40: 51–56.

Lenzer, G. (1975). On masochism: A contribution to the history of a phantasy and its theory. *Signs* 1: 277–324.

Lerner, M.J. (1965). Evaluation of performance as a function of performer's reward and attractiveness. *Journal of Personality and Social Psychology* 1: 355–360.

Lerner, M.J., and Miller, D.T. (1978). Just world research and the attribution process: Looking back and ahead. *Psychological Bulletin* 85: 1030–1051.

Lesieur, H.R., and Rosenthal, R.J. (1991). Pathological gambling: A review of the literature (prepared for the American Psychiatric Association task force on DSM-IV committee on disorders of impulse control not elsewhere classified). *Journal of Gambling Studies* 7: 5–39.

Lesieur, H.R., and Rosenthal, R.J. (1998). Analysis of pathological gambling. In: *DSM-IV Sourcebook*, Volume 4, eds. T.A. Widiger, A.J. Francis, H.A. Pincus, R. Ross, M.B. First, W. Davis, and M. Kline, pp. 393–401. Washington, DC: American Psychiatric Association.

Levine, H.B. (1997). Men at work: Work, ego, and identity in the analysis of adult men. In: *Work and Its Inhibitions: Psychoanalytic Essays*, eds. C.W. Socarides and S. Kramer, pp. 143–158. Madison, CT: International Universities Press.

Levy, S.T. (1987). Therapeutic strategy and psychoanalytic technique. *Journal of the American Psychoanalytic Association* 35: 447–466.

Lewes, K. (2005). Homosexuality, homophobia, and gay-friendly psychoanalysis. *Fort-DA* 11: 13–34.

Lewis, A. (1936). Problems of obsessional illness. *Proceedings of the Royal Society of Medicine* 29: 325–328.

Li, J., Vestergaard, M., Cnattingius, S., Gissler, M., Bech, B., Obel, C., and Olsen, J. (2014). Mortality after parental death in childhood: A nationwide cohort study from three Nordic countries. *PLOS/Medicine* 10: e1001679.

Lidz, T. (1983). *The Person: His and Her Development Throughout the Life Cycle*. New York: Basic Books.

Lindner, R.M. (1950). The psychodynamics of gambling. *Annals of the American Academy of Political and Social Science* 269: 93–107.

Linn, L. (1953). The role of perception in the mechanism of denial. *Journal of the American Psychoanalytic Association* 1: 690–705.

Mack, J. (1981). Alcoholism, AA, and the governance of the self. In: *Dynamic Approaches to the Treatment of Addictions*, eds. M.H. Bean, E.J. Khantzian, J. Mack, and N. Zinberg, pp. 128–162. New York, NY: Free Press.

Maleson, F.G. (1984). The multiple meanings of masochism in psychoanalytic discourse. *Journal of the American Psychoanalytic Association* 32: 325–356.

Matyszczyk, C. (2015, May 9). 17 percent take selfies or other photos while driving, AT&T study says. Retrieved December 1, 2018, from https://www.cnet.com/news/17-percent-take-selfies-while-driving-at-t-study-says/

Marcus, C.R., Rogers, P.J., Brouns, F., and Schepers, R. (2017). Eating dependence and weight gain; no human evidence for a "sugar-addiction" model of overweight. *Appetite* 114: 64–72.

Markson, E.R. (1993). Depression and moral masochism. *International Journal of Psychoanalysis* 74: 931–940.

McDougall, J. (1974). The psychosoma and the psychoanalytic process. *International Review of Psycho-Analysis* 1: 437–459.

McDougall, J. (1984). The "dis-affected" patient: Reflections on affect pathology. *Psychoanalytic Quarterly* 53: 386–409.

McDougall, J. (1985). *Theaters of the mind: Illusion and truth on the psychoanalytic stage.* New York: Basic Books.

McDougall, J. (1986). Identifications, neoneeds and neosexualities. *International Journal of Psychoanalysis* 67: 19–31.

McDougall, J. (1989). *Theaters of the Mind.* New York: Basic Books.

McDougall, J. (2001). The psychic economy of addiction. In: *Hungers and Compulsions: The Psychodynamic Treatment of Eating Disorders and Addictions*, eds. J. Petrucelli and C. Stuart, pp. 5–26. Northvale, NJ: Jason Aronson.

McElroy, S.L., Keck, P.E., Jr., and Phillips, K.A. (1995). Kleptomania, compulsive buying and binge eating disorder. *Journal of Clinical Psychiatry* 56: 14–26.

McElroy, S.L., Keck, P.E., Pope, H.G., Smith, J.M., and Strakowski, S.M. (1994). Compulsive buying: A report of 20 cases. *Journal of Clinical Psychiatry* 55: 242–248.

McNicol, M.L., and Thorsteinsson, E.B. (2017). Internet addiction, psychological distress, and coping responses among adolescents and adults. *Cyberpsychology, Behavior, and Social Networking* 20: 296–304.

Meerkerk, G.-J., Van Den Eijnden, R.J., Vermulst, A.A., and Garretsen, H.F. (2009). The Compulsive Internet Use Scale (CIUS): Some psychometric properties. *CyberPsychology and Behavior* 12: 1–6.

Meissner, W.W. (1997). The self and the principle of work. In: *Work and Its Inhibitions: Psychoanalytic Essays*, eds. C.W. Socarides and S. Kramer, pp. 35–60. Madison, CT: International Universities Press.

Menninger, K. (1942). Work as sublimation. *Bulletin of the Menninger Clinic* 6: 170–182.

Mihajlov, M., and Vejmelka, L. (2017). Internet addiction: A review of the first twenty years. *Psychiatria Danubina* 29: 260–272. https://doi.org/10.24869/psyd.2017.260.

Mikulincer, M., and Shaver, P.R. (2005). Attachment theory and emotions in close relationships: Exploring the attachment-related dynamics of emotional reactions to relational events. *Personal Relationships* 12: 149–168.

Milkman, H., and Frosch, W.A. (1973). On the preferential abuse of heroin and amphetamines. *Journal of Nervous and Mental Disease* 156: 242–248.

Miniwatts Marketing Group. (2018, September 25). World Internet Users Statistics and 2018 World Population Stats. Retrieved December 1, 2018, from https://www.internetworldstats.com/stats.htm#link.

Mitchell, S.A. (1988). *Relational Concepts in Psychoanalysis: An Integration.* Cambridge, MA: Harvard University Press.

Mottram, A.J., and Fleming, M.J. (2009). Extraversion, impulsivity, and online group membership as predictors of problematic internet use. *CyberPsychology and Behavior* 12: 319–321.

Naskar, S., Victor, R., Nath, K., and Sengupta, C. (2016). "One level more": A narrative review on internet gaming disorder. *Industrial Psychiatry Journal* 25: 145–154.

Natraraajan, R., and Goff, B. (1992). Manifestations of compulsiveness in the consumer-marketplace domain. *Psychology and Marketing* 9: 31–44.

Niederland, W. (1968). Clinical observations on the "survivor syndrome". *International Journal of Psychoanalysis* 49: 313–315.

Novick, J., and Novick, K.K. (1991). Some comments on masochism and the delusion of omnipotence from a developmental perspective. *Journal of the American Psychoanalytic Association* 39: 307–331.

Novick, K.K. and Novick, J. (1987). The essence of masochism. *Psychoanalytic Study of the Child* 42: 353–384.

Oates, W. (1971). *Confessions of a Workaholic*. New York: World.

Oberst, U., Wegmann, E., Stodt, B., Brand, M., and Chamarro, A. (2017). Negative consequences from heavy social networking in adolescents: The mediating role of fear of missing out. *Journal of Adolescence* 55: 51–60.

Ogden, T.H. (1986). *The Matrix of the Mind: Object Relations and the Psychoanalytic Dialogue*. New York: Jason Aronson, Inc.

Olmsted, C. (1962). *Heads I Win: Tails You Lose*. New York: Macmillan.

Ornstein, A. (2012). Self-abuse and suicidality: Clinical manifestations of chronic narcissistic rage. In: *The Clinical Problem of Masochism*, eds. D. Holtzman and N. Kulish, pp. 113–127. Lanham, MD: Jason Aronson.

Osada, H. (2013). Internet addiction in Japanese college students: Is Japanese version of Internet Addiction Test (JIAT) useful as a screening tool? *Bulletin of Senshu University School of Human Sciences* 3: 71–80.

PDM Task Force. (2006). *Psychodynamic Diagnostic Manual*. Silver Spring, MD: Alliance of Psychoanalytic Organizations.

Perlman, D. (2016, September 15). How many cardboard boxes does Amazon ship each day? Retrieved December 1, 2018, from https://www.linkedin.com/pulse/how-many-cardboard-boxes-does-amazon-ship-each-day-david-perlman/

Petrucelli, J. (2004). Treating eating disorders. In: *Handbook of Addictive Disorders*, ed. R. Coombs, pp. 310–324. Hoboken, NJ: John Wiley and Sons.

Petrucelli, J. (2010). Things that go bump in the night: Secrets after dark. In: *Knowing, Not-Knowing and Sort-of-Knowing: Psychoanalysis and the Experience of Uncertainty*, ed. J. Petrucelli, pp. 135–150. London: Karnac Books.

Petrucelli, J. (2015a). Mermaids, mistresses and Medusa: "Getting inside out and outside in" the relational montage of eating disorders. In: *Body-States: Interpersonal/Relational Perspectives on the Treatment of Eating Disorders*, ed. J. Petrucelli, pp. 13–34. London: Routledge.

Petrucelli, J. (2015b). My body is my cage: Interfacing interpersonal neurobiology, attachment, affect regulation, self-regulation, and the regulation of relatedness in treatment with patients with eating disorders. In: *Body-States: Interpersonal/Relational Perspectives on the Treatment of Eating Disorders*, ed. J. Petrucelli, pp. 35–56. London: Routledge.

Petry, N., ed. (2005). *Behavioral Addictions: DSM-V and Beyond*. New York: Oxford University Press.

Pew Research Center. (2016). Smartphone ownership and Internet usage continues to climb in emerging economies (fact sheet). Washington D.C.: Pew Research Center. Retrieved from February 22, 2016, http://www.pewglobal.org/2016/02/22/smartphone-ownership-and-internet-usage-continues-to-climb-in-emerging-economies/

Pew Research Center. (2018). Demographics of Internet and home broadband usage in the United States (fact sheet). Washington D.C.: Pew Research Center. Retrieved from http://www.pewinternet.org/fact-sheet/internet-broadband/

Phillips, A. (2010). On getting away with it: On the experiences we don't have. In: *Knowing, Not-Knowing and Sort-of-Knowing: Psychoanalysis and the Experience of Uncertainty*, pp. 165–174. London: Karnac Books.

Pine, F. (1988). The four psychologies of psychoanalysis and their place in clinical work. *Journal of the American Psychoanalytic Association* 36: 571–596.

Pine, F. (1997). *Diversity and Direction in Psychoanalytic Technique*. New Haven, CT: Yale University Press.

Polivy, J., Coleman, J., and Herman, C.P. (2005). The effect of deprivation on food cravings and eating behavior in restrained and unrestrained eaters. *International Journal of Eating Disorders* 3: 301–309.

Polivy, J., and Herman, C.P. (1985). Dieting and bingeing: A causal analysis. *American Psychologist* 40: 193–201.

Portis, S.A., ed. (1946). *Diseases of the Digestive System*, 2nd Edition. Philadelphia, PA: Lea and Febinger.

Potenza, M.N. (2006). Should addictive disorders include non-substance-related conditions? *Addiction* 101S: 142–151.

Poushter, J., Bishop, C., and Chwe, H. (2018). Social media use continues to rise in developing countries but plateaus across developed ones. *Pew Research Center*, June 19. Retrieved July 30, 2018, from assets.pewresearch.org.

Pressman, P., Clemens, R.A., and Rodriguez, H.A. (2015). Food addiction: Clinical reality or mythology. *The American Journal of Medicine* 128: 1165–1166.

Przybylski, A.K., Murayama, K., DeHaan, C.R., and Gladwell, V. (2013). Motivational, emotional, and behavioral correlates of fear of missing out. *Computers in Human Behavior* 29: 1841–1848.

Radó, S. (1926). The psychic effects of intoxicants: An attempt to evolve a psycho-analytical theory of morbid cravings. *International Journal of Psychoanalysis* 7: 396–413.

Radó, S. (1933). The psychoanalysis of pharmocothymia. *Psychoanalytic Quarterly*: 1–23.

Rasmussen, P. (2008). *When Work Takes Control: The Psychology and Effects of Work Addiction*. London: Karnac Books.

Reich, W. (1949). *Character Analysis*. New York: Farrar, Straus and Giroux.

Reid Chassiakos, Y., Radesky, J., Christakis, D., Moreno, M.A., and Cross, C. (2016). Children and adolescents and digital media. *Pediatrics* 138: e20162593.

Reik, T. (1941). *Masochism in Modern Man*. New York: Farrar and Strauss.

Rendon, M. (1991). Money and the left in psychoanalysis. In: *Money and Mind*, eds. S. Klebanow and E.L. Lowenkopf, pp. 135–148. New York: Plenum Press.

Rifkin, J., Cindy, C., and Kahn, B. (2015). Fomo: How the fear of missing out leads to missing out. *ACR North American Advances*, *NA-43*. Retrieved July 30, 2018, from acrwebsite.org/.

Robins LN, Helzer JE, Davis DH. Narcotic use in Southeast Asia and afterward. Archives of General Psychiatry (1975) 32:955–6110.1001

Robinson, B.E. (1989). *Work-Addiction: Hidden Legacies of Adult Children*. Deerfield Beach, FL: Health Communications Inc.

Robinson, B.E. (2014). *Chained to the Desk*. New York: New York University Press.

Rose, M. (2001). The body doesn't lie: Five tales of superobesity as somatic language. *Psychoanalytic Inquiry* 21: 337–355.

Rosen, I.C. (1993). Relational masochism: The search for a "bad-enough" object. Paper presented to the Topeka Psychoanalytic Society, October 14.

Rosen, I.C. (2007). Revenge: The hate that dare not speak its name: A psychoanalytic perspective. *Journal of the American Psychoanalytic Association* 55: 595–619.

Rosenberg, K.P., and Feder, L.C. (2014). *Behavioral Addictions: Criteria, Evidence, and Treatment*. Waltham, MA: Academic Press.

Rosenthal, R.J. (1986). The pathological gambler's system for self-deception. *Journal of Gambling Behavior* 2: 108–120.

Rosenthal, R.J. (1987). The psychodynamics of pathological gambling: A review of the literature. In: *Essential Papers on Addiction*, ed. D.L. Yalisove, pp. 184–212. New York: New York University Press.

Rosenthal, R.J. (1988). Transparent screens. *Journal of the American Psychoanalytic Association* 36: 295–317.

Rosenthal, R.J. (1997). The gambler as case history and literary twin: Dostoevsky's false beauty and the poetics of perversity. *Psychoanalytic Review* 84: 593–616.

Rosenthal, R.J. (2005). Staying in action: The pathological gambler's equivalent of the dry drunk. *Journal of Gambling Issues*, March 13. DOI: 10.4309/jgi.2005.13.12.

Rosenthal, R.J. (2008). Psychodynamic psychotherapy and the treatment of pathological gambling. *Brazilian Journal of Psychiatry (Revista Brasileira de Psiquiatria)* 30S: 41–50.

Rosenthal, R.J., and Lesieur, H.R. (1992). Self-reported withdrawal symptoms and pathological gambling. *American Journal on Addictions* 1: 150–154.

Rosenthal, R.J., and Rugle, L.J. (1994). A psychodynamic approach to the treatment of pathological gambling, part I: Achieving abstinence. *Journal of Gambling Studies* 10: 21–42.

Rosewater, L.B. (1987). A critical analysis of the proposed self-defeating personality disorder. *Journal of Personality Disorders* 1: 190–195.

Rubin, T.I. (1973). Discussion. *American Journal of Psychoanalysis* 33: 39–41.

Ryan, M. (1995). *Secret Life*. New York: Vintage Books.

Sacher-Masoch, L. von. (1870). *Venus in Furs*. New York: Belmont Books, 1965.

Salimpoor, V.N. (2011). Anatomically distinct dopamine release during anticipation and experience of peak emotion to music. *Nature Neuroscience* 14: 257–262.

Salmon, A. (2010, April 2). Couple: Internet gaming addiction led to baby's death. *CNN*. Retrieved from http://www.cnn.com/2010/WORLD/asiapcf/04/01/korea.parents. starved.baby/index.html

Sands, S.H. (1989). Eating disorders and female development: A self-psychological perspective. *Progress in Self Psychology* 5: 75–103.

Savelle-Rocklin, N. (2016). *Food for Thought: Perspectives on Eating Disorders*. Lanham, MD: Rowman and Littlefield.

Savitt, R.A. (1963). Psychoanalytic studies on addiction: Ego structure in narcotic addiction. *Psychoanalytic Quarterly* 32: 43–57.

Schafer, R. (1984). The pursuit of failure and the idealization of unhappiness. *American Psychologist* 39: 398–405.

Schafer, R. (1988). Those wrecked by success. In: *Masochism: Current Psychoanalytic Perspectives*, eds. R.A. Glick and D.I. Meyers, pp. 81–91. Hillsdale, NJ: Analytic Press.

Scharff, J., and Scharff, D. (1997). Object relations couple therapy. *American Journal of Psychotherapy* 51: 141–173.

Schimmenti, A., and Caretti, V. (2010). Psychic retreats or psychic pits?: Unbearable states of mind and technological addiction. *Psychoanalytic Psychology* 27: 115–132.

Schlosser, S., Black, D.W., Repertinger, S., and Freet, D. (1994). Compulsive buying: Demography, phenomenology, and comorbidity in 46 subjects. *General Hospital Psychiatry* 16: 205–212.

Scott, J. (1974). Early childhood influences. In: *Women and success: The anatomy of achievement*, ed. J. Kundsin. New York: Morrow.

Segal, H. (1978). On symbolism. *International Journal of Psychoanalysis* 59: 315–319.

Shaffer, H.J. (1999). Strange bedfellows: A critical view of pathological gambling and addiction. *Addiction* 94: 1445–1448.

Shah, D. (2015). Hopelessness in the countertransference. In: *Hopelessness: Developmental, Cultural, and Clinical Realms*, eds. S. Akhtar and M.K. O'Neil, pp. 181–201. London: Karnac Books.

Shainess, N. (1997). Masochism revisited: Reflections on masochism and its childhood antecedents. *American Journal of Psychotherapy* 51: 552–568.

Shapiro, S. (2012). Therapeutic change from the perspective of integrative trauma treatment. *Psychoanalytic Perspectives* 9: 51–65.

Sifneos, P. (1973). The prevalence of "alexithymic" characteristics in psychosomatic patients. *Psychotherapy and Psychosomatics* 22: 255–262.

Sifneos, P. (1975). Problems of psychotherapy with patients with alexithymic characteristics and physical disease. *Psychotherapy and Psychosomatics* 26: 65–70.

Simmel, E. (1920). Psychoanalysis of the gambler. *International Journal of Psychoanalysis* 1: 352–353.

Simmel, E. (1948). Alcoholism and addiction. *Psychoanalytic Quarterly* 17: 6–31.

Skodol, A.E., Oldham, J.M., Gallaher, P.E., and Bezirganian, S. (1994). Validity of self-defeating personality disorder. *American Journal of Psychiatry* 151: 560–567.

Slater, E., and Roth, M. (1969). *Clinical Psychiatry*, 3rd Edition. Baltimore, MD: William and Wilkins.

Socarides, C. and Kramer, S. (1997). *Work and Its Inhibitions: Psychoanalytic Essays*. Madison, CT: International Universities Press.

Spring, B., Schneider, K., Smith, M., Kendzor, D., Appelhans, B., Hedeker, D., and Pagoto, S. (2008). Abuse potential of carbohydrates for overweight carbohydrate cravers. *Psychopharmacology* 197: 637–647.

Spruiell, V. (1975). Three strands of narcissism. *Psychoanalytic Quarterly* 44: 577–595.

Stekel, W. (1924). The gambler. In: *Peculiarities of Behavior*, Volume 2, ed. J.S. Van Teslaar, pp. 233–255. New York: Liveright.

Stern, D. (1997). *Unformulated Experience: From Dissociation to Imagination in Psychoanalysis*. Hillsdale, NJ: Analytic Press.

Stern, D. (2004). *The Present Moment In Psychotherapy and Everyday Life*. New York, NY: W.W. Norton & Co Ltd.

Stoller, R.J. (1975). *Perversion: The Erotic Form of Hatred*. New York: Pantheon.

Stolorow, R.D. (1975). Toward a functional definition of narcissism. *International Journal of Psycho-Analysis* 56: 179–185.

Stolorow, R.D., and Atwood, G.E. (1991). The mind and the body. *Psychoanalytic Dialogues* 1: 181–195.

Stone, M. (1972). Treating the wealthy and their children. *International Journal of Child Psychotherapy* 1: 15–46.

Stone, M.H. (1979). Upbringing in the super-rich. In: *Modern Perspectives in the Psychiatry of Infancy*, ed. J. Howells. New York: Brunner/Mazel.

Stone, M.H. (2012). Disorder in the domain of the personality disorders. *Psychodynamic Psychiatry* 40: 23–46.

Stuart, C. (2001). Addictive economies: Intrapsychic and interpersonal discussion of McDougall's chapter. In: *Hungers and Compulsions: The Psychodynamic Treatment of Eating Disorders and Addictions*, eds. J. Petrucelli and C. Stuart, pp. 29–38. Northvale, NJ: Jason Aronson.

Suissa, A.J. (2014). Cyber addictions: Toward a psychosocial perspective. *Addictive Behaviors* 43: 28–32.

Sussman, C.J., Harper, J.M., Stahl, J.L., and Weigle, P. (2018). Internet and video game addictions. *Child and Adolescent Psychiatric Clinics of North America* 27: 307–326.

Tang, D., Wei, F., Qin, B., Liu, T., and Zhou, M. (2014a). Coooolll: A deep learning system for twitter sentiment classification association for computational linguistics. Proceedings of the 8th International Workshop on Semantic Evaluation, pp. 208–212, Dublin, Ireland, August 23–24.

Tang, J., Yu, Y., Du, Y., Ma, Y., Zhang, D., and Wang, J. (2014b). Prevalence of internet addiction and its association with stressful life events and psychological symptoms among adolescent internet users. *Addictive Behaviors* 39: 744–747.

Target, M., and Fonagy, P. (1996). Playing with reality: II. The development of psychic reality from a theoretical perspective. *International Journal of Psychoanalysis* 77: 459–479.

Taubes, G. (2016). *The Case against Sugar*. New York: Anchor Books.

Taylor, G.J., and Bagby, R.M. (2013). Psychoanalysis and empirical research: The example of alexithymia. *Journal of the American Psychoanalytic Association* 61: 99–133.

Tepper, M., Dodes, L.M., Wool, C., and Rosenblatt, L. (2006). A psychotherapy dominated by separation, termination, and death. *Harvard Review of Psychiatry* 14: 257–267.

Thoreau, H.D. (1854). *Walden; or, Life in the Woods*. Boston, MA: Ticknor and Fields.

Tibon, S., and Rothschild, L. (2009). Dissociative states in eating disorders: An empirical Rorschach study. *Psychoanalytic Psychology* 26: 69–82.

Tolpin, P. (1983). A change in the self: The development and transformation of an idealizing transference. *International Journal of Psycho-Analysis* 64: 461–483.

Treece, C., and Khantzian, E.J. (1986). Psychodynamic factors in the development of drug dependence. *Psychiatric Clinics of North America* 9: 399–412.

Tustin, F. (1972). *Autism and Childhood Psychosis*. London: Hogarth Press.

UKOM Insights. (2018). Facebook and Snapchat: Age profiles. Retrieved July 30, 2018, from http://www.comscore.com/Insights/Presentations-and-Whitepapers/2018/Facebook-Snapchat-Age-Profiles.

Urbszat, D., Herman, C.P., and Polivy, J. (2002). Eat, drink, and be merry, for tomorrow we diet: Effects of anticipated deprivation on food intake in restrained and unrestrained eaters. *Journal of Abnormal Psychology* 3: 396–401.

van Schoor, E. (1992). Pathological narcissism and addiction: A self-psychology perspective. *Psychoanalytic Psychotherapy* 6: 205–212.

Von Hattingberg, H. (1914). Analerotik, angstlust und eigensinn. *Internationale Zeitschrift fur Psychoanalyse* 2: 244–258.

Waelder, R. (1936). The principle of multiple function: Observations on multiple determination. *Psychoanalytic Quarterly* 41: 283–290.

Wahl, C. (1974). Psychoanalysis of the rich, the famous, and the influential. *Contemporary Psychoanalysis* 10: 71–85.

Walker, L. (1987). Inadequacies of the masochistic personality disorder diagnosis for women. *Journal of Personality Disorders* 1: 183–189.

Wallerstein, R.S. (1983). Self psychology and "classical" psychoanalytic psychology: The nature of their relationship. In: *The Future of Psychoanalysis*. ed. A. Goldberg, pp. 19–63. New York, NY: International Universities Press.

Wanat, M.J., Kuhnen, C.M., and Phillips, P.E.M. (2010). Delays conferred by escalating costs modulate dopamine release to rewards but not their predictors. *Journal of Neuroscience* 30: 12020–12027.

Wang, Y., Wu, L., Wang, L., Zhang, Y., Du, X., and Dong, G. (2017). Impaired decision-making and impulse control in internet gaming addicts: Evidence from the comparison with recreational internet game users. *Addiction Biology* 22: 1610–1621. https://doi.org/10.1111/adb.12458.

Wangh, K. (1962). The evocation of a proxy: A psychological maneuver, its use as a defense, its purpose and genesis. *Psychoanalytic Study of the Child* 17: 451–472.

Wegmann, E., and Brand, M. (2016). Internet-communication disorder: It's a matter of social aspects, coping, and internet-use expectancies. *Frontiers in Psychology* 7: 1747–1749.

Weinstein, A., and Lejoyeux, M. (2015). New developments on the neurobiological and pharmaco-genetic mechanisms underlying internet and videogame addiction. *American Journal on Addictions* 24: 117–125.

Weissman, P. (1963). The effects of preoedipal paternal attitudes on development and character. *International Journal of Psychoanalysis* 44: 121–131.

Westwater, M.L., Fletcher, P.C., and Ziauddeen, H. (2016). Sugar addiction: The state of the science. *European Journal of Nutrition* 55S: 55–69.

Wheelis, A. (1975). *On Not Knowing How to Live*. New York: Harper and Row.

White, R.W. (1963). *Ego and Reality in Psychoanalytic Theory*. New York: International Universities Press.

Whitebook, J. (1995). *Perversion and Utopia*. Cambridge, MA: Massachusetts Institute of Technology Press.

Wieder, H., and Kaplan, E.H. (1969). Drug use in adolescents. *Psychoanalytic Study of the Child* 24: 399–431.

Williams, D., Kennedy, T.L.M., and Moore, R.J. (2011). Behind the Avatar: The patterns, practices, and functions of role playing in MMOs. *Games and Culture* 6: 171–200.

Winestine, M.C. (1985). Compulsive shopping as a derivative of childhood seduction. *Psychoanalytic Quarterly* 54: 70–72.

Winkler, D.F., and Webster, J.L. (1997). Searching The Skies: The Legacy of the United States Cold War Defense Radar Program. U. S. Army Construction Engineering Research Laboratories (USACERL). Langley AFB: U.S. Air Force Air Combat Command. https://doi.org/10.1177/1555412010364983.

Winnicott, D.W. (1949). Mind and its relation to the psyche-soma. *British Journal of Medical Psychology* 27: 201–209.

Winnicott, D.W. (1953). Transitional objects and transitional phenomena: A study of the first not-me possession. *International Journal of Psychoanalysis* 34: 89–97.

Winnicott, D.W. (1960). Ego distortion in terms of true and false self. In: *The Maturational Processes and the Facilitating Environment*, pp. 140–157. New York: International Universities Press.

Winnicott, D.W. (1968). The use of an object and relating through identifications. New York Psychoanalytic Society Meeting, New York.

Wolf, E. (1988). *Treating the Self: Elements of Clinical Self Psychology*. New York: Guilford Press.

Wolf, E. (1997). A self psychological perspective of work and its inhibitions. In: *Work and Its Inhibitions: Psychoanalytic Essays*, eds. C.W. Socarides and S. Kramer, pp. 99–114. Madison, CT: International Universities Press.

Wood, H. (2013). The nature of the addiction in "sex addiction" and paraphilias. In: *Addictive States of Mind*, eds. M. Mower, R. Hale, and H. Wood, pp. 151–174. London: Karnac Books.

World Health Organization [WHO]. (2018, September 13). ICD-11 for mortality and morbidity statistics. Retrieved from https://icd.who.int/browse11/l-m/en#/http://id.who.int/icd/entity/1448597234.

Wulff, M. (1932). On an interesting oral symptom complex and its relationship to addiction: Lecture in the German Psychoanalytic Society, April 12, 1932, transl. *International Journal of Psychoanalysis* 18: 281–302.

Wurmser, L. (1974). Psychoanalytic considerations of the etiology of compulsive drug use. *Journal of the American Psychoanalytic Association* 22: 820–843.

Wurmser, L. (1980). Drug use as a protective system: Theories on drug abuse: Selected contemporary perspectives. *NIDA Research Monograph* 30: 71–74.

Wurmser, L. (1984a). The role of superego conflicts in substance abuse and their treatment. *International Journal of Psychoanalysis* 10: 227–258.

Wurmser, L. (1984b). More respect for the neurotic process. *Journal of Substance Abuse Treatment* 1: 37–48.

Wurmser, L. (1985). Denial and split identity: Timely issues in the psychoanalytic psychotherapy of compulsive drug users. *Journal of Substance Abuse and Treatment* 2: 89–96.

Wurmser, L. (1995). Compulsiveness and conflict: The distinction between description and explanation in the treatment of addictive behavior. In: *The Psychology and Treatment of Addictive Behavior*, ed. S. Dowling, pp. 133–145. Madison, CT: International Universities Press.

Wurmser, L. (2007). *Torment Me, But Don't Abandon Me: Psychoanalysis of the Severe Neuroses in a New Key*. Lanham, MD: Jason Aronson.

Wurmser, L., and Zients, A. (1982). The return of the denied superego. *Psychoanalytic Inquiry* 2: 539–580.

Xiuqin, H., Huimin, Z., Mengchen, L., Jinan, W., Ying, Z., and Ran, T. (2010). Mental health, personality, and parental rearing styles of adolescents with internet addiction disorder. *Cyberpsychology, Behavior, and Social Networking* 13: 401–406.

Yablonsky, L. (1991). *The Emotional Meaning of Money*. London: Gardner Press.

Young, K.S. (1998). Internet addiction: The emergence of a new clinical disorder. *CyberPsychology & Behavior* 1: 237–244. https://doi.org/10.1089/cpb.1998.1.237.

Young, K.S. (2004). Internet addiction: A new clinical phenomenon and its consequences. *American Behavioral Scientist* 48: 402–415. https://doi.org/10.1177/0002764204270278.

Young, K.S., and Brand, M. (2017). Merging theoretical models and therapy approaches in the context of internet gaming disorder: A personal perspective. *Frontiers in Psychology* 8: 153–158.

Yuan, K., Cheng, P., Dong, T., Bi, Y., Xing, L., Yu, D., and Tian, J. (2013). Cortical thickness abnormalities in late adolescence with online gaming addiction. *PLoS One* 8: e53055.

Zerbe, K. (1993). *The Body Betrayed: Women, Eating Disorders, and Treatment*. Washington, DC: American Psychiatric Press, Inc.

Zhou, Y., Lin, F., Du, Y., Qin, L., Zhao, Z., Xu, J., and Lei, H. (2011). Gray matter abnormalities in internet addiction: A voxel-based morphometry study. *European Journal of Radiology* 79: 92–95.

Ziauddeen, H., Farooqi, I.S., and Fletcher, P.C. (2012). Obesity and the brain: How convincing is the addiction model? *Nature Reviews Neuroscience* 13: 279–286.

Ziauddeen, H., and Fletcher, P.C. (2013). Is food addiction a valid and useful concept? *Obesity Review* 14: 19–28.

Zinczenko, D., and Perrine, S. (2016). *Zero Sugar Diet: The 14-Day Plan to Flatten Your Belly, Crush Cravings, and Help Keep You Lean for Life*. New York: Ballantine Books.

Zizek, S. (1994). *The Metastases of Enjoyment*. London: Verso Books.

Zynga Inc. (2018). FarmVille 2: Country Escape. Retrieved December 1, 2018, from https://itunes.apple.com/us/app/farmville-2-country-escape/id824318267?mt=8

Index

addiction: as "action disorder" 83; affect-based explanation for 120; balkanization of 4; behavioral 122–124, 135, 148; as chronic brain disease 20; clinical vignettes 8–14; and compulsion 14, 15, 20, 28–29, 81, 86, 143, 150–152; defined 135; and denial 17–18; diagnosis of 18; as displacement 8, 12–14, 16; and early psychoanalytic theory 27; historical perspective 27–29; neurobiological mechanism of 8, 12–14, 16, 104–105, 146; non-drug 6; as perversion 47, 121, 151–152; pregenital foundation of 119; psychological nature of 5, 16; relative to work 119–121; as response to helplessness/powerlessness 7, 28–29; as reward-seeking 20; to substances 135; theories of 5–7; treatment for 135, 152; *see also* compulsive shopping; drug addiction; food addiction; gambling addiction; internet addiction; sex addiction; work addiction
addictive search 7
addictive urges 7, 18–19, 28
Adler, Alfred 78
affect: denial of 120; dysregulation of 88; intense 30, 69; intolerable 49, 59, 71; negative 72; overwhelming 7, 28, 84; painful 27–28, 119; primitivization of 120; regulation and management of 73, 74, 82–83, 89, 108, 121, 143, 148; somatization of 82–85, 143–144
affect intolerance 87
affective flooding 7, 15
aggression 10, 15, 27, 40, 58, 62, 75, 90, 108, 118, 120, 152
alcoholism 5, 6, 8, 28, 59, 76, 80, 121, 124, 151; clinical vignettes 9–14; as masochism 59

alexithymia/alexithymic 34, 82, 83, 84, 86, 87, 90, 144
alimentary orgasm 27, 30
ambient intimacy 100
anal eroticism 77
anal phase 76
anal regression 125
anal sadism 125, 148, 149
anxiety 7, 18, 26, 27, 61, 65, 80, 83, 88, 102, 103, 106, 110, 121, 138, 142, 150; moral 125; separation 36–37; social 102, 110
attachment 36, 71, 78, 92, 93, 104, 111, 112, 113, 126, 138, 139, 145; avoidant 107; insecure 89, 106; and object relatedness 106–107, 146–147; preoedipal 37
attention deficit hyperactivity disorder (ADHD) 102, 105
autoeroticism 119–120

basal ganglia 104–105, 114n5
Begent, Jo 110
behavioral addictions 122–124, 135, 148
big data 113, 114n6
binge-eating 23, 25, 29, 30, 83; as expression of object hunger 36–37; as means of dissociation 30–32; as means of self-soothing 30–32; psychological motives for 26–27; as way of filling a void 41–42; *see also* food addiction
Bleuler, E. 80
borderline personality disorder *see* personality disorders
Bruch, Hilda 34
buying maniacs 80; *see also* shopping addiction

castration 48, 49
Center for Internet Addiction Recovery 104